D0127788

A PIONEER'S SEARCH
for AN IDEAL HOME

By

PHOEBE GOODELL JUDSON
*who crossed the Plains in 1853 and became
a resident on Puget Sound before the
organization of Washington
Territory*

A Book of Personal Memoirs

Foreword by Susan Armitage

University of Nebraska Press
Lincoln and London

Foreword copyright 1984 by the University of Nebraska Press
All rights reserved
Manufactured in the United States of America

First Bison Book printing: November 1984

Reprinted from the original 1925 edition.

Library of Congress Cataloging in Publication Data
Judson, Phoebe Goodell, 1832–1926.
   A pioneer's search for an ideal home.
   Reprint. Originally published: Bellingham, Wash. :
Printed by Union Printing, Binding, and Stationary Co.,
1925.
   Includes bibliographical references.
   1. Judson, Phoebe Goodell, 1832–1926. 2. Overland
journeys to the Pacific. 3. West (U.S.)—Description and
travel—1848–1860. 4. Pioneers—Washington (State)—
Puget Sound Region—Biography. 5. Puget Sound Region
(Wash.)—Biography. 6. Frontier and pioneer life—
Washington (State)—Puget Sound Region. I. Title.
F897.P9J83 1984   979.7'03'0924 [B]   84-7478
ISBN 0-8032-2563-6
ISBN 0-8032-7559-5 (pbk.)

⊛

Foreword
By Susan Armitage

Phoebe Judson was twenty when she crossed the plains to Oregon Territory. She was ninety-five when this book was first published in 1925. The years between were spent, as she says, in "a pioneer's search for an ideal home" and in living there, once found. This delightful reminiscence tells that story.

Phoebe and Holden Judson crossed the plains from Vermillion, Ohio, to search for their ideal home in the Puget Sound area of western Washington. They first lived at the extreme southern tip of the Sound, in and near Olympia, the territorial capital, which was then just a small muddy village of approximately twenty-five log cabins and some Indian dwellings. Later the Judsons pioneered in the Nooksack Valley, inland from Bellingham, the northernmost American settlement on Puget Sound. Seattle, now the largest and best-known of the Puget Sound cities, was then only a straggling cluster of cabins at the water's edge.

Phoebe and Holden Judson traveled west on the Overland Trail in 1853. In that year, an estimated 27,500 people crossed the plains.[1] The majority of them went to California, not to Oregon. Of the Oregon-bound, only a few settled north of the Columbia River in the newly created Washington Territory, which was estimated in 1853 to have an American population of only 4,000.

By the time the Judsons headed west in 1853, earlier pioneers had preceded them for a decade. The Overland Trail itself was in better physical shape than in the beginning, and the major part of the route was better known (although, as Phoebe notes, people were still getting lost and in trouble as they explored alternative routes across the rugged Cascade Mountains in Washington). Furthermore, some of the earlier political uncertainties in Oregon Territory had been resolved. The boundary dispute with England, which had at several times threatened war, was settled diplomatically in 1846. The land that England once had claimed became Washington Territory in 1853.

That year Congress appointed Isaac Stevens the first territorial governor. There was urgent business for Stevens to attend to, for while the international question had been settled, relations with the Indians had not. The pioneering missionary efforts led by Marcus and Narcissa Whitman and Henry and Eliza Spalding in 1837 had come to a disastrous conclusion with the killing of the Whitmans at Waiilatpu in 1847 and the outbreak of the Cayuse War. Stevens was charged with responsibility to settle the "Indian question," which he did brusquely, efficiently, and, as it turned out, badly. The diminutive man with his turned-up pants cuffs, as Phoebe so appealingly describes him, was a stern negotiator with the Indian tribes of Washington Territory. Stevens rapidly concluded a series of treaties that cleared land for American settlement by offering the Indians limited reservations and the promise of permanent assistance. He ignored the fact that the reservation policy, fairly suitable for the relatively settled Puget Sound tribes, was inappropriate for the more nomadic eastern tribes. Those tribes—the Yakima, Nez Perce, Cayuse, Walla Walla, and Palouse—accepted the treaties unwillingly. The general Indian attitude, both east and west of the Cascades, was one of confusion and resentment as whites continued to encroach on their lands, even before the treaties had been ratified by Congress.[2] As Phoebe Judson recounts, trouble inevitably occurred: the Indian Wars began with an incident in 1855 and dragged on for three years before the Americans finally ended Indian resistance. The Indian Wars forced many American settlers to abandon their farms and live together in fortified stockades for longer than a year. Although Phoebe paints a lovely portrait of fort life, describing the inhabitants "as thick as bees in a hive, and in perfect harmony," the fact is that the Indian Wars were a serious economic setback for many American settlers, the Judsons among them.

The Civil War, following close on the Indian Wars, further discouraged rapid settlement of Washington Territory. The Judsons, who abandoned farming in favor of a small business in Olympia, were unable to prosper. So it was that after eighteen years in Washington Territory, Phoebe and Holden Judson once again pioneered, taking up land in a remote location at the head of the Nooksack River, almost on the Canadian border. They found themselves in the most isolated and primitive conditions they had ever experienced. Phoebe was unhappy with the isolation and longed for the companionship she had had in Olympia. So far her story is not the stereotypically successful one of western legend! At this point, however, the Judsons' luck turned. They had found their ideal home, as it turned out, and were able to shape it to their liking. The couple founded a prosperous town, Lynden, and received wide recognition as founders. Holden was the first mayor, and Phoebe was called "the mother of Lynden."

Phoebe Judson's reminiscence is a classic pioneering account: concerned with getting there, searching for favorable economic circumstances, and eventual permanent settlement. Phoebe's account of the westward journey in 1853, which took approximately six months, consumes nearly a quarter of her memoirs. The following eighteen years, when the Judsons moved four times in their search for an ideal home, take up about a third of the book. The remainder is devoted to the Judsons' life in the Nooksack Valley, where they moved in 1871. Most of this section deals with events before 1899, when Holden Judson died, four months after their golden wedding anniversary.

The relative weighting of topics within the reminscence tells us a good deal about the pioneer memoir as a genre. The Overland Trail journey takes up much more space than the actual expenditure of time would warrant, were it not that these travel accounts had become a recognized literary form by the time Phoebe Judson wrote her reminiscence. Phoebe's detailed account of the journey, evidently based on a diary she kept at the time, is an informative addition to existing trail literature. A good storyteller, she clearly conveys the fear and excitement of the start as well as the dragging exhaustion of the last leg of the journey from Fort Boise on. She provides us with much good, homey detail, including instructions for baking light bread on the trail. In return, we must accept some common nineteenth-century reticences, such as the unheralded birth of Phoebe's second child, Charles, on the journey. When we realize that she left Kansas City, their "jumping-off place," more than seven months pregnant, her early worries seem very restrained. It should be noted that, although the Judsons joined a fast and well-managed party, the group nevertheless experienced a death, a serious accident, and at least one serious illness. Moreover, they had to leave many household goods and belongings behind.

Following their arrival in Washington Territory, Phoebe's emphasis is on the exciting, unusual, and picturesque in the settlement experience rather than on the details of daily living. Although, for example, we learn a good deal about Indians and the Indian Wars, we never learn how the Judsons supported themselves. We do not know what crops they grew in Lewis County, what goods they sold in their Olympia store (or, indeed, what happened to that business), or even how they lived in Lynden, although we know from other sources that they had a large dairy farm. Once past the adventure of early settlement, the account becomes very sketchy. These gaps in the record, characteristic of the pioneer genre, have affected the writing of western history. Historians are still struggling to make connections between the pioneering phase and subsequent development—to fill in the information that the pioneer generation thought was too ordinary to write about.

Given the limitations of the pioneer genre, what do we learn from Phoebe Judson's reminiscence? Above all, we learn about human relationships. Family was the most important thing in Phoebe Judson's life. Family brought her west and sustained her, once there. As she recounts, her parents and sister had traveled west in 1852. So, although parting with Holden's family was difficult (they were to follow in the migration of 1854), Phoebe had a family to look forward to at the end of the journey. In fact, she speaks of "going home" to her parents in their newly settled location in Grand Mound. Throughout her reminiscence, the experiences of members of a widespread family network are of major importance. On occasions when she lacked a kinship network, Phoebe either found one, for example, by joining the Hines party on the Overland Trail, or created one, as she did in Lynden by adopting several groups of mixed-blood children, and by treating the sparse population in the Nooksack Valley "like one family." It was indeed fitting that she should end her life recognized as "the mother of Lynden."

Historians are just beginning to realize fully the importance of family and kinship networks in western settlement. Many couples, like Holden and Phoebe Judson, followed family west and then encouraged other kin to follow. In the small world of pioneer settlers, kinship— and, by natural extension, old acquaintance—remained a powerful connection that was not only personally satisfying (like Phoebe's visits with her old friend Elizabeth Roeder in Bellingham) but politically useful (as some of the Judson connections must have been to Holden). Women's diaries and reminiscences such as this are an important source for documenting the importance of family connections.

Surely the most unusual aspect of Phoebe Judson's story is her attitude toward Indians. Although she never completely shook off the ingrained American fear of "the treacherous savage," her natural curiosity and friendliness soon led her to adopt a more open attitude. Repeatedly, both on the Overland Trail and later, we see her trying to understand the Indian side of things, even when she is afraid and her own property is threatened. Upon arrival in Washington, she immediately began to learn Chinook so that she could understand Indian legends and customs. As she remarks, "As I became better acquainted with them my fears were, in a measure, dissipated." Her attitude remained sympathetic even when the Indian Wars drove the Judsons from their homestead. Phoebe's account of the wars, and especially the capture and eventual death of Leschi, a leader of the Nisqually Indians, is very fair. The later move to the Nooksack Valley made Phoebe fearful at first: "The scene in this place of gloomy solitude, where white women's feet never before trod, was inexpressibly dreary and saddening." But her spirits soon rebounded, and she developed real feelings of warmth toward one particular Indian couple, Sally and Old Joe. However, a distance always remained. Phoebe was most comfortable dealing with Indians as servants or when she adopted the role of a quasi-anthropological observer noting their "interesting customs." She thoroughly approved of the Indian school later established in Lynden, which trained young Indians "to be industrious farmers, tidy housekeepers and skillful needle women." She seems never to have considered the feelings of the young Indians forcibly removed from their own families, harshly required to learn alien and meaningless ways. Never-

theless, for her time, Phoebe Judson was an unusually open and toler-
ant person. Surely there were many western frontiers where, as in the
Nooksack Valley, Indians and whites lived peaceably together for long
periods of time. Women like Phoebe Judson were part of what made
that mutual accommodation possible.

Phoebe Judson also believed in women's rights. She praised the
Oregon Donation Land Act of 1851, which allowed married women to
claim 160 acres in addition to the husband's 160 as a "just and righteous law." In 1883–87, Washington Territory extended the suffrage to
its female citizens. Phoebe served on juries, worked on election boards,
and voted proudly, "not feeling any more out of my sphere than when
assisting my husband to develop the resources of our country." In 1888,
when women's suffrage was rescinded in Washington Territory,
Phoebe asserted that the rescission occurred because Washington
women, once enfranchised, had promptly passed local measures for
prohibition, alarming the liquor interests and many drinking men.
Washington women did not regain the right to vote until 1910. In the
meantime, voteless Phoebe Judson looked on helpless in horror as
saloons opened in her "fair Lynden." Prohibition, very much a
"women's issue" in the late nineteenth century, was a major topic in the
women's suffrage campaigns of the Pacific Northwest. Suffrage leader
Abigail Scott Duniway of Oregon always believed that women's vigorous promotion of prohibition harmed the suffrage cause, and the
Washington experience certainly seemed to prove her point.[3]

Many of the most interesting parts of this reminiscence are subjects
that fell into "woman's special sphere" as nineteenth-century Americans defined it. The concern with personal relationships, both with
family and with the Indians, the issue of women's rights (infrequently
mentioned in men's memoirs), and much of the domestic detail are
characteristically female. One reason to republish Phoebe Judson's
account, then, is to "round out the record" so that the female side of the
pioneering experience becomes more widely known. But there are
other reasons as well. Above all, in the pages of this reminiscence we
have the opportunity to meet a kindly, cheerful, and observant woman.
We can all enjoy Phoebe Judson's charming and informative account of
her search for her "ideal home."

Notes

1. John Unruh, *The Plains Across* (Urbana: University of Illinois Press,
1979), p. 120.

2. Kent Richards, *Isaac I. Stevens, Young Man in a Hurry* (Provo, Utah:
Brigham Young University Press, 1979), pp. 181–272.

3. Ruth Moynihan, *Rebel for Rights: Abigail Scott Duniway* (New Haven:
Yale University Press, 1983), pp. 131–47, 206–19.

PREFACE

The manuscript written by Mrs. Judson telling of her trip across the plains and mountains to the Pacific, with the perils and hardships that attended such a trek in the early fifties, together with her pioneering experiences in the new land has been read with keen interest and appreciation by her friends. Others have sought it for the rich fund of historical data interwoven with the life story of this remarkable woman. It was the opinion of all that this manuscript, limp and worn by much passing around and reading and re-reading, should be preserved in a more durable form. Hence this book.

All who read the manuscript marveled at the facility with which this pioneer woman, in the evening of a long life of hardship and toil, had turned to the pen and written a narrative of such high literary merit and compelling interest.

These memoirs of Phoebe Judson profess to tell the story of an ordinary woman, but unwittingly reveal a most extraordinary character. Her fine Christian spirit and inherent refinement were never dimmed by the rough life that surrounded her in the primitive days before civilization came to the West.

It is a fortunate people whose civic foundation was laid by such indomitable Christian spirits as the author of this book.

*—By an Appreciative Reader of the
Original Manuscript.*

A PIONEER'S SEARCH
for AN IDEAL HOME

CHAPTER I

It is the oft repeated inquiry of my friends as to what induced me to bury myself more than fifty years ago in this far-off corner of the world, that has determined me to take my pen in hand at this late day.

Did I come around the Horn, cross the Isthmus, or come across the plains? Was I not afraid of the Indians, and much more they ask. So I have decided to answer them all and singly by writing a short history of our pioneer life, and to affectionately dedicate my book to the memory of the late Holden A. Judson, my dear husband, who journeyed with me for half a century in the wilderness.

This will be but a condensed narrative of events which I shall endeavor to recall out of the mists of the past, written with no attempt at literary display, containing no fiction, but simply a record of the homely, everyday incidents of a plain woman, who has now exceeded her three score years and ten, and who has roughed it in the early fifties on the extreme northwestern frontier.

Time has passed so rapidly I can scarcely realize that I have already attained the number of years allotted to mortals on earth.

The romance of frontier life beyond the confines of civilization with its varied, exciting and interesting experiences among the children of nature—both human and brute —has caused the years to fly swiftly, as on the wings of the wind.

If I am permitted to occupy the body that has served me well for so many years until this chronicle is completed, I shall be satisfied, and consider my work upon this planet finished.

Our pioneer story begins where love stories (more is the pity) frequently terminate, for Holden Allen Judson and Phoebe Newton Goodell had been joined in the holy bonds of matrimony three years before we decided to emigrate to the vast and uncultivated wilderness of Puget Sound, which at that time was a part of Oregon.

Little did I realize how much it meant when I promised the solemn, but kindly faced, minister in the presence of a large assembly of friends, to obey, as well as to love, the one whom I had chosen for a partner through life, for the thought of becoming a pioneer's wife had never entered my mind; but it is not surprising that a girl of only seventeen summers, romantically inclined, should have chosen from among her suitors one possessing a spirit of adventure.

Mr. Judson was five years my senior. Seldom were two more congenially mated to travel the rough voyage of life. Both were endowed with vigorous health, fired with ambition and a love of nature.

Our childhood days were spent together in the little town of Vermillion, Ohio, located midway between Cleveland and Sandusky, on the shores of Lake Erie, on whose beaches we strolled, and on whose blue waters we sailed in company, little dreaming our future lives were destined to be passed together on the far away shore of Puget Sound.

We attended the same church and the same district school. It was "Hopkins' choice," for there was only one of each in town. These two buildings stood side by side.

The motive that induced us to part with pleasant associations and the dear friends of our childhood days, was to obtain from the government of the United States a grant of land that "Uncle Sam" had promised to give to the head of each family who settled in this new country. This, we hoped, would make us independent, for as yet we did not possess a home of our own—all of which meant so much to us that we were willing to encounter dangers, endure hardships and privations in order to secure a home that we might call "ours."

The many air castles that I built concerning my "ideal home" while the preparations for our long journey were being made, are still fresh in my memory.

It should be built by a mountain stream that flowed to the Pacific, or by some lake, or bay, and nothing should obstruct our view of the beautiful snow-capped mountains.

True, it would be built of logs, but they would be covered with vines and roses, while the path leading to it should be bordered with flowers and the air filled with their sweet perfume.

> "*Home, home, sweet home;*
> *Be it ever so humble,*
> *There's no place like home.*"

My parents had already found a home on the banks of the Willamette, in Oregon.

The parting with my husband's parents and only sister was very affecting, as he was their only son and brother, and our little two-year-old Annie their idol.

The time set for our departure was March 1st, 1853. Many dear friends gathered to see us off. The tender "good-byes" were said with brave cheers in the voices, but many tears from the hearts. After we were seated in the stage that was to carry us forth on the first part of our journey into the "wide, wide world," little Annie put out her hands and asked "Fazzer," as she called her grandpapa, to take her. He begged us to leave her with them—mother and Lucretia seconding his request with tearful eyes. Her sweet young life was interwoven with theirs, and well I knew the anguish that rent their hearts at the parting with their little darling. Deeply we sympathized with them in their grief, but how could we part with our only treasure?

Amid the waving of handkerchiefs and the lingering "God bless you" the stage rolled away—and we were embarked on our long and perilous journey.

Our route lay along the lake shore road as we journeyed, and as the distance increased between our loved ones—father, mother, sister and the dear home environments, my heart grew heavy. I realized we were for the last time gazing upon the waters of beautiful Lake Erie, upon whose sandy beaches I, with my twin sister, had whiled away many, many happy hours gathering the little periwinkles and other shells, or rowing upon its placid waters; never tiring of watching the steamers and other vessels sail into the harbor, or hastening to the islands of Put In Bay for protection in time of storm.

These beautiful islands were a place of resort, and also of renown—steamers making many delightful "picnic" excursions to the place where Commodore Perry captured the British fleet, about which he sent the famous laconic message to General Harrison, "We have met the enemy, and they are ours."

My mind was occupied with many sad reflections until we reached Sandusky City, where we boarded the train for Cincinnati. 'Twas here we parted with my dear brother, William, who had accompanied us this far on our journey. From my car window I saw he was weeping, while I could scarcely refrain from sobbing aloud. He was but two years my senior, and we were both much attached to each other. He was married a few days before our departure, that we might attend his wedding, and with his young wife emigrated to this coast the following year.

Riding on the train was a new experience for me—the interest and novelty of the trip served in a measure to alleviate the sadness of parting. It was before the day of fast trains, and, though owing to my inexperience, we seemed to be moving very rapidly, the trip consumed the entire day; and it was long after dusk when we reached Cincinnati. The depot was some distance from our hotel and the deafening rattle of the cab wheels over the cobble stones frightened little Annie, and she cried piteously to be carried back home.

The hotel accommodations were luxurious. As we rested in the pleasant parlor a short time before retiring to our rooms, a lady played the piano and sang that pathetic song, "The Old Folks at Home."

The sentiment of the sweet old song harmonized with my feelings and caused the tears to flow afresh, as I thought of the dear father and mother we had left in their lonely home. The music soothed Annie's fears. She sat in my lap and talked about poor "Fazzer, mozzer and Aunt Trecia," as she called them, until she fell asleep.

In the morning we boarded a steamer. I have forgotten her name, but she was a floating palace for those days, and was loaded with passengers bound for the "far west."

We steamed rapidly down the Ohio and up the Mississippi. The pleasure of this voyage would have been without alloy, but the third day little Annie was taken very ill, and for a time we were much alarmed; but with simple remedies and good nursing she recovered without the aid of a physician.

The deafening whanging and banging of the gong startled us from our slumbers in the morning, calling us to a bountifully spread table. We greatly enjoyed the luxurious meals with which we were served on these river boats.

To while away the time, many of the passengers indulged in dancing and simple games of cards, which seemed innocent amusements; but after awhile, to my horror, I learned that others were gambling—risking their fortunes, many times beggaring their innocent families by a single throw of the dice. Although there were no bloody affrays on the boat, still I knew that gambling frequently led to murders, and the iniquity of this awful practice filled my soul with terror and I was in constant dread that the vengeance of an angry God would be visited upon us, by the blowing up, or sinking, of the boat, with all on board. My religious training had taught me fear, instead of trust. My heart was filled with thankfulness when we reached St. Louis in safety, where we remained but one day and night.

Transferring our baggage to the little steamer "Kansas," we began the ascent of the Missouri river, which we found was a very difficult and dangerous stream to navigate. Only light draft steamers were able to stem the current of its turbulent waters and make their way around the many jams and snags with which it was obstructed, and over the logs which made the little steamer bend and creak as though she was breaking in two. Our progress was slow and we were ten long days in reaching our destination, feeling greatly relieved when we disembarked at what was then called "Kansas Landing," where now stands the large and flourishing city of Kansas City.

A number of our fellow travelers, who were emigrating to California and Oregon, went on to Council Bluff to purchase their "outfit" for the journey over the plains. They urged us to go on with them, which would have pleased us well, for they were enterprising and intelligent people, with congenial qualities, well fitting them for good citizens in a new country. But we were only too glad to leave the muddy Missouri.

We had made our arrangements, before leaving home, to purchase our outfit for our journey at this place, which seems quite providential, for the news came to us here that the steamer Kansas struck a snag and sank before reaching her destination—the unfortunate emigrants losing all of their baggage.

We were thankful to get this far without accident, not knowing what lay before us. We little realized this was a pleasure trip in comparison with the journey across the plains.

CHAPTER II

The emigrant rendezvous was at a small trading post called West Port, two miles from the landing, but is now included in the great city of Kansas City. Here we found a comfortable boarding place, where all the work was performed by slaves. Eggs were only five cents per dozen, and were served to us in some shape at every meal by the black waiters. The cook was a large, good-natured negress, who prepared all the food in a little shanty separated from the main building, where she lived with her husband and pickaninnies.

This was my first, and only, experience in a slave state, and as "Uncle Tom's Cabin" had just been published, my sympathies were so strongly excited in behalf of the poor slaves in their hopeless bondage, and consequent afflictions, that I became engaged in some warm discussions with the landlady of the hotel.

Here we were occupied five weeks in making the final preparations for our journey. Mr. Judson ordered our wagon made with a projection on each side of one foot in width, which enabled us to cord up our bed in the back end and to stow away our provisions under it, leaving room in front for our cooking utensils, where they would be convenient to lift out and into the wagon.

Straps were attached to the hoops, overhead, for the rifle. Our wagon cover was made of white cotton drilling, which I lined with colored muslin to subdue the light and heat of the sun while crosing the desert plains.

Cattle were brought here for sale from New Mexico. Mr. Judson purchased two yoke of well broken oxen, and a cow. A young Scandinavian who had offered to go with us and help to drive the team, to which we had consented, bought two yoke of unbroken steers for leaders.

We now considered ourselves fully equipped and in readines to roll out to the emigrant road and join some company, without the most remote idea as to who would be our fellow travelers, when one day, while arranging things in the wagon to make it, if possible, more "home-like," two gentlemen came to us and introduced themselves as Revs. Gustavus Hines and Harvey Hines, brothers, Methodist missionaries from New York. On hearing the name of Gustavus Hines we surmised at once that he was the author of a history of Oregon in which we were much interested before leaving home, and upon inquiry found we were not mistaken. He informed us that he was returning to Oregon with his family, accompanied by his two brothers and their families, and were camping out while waiting for a better growth of grass.

When they invited us to join their company we were much pleased and gladly accepted their invitation. Mr. Judson and young Nelson managed, after many vain attempts, to yoke the cattle, hitch them to the wagon, and drive around to the door of our boarding place, where Annie and myself were waiting to take possession of this house on wheels, that was to be our abode for a number of months.

After bidding "good-bye" to our landlady and the black waiters, who had been very kind to us, and in whom we had become much interested, we climbed up over the heavy wheels, entered our tiny house and were off, headed for Hines' camp.

The greater portion of our journey across the plains seems more like a dream than reality, but this, my first ride in a "prairie schooner," is as fresh in my memory as though it had occurred yesterday.

The yoke of leaders were wild steers and were bent on running away. For a time all four yoke were on the stampede. Mr. Judson on one side of the team and Nelson on the other made free use of their great ox goads, and succeeded in controlling them. I held on to little Annie with one hand and the wagon hoops with the other, while she was struggling to hold a pet kitten in her lap; and the old cow that was hitched to the back end of the wagon, in her vain efforts to keep it from moving forward, shook her bell furiously.

Although much amused at the novelty of the experience, we were somewhat relieved to reach Hines' camp without further accident than the loss of Annie's pet kitten, over which she was much grieved.

Hines' camp was on a lovely prairie in the Indian Territory. The hills were green and dotted with cattle. The absence of human dwellings and the improvements of civilization made the scene one of a wild, weird nature, to which we must now become accustomed.

The three Hines brothers and their families, together with another New York family by the name of Bryant, gave us a hearty welcome.

There were three young ladies in the company. One, the daughter of Jeddadiah Hines, the eldest of the three brothers, and the other two were sisters of the wives of the younger brothers. And then there was Lucy Ann Lee, the sweet ten-year-old child of Rev. Jason Lee. The little one

was bereft of its mother when a tiny babe, and her father
died soon after. She was fortunate in finding loving and
devoted parents in Gustavus Hines and his wife, who
adopted her as their own. Lucy Ann's father and mother
were among the first missionaries to Oregon.

We had but three small children in the company, Alta
and Lee Bryant and Annie Judson. Alta and Annie were
of the same age and proved loving companions during the
journey. Three young men completed our number.

Before breaking camp, another family by the name of
Leonard, from Missouri, joined the "caravan," but only
remained with us a few days.

It was now the first of May—two months since we left
home, and we were becoming impatient to get started on
our journey "over the plains."

CHAPTER III

At length, early one bright morning, our camp became a scene of great commotion. The final preparations for our departure were in progress. Tents were taken down, tin dishes and cooking utensils were packed away. Men were excitedly running to and fro, hallooing at the cattle, who decidedly objected to being caught, as if they suspected what was before them—as some of them were unbroken steers, and there was not a practical ox driver in the crowd. With much difficulty they were finally collected, yoked and attached to the wagons.

The sunbonneted women watched the operations with intense interest, patiently awaiting the time to move forward.

It was nearly noon before the whole train, consisting of six wagons, each drawn by four yoke of oxen, one carriage drawn by a span of mules, and a band of loose cattle driven by the young men on horseback, were ready to begin the journey. At last the teamsters began shouting "gee Tom," "haw Buck," "up there Tom and Jerry,' with various other names they had given to their oxen—and the start was made.

What a sense of relief possessed our hearts as the heavy wheels made their first revolution on the forward march.

Each advanced step of the slow, plodding cattle carried us farther and farther from civilization into a desolate, barbarous country, where for several months we would be at the mercy of the treacherous savage. But our "new home" lay beyond all this and was a shining beacon that beckoned us on, inspiring our hearts with hope and courage.

This hope was mingled with fear, for I had many forebodings, with but little trust in those days that "He who gives his angels charge over us, would keep us in all our days." I could only hope that we would get through safely, and was much gratified that we were at length en-route for Puget Sound—our watchword "Westward Ho!" A few hours' travel brought us to Kansas river crossing, just at nightfall, where we camped on its banks, amid the cottonwood trees. As we were in the forests, the horses and mules were tethered to the trees, and the cattle gathered into a body and guarded by the men to prevent their straying.

The men soon had the tents pitched, and the cheering blaze of the camp fires cast their fantastic shadows high among the dark cottonwoods. Our bed was so comfortably arranged that we preferred sleeping in our wagons.

I prepared the food in the wagon, then passed it down to Mr. Judson, who cooked it over the camp fire. When the bacon was fried and the tea steeped our meal was ready. A flat top trunk in the front of the wagon served as our dining table, and the foot of the bed for seats for Annie and myself. Mr. Judson and Nelson made themselves as comfortable as possible on the front board of the wagon.

There was but little sleep in the camp that night. The novelty and excitement of our environments drove slumber from our eyelids. My excited nerves kept me wide awake; the shouting of the men to the cattle, and the jingling ox chains on our journey during the day still rang in my ears, mingled with the noises of the camp, the steady tread of the guard, the stamping of the horses, the continued, though subdued movement all through the camp, and the occasional braying of the mules—all combined, were not conducive to sleep.

Oh, those mules; every tortured nerve of my being cried out in protest as their ear-splitting brayings rent the air. Our camp lay on the reservation of the Delaware Indians, who owned the ferry.

The next morning we, the women and children, with the wagons, were safely ferried across, while the men swam the stock. This was a difficult undertaking and not without dangers, as the river was much swollen by the melting snow, being about three hundred yards wide at this point, with a very rapid current.

One of our large wheel oxen, in some way, got one foot over the yoke. We were afraid he would drown; it seemed almost impossible for him to escape that fate, but greatly to our joy he managed to swim out, in spite of his awkward position.

Years after, while recalling this incident, I attributed this remarkable feat to "old Tom," but Mr. Judson said no, it was "old Jerry." Well, it does not matter, they were both faithful creatures, and we depended more upon them than any other yoke in our team to carry us safely over the rough and dangerous places, for they were very large, strong and obedient.

It was nearly night before the arduous task of swimming the stock was accomplished, and with thankful hearts we again took up our line of march, only traveling one mile, when the falling shades of night compelled us once more to make our camp among the cottonwood trees that fringed the Kansas. Although still among friendly Indians, we

were obliged to guard our stock to keep them from straying. In spite of our vigilance, the mules made their escape from the camp. It was two days before they were restored to us by a friendly Indian, named "Grey Eyes"—
he had tracked them twelve miles. Though my nerves rejoiced in the absence of their discordant voices, I' was
pleased that their owners did not suffer loss. Only six
miles of our journey had thus been accomplished. Here
the organization of our company was affected.

Gustavus Hines was elected captain; we could not have
made a better choice. As a leader, he was qualified by experience, and his personal appearance and manners commanded our admiration and respect, inspiring our little
band with hope and courage. When leading the train,
mounted on a magnificent gray horse, I looked upon him
more as a general than a captain—often mentally compar-
ing him to General Winfield Scott. On him devolved the
duty of selecting our camping places. On Saturdays he
was particularly careful to select a suitable situation for
our Sabbath encampment, which would afford water and
grass for our cattle, these being of the first importance.

Our route for the first hundred miles lay westward, up
the Kansas river, away from the great line of emigrant
travel. During the first week we crossed four small rivers,
the Kansas, the Stranger, Soldier and Grasshopper.

Over the last named river our wagons and provisions
were carried in a very large canoe. The entire day was
consumed in the tedious operation of unloading, crossing
and reloading the wagon.

CHAPTER IV

The first Sabbath of our journey over the plains found us encamped on a beautiful rolling prairie, covered with a luxuriant carpet of grass, as green as a meadow. The wide spreading plains, as far as the eye could reach, presented a picturesque scene—whose silent beauty awakened solemn thoughts—that impressed one with awe and reverence. Here we were isolated from the world, and in this secluded, romantic spot we were free to worship our Maker according to the dictates of our conscience. It is Emerson who says, "We are as much strangers to nature as we are aliens from God."

Only one incident occurred to mar the harmony of the day of rest. Our Missouri family, though good Methodists at home, seemed to think they could not afford to keep the Sabbath day holy while traveling on the plains. When they found they could not prevail upon our good captain to break the Sabbath, they gathered up their stock, and, after saying "good-bye," pulled out." We were sorry to have them leave us, as they had the appearance of being a very nice family. Mr. Judson and I were as much opposed to camping two nights in the same place as they were, and our fears greatly inclined us to go with them, but we decided to abide by the decision of our captain, in whom we had much confidence, and afterward during our long journey were very thankful that we were so providentially led into his company.

During the week our men had been very busily employed driving their oxen, yoking and unyoking their cattle, standing guard at night, unloading and reloading the wag-

ons at the ferries, and swimming the stock. Saturday night
found them very tired and much in need of physical rest, so
they lolled around in the tents and on their blankets spread
on the grass, or under the wagons out of the sunshine,
seeming to realize that the "Sabbath was made for man."

But the women, who had only been anxious spectators
of their arduous work, and not being weary in body, could
not fully appreciate physical rest, and were rendered more
uneasy by the continual passing of emigrant trains all day
long—most of them much larger than our own. To me,
much of the day was spent in meditating over the past and
in forebodings for the future. In my reveries I was carried
back home to my childhood days, and listened to the waves
of beautiful Lake Erie as they softly lapped the sandy
beach. I saw the barefooted children splashing in its lim-
pid waters. Happy children; childhood days are only too
short. The snowballs and lilacs in mother's yard were in
full bloom; how lovely they looked. The ringing of the
church bell greeted my ear, and in fancy I joined the
throng that wended its way to the church, and, ascending
the flight of stairs that led to the gallery, mingled my voice
as of yore with the choir in singing Old Hundred, Corona-
tion, Boylston, and other grand old tunes. At the singing
of each song the whole congregation rose to their feet,
turned in their pews in order to face the choir, and listened
attentively to the music. When again seated, the minister,
with a dignified air and solemn countenance, arose in the
pulpit (my father, the Rev. J. M. Goodall, pastor of the
Presbyterian church, arose in the pulpit)—and announced
his text: "Known unto God are all His works from the
beginning of the world." By the time he had finished his

discourse on creation, transgression, effectual calling, election, redemption, justification, adoption and sanctification —with all the benefits derived from firstly to last, I was aroused from my reverie, and, looking out upon God's glorious works of creation, concluded with Whittier "that the book, the church, the day, were made for man, not God, for earth, not heaven."

Although so remote from civilization and haunted by many fears of the calamities that might overtake us on our journey through the wilderness, we passed a very pleasant day. It gave us a better opportunity to become acquainted with our fellow travelers.

Monday morning we were up bright and early, our men much refreshed by their day of rest, and all were in fine spirits. After camp duties were performed and the oxen yoked and attached to the wagons, we were ready to jog along on our journey.

By the departure of our Missouri family our train was reduced to five wagons, and each took its turn in leading the train, like an old fashioned spelling class—the one that was head at night took its place at the foot next morning.

In a few hours we reached the Big Blue river and were somewhat crestfallen when we found there were several large trains ahead of us awaiting their turn to be ferried over. The facilities for crossing were so inadequate that we were detained five days, awaiting our turn to be ferried over.

The time seemed long to wait, and I, for one, was quite impatient at the delay, but not a murmur was heard censuring "our Moses," who, no doubt, had he known the situation, would have made another day's travel and not allowed so many trains to pass us. There was nothing for us to do but "possess our souls in patience" and wait.

One would naturally suppose that traveling after the slow, plodding cattle would have been sufficient to thoroughly inculcate that Christ-like quality, but it was evident, at least in our case, that additional lessons were required. So here we were, mixed up with other trains in the greatest confusion on the sandy banks of the Blue, where a perfect bedlam reigned. Men hallooing from one side of the river to the other, cattle bellowing, calves bawling, and a woman on the opposite side of the river screaming at the top of her voice, "Oh, papa, mam says them cows can't swim with their bags full of milk." The poor woman was nearly frantic for fear the cows would drown. The prolonged sound of the "O" indicated that they were western people, or at least were not Yankees.

Many trains were distinguished by having the names of their states painted on the covers of their wagons, and some were loaded with "a right smart chance of truck," with many of the belongings of its inmates dangling from the outside.

The women and children of each train were ferried over on the flatboat with the wagons, where they anxiously awaited the swimming of the stock. The river was much swollen from the melting snow, and it seemed utterly impossible to drive the poor, dumb brutes into the cold water of the rapid stream.

Our captain finally devised a successful plan which proved a solution of the difficulty. Placing three young calves on the stern of the ferry boat, he huddled the cattle together on the bank, and when the boat started the calves bawled for their mothers, who plunged into the river after them—the other cattle following. They were all soon over on the opposite bank of the river, when a shout of victory went up for the shrewd "Yankee" captain.

One of the Missourians was so pleased with this successful scheme of the captain that he gave utterance to this encouraging prophecy, "You ones will git to Oregon," which implied that he had some lingering doubts that the others would attain the goal of their ambition.

The expense of the ferriage was three dollars per wagon, but we did not stop to parley—we were only too glad to take up our line of march again at any price.

CHAPTER V

All were in fine spirits and we were making good time, when all at once, just as we were about to camp on a little creek for our noon lunch, every spoke in the hind wheel of Harvey Hines' wagon gave away at once. "There," ruefully remarked my husband, "is one wagon already that will have to be left behind." But the owner of the wagon had not given up hope. After dinner he went up the creek to a thicket of ash which we had passed a short time before and brought some of the wood to the camp, with which, and the aid of willing hands, he had the wheel filled, and the tire reset ready to resume our journey with thankful hearts in the morning.

The prairie over which we moved so slowly with our horned steeds was covered with a coat of living green. Springs of pure, cold water came bubbling forth from ravines in abundance. An occasional patch of timber, snow-capped mountains, lake or bay, I fancied, until we had experienced one of the terrific thunder storms and hurricanes peculiar to that locality, would have made it the "ideal home" of my dreams.

So far we had been free from the fear of Indians. We had passed through the territory occupied by three tribes— the Shawnees, Delawares and the Potawotamies, all of whom were friendly. One of the Delawares had been the faithful guide of the explorer, Fremont. He was with him when his party was so nearly annihilated by a treacherous tribe.

This same friendly Indian kindly warned our captain to beware of the Pawnees, as we were now entering their territory, which lay between the Blue and Republican rivers. Now that we had entered the Pawnees' hunting grounds, it behooved us to exercise great vigilance. Our company was so small that two of our men had to take their turn standing guard six hours every other night. Each was armed with a rifle and revolver, which they kept in readiness for instant use, in case of attack. We kept aloof from the great body of emigrants, that we might have the advantage of the little patches of grass and pools of water that lay along our way—which enabled us to advance more rapidly than in a larger company.

One night, while encamped in a rather exposed place, and all were asleep, with the exception of the guard, we were suddenly aroused from our slumbers by the stampeding of our stock. Oxen, cows and horses came rushing "pell mell" through the camp, making a terrifying noise which threw us into the wildest consternation. The men rushed after the frightened animals, and fortunately found there were none missing. The Indians, after they had stampeded them, were foiled in their purpose of securing any. They are cowardly, and seldom fight without a decided advantage in position and numbers. After this alarm we were more vigilant in watching for these stealthy miscreants, for pitiable indeed would have been our plight had they succeeded in capturing our teams.

Not long after our first alarm, while all were enjoying a sermon from our captain on a fine Sabbath day, and at the same time keeping an eye out for the stock, which were feeding but a short distance away, Indians were spied crawling stealthily upon them. For that once the "Doxology" was omitted, and our men went full speed after them, with their firearms—in time to save them from stampeding. These alarming incidents were quite frequent in this region of the country.

A few more days of travel, going through the same monotonous line of camp duties, brought us to the Platte river valley. We made our encampment opposite Grand Island, some ten miles below Fort Kearney, whose adobe building could be seen in the distance, and as this was the first land mark of importance it was a satisfaction to know we had reached this noted point in our journey.

The river extended at the head of the island into a broad, shallow stream, flowing over a bed of sand, making the water very roily. We were compelled to allow it to settle before using. We found water and grass in abundance, but wood was very scarce, except in places near the margin of the river. The river bottom land was so soft and muddy that we were in constant fear of losing our teams, and for many days the cool north wind made traveling very unpleasant.

As our guide book pointed to the places where we would be obliged to make our camp without wood, we managed to carry a few sticks along with us—just enough to boil the coffee and fry the bacon. When out of bread we made "hard tack" and crackers take its place.

How much we missed our camp fires at night in these cheerless places, not only for culinary purposes, but to brighten the dreariness of the way. But my sympathies were more with our men, who were wading through the mud and sloughs, day after day, driving their teams. There seemed but little rest for them night or day, except when we were camped for the Sabbath.

Buffaloes were often seen at a distance, in droves, but we had no time to capture them. One day we were so fortunate as to come across two that had been slain by the train ahead of us, and as they had carried away but a small portion, we helped ourselves and left an abundant supply for the next train. Our buffalo steak compared favorably with beef, and better relished on account of it being the first fresh meat we had tasted since we began our journey.

Antelopes were frequently seen, but were so fleet of foot we did not get a shot at them.

The captain's youngest brother, Rev. Harvey K. Hines, who possessed a daring spirit of adventure, wandered off one pleasant afternoon, accompanied by a young man of the train. Ascending a high hill they were lured so far away by the grandeur of the scenery that on their return they were overtaken by darkness, and it was midnight before they found their way into camp, where we were still up, anxiously waiting with lanterns on the wagons for beacon lights. Mr. Hines found his young wife in tears, and indeed we were all terror stricken for fear they had been captured by the Pawnees. This was the only time that any of our party ventured on so hazardous an expedition.

CHAPTER VI

For many days we traveled in sight of long emigrant trains on the opposite side of the river, and we judged that the heaviest portion of the emigration was on the north side of the Platte, which made it all the better for our stock. The white tops of these "prairie schooners" creeping so slowly in the distance reminded me of the sailing vessels that I had so often seen on Lake Erie, beating against a light head wind. They were the trains that had fitted out at Council Bluffs, and I presume were making as good time as ourselves.

On reaching the south fork of the Platte we found that the river was rising caused by the melting snows from the Rocky mountains, and was one and a half miles wide. Many of the trains went farther up the river before crossing, but our captain concluded it was best to cross here. We were obliged to double teams, making eight yoke of oxen to each wagon. The beds of the wagons were raised a number of inches by putting blocks under them. When all was in readiness we plunged into the river, taking a diagonal course. It required three quarters of an hour to reach the opposite shore. After starting in we never halted a moment, for fear of sinking in the quicksand, of which there was much danger. We found the river so deep in places that, although our wagon box was propped nearly to the top of the stakes, the water rushed through it like a mill race, soaking the bottom of my skirts and deluging our goods. The necessity of doubling the teams for each wagon required three fordings, consequently by the time the last wagon was brought across the whole day was consumed. Thankful were we when night found us all safely encamped on the west side of the Platte, where we remained a day in order to dry our goods.

One of the dreaded obstacles on the journey had been successfully overcome, and we proceeded on our way up the valley of the North Platte with lighter hearts. We found the water, if possible, more roily than that of the South Platte.

Most melancholy indeed was the scene revealed as we journeyed through this valley—the road was lined with a succession of graves. These lonely resting places were marked with rude head boards, on which were inscribed their names, and "Died of cholera, 1852."

Many of these graves bore the appearance of being hastily made. Occasionally we passed one marked "killed by lightning," which was not surprising to us after having witnessed one of the most terrific thunder storms it had been our fortune to experience. This storm broke upon us after we had retired for the night. One after another, terrific peals of thundred rending the heavens in quick succession, roaring, rolling and crashing around, above and below, accompanied by blinding flashes of lightning, illuminating our wagons with the brightness of noonday, while the rain came beating down upon our wagon covers in great sheets. It was simply awful. Annie cried piteously to be "carried back home of Fazzer's house."

Our guard, being insufficiently protected, fled to the camp. The captain and his brother, having gum coats and everything necessary for such an emergency, sallied forth, and by indefatigable efforts succeeded in keeping the frightened animals from stampeding. I have often thought of this noble deed of these courageous missionaries braving the terrors of that appalling storm for the welfare of the company who were sheltering themselves as best they could from the raging elements.

In the morning we found there was not a head of our stock missing, while other trains that were camped near us had allowed theirs to be scattered for miles away. Our bedding and clothing were as wet as water could make them, but the sun came out brightly in the morning, and we were again compelled to lay over a day to dry them.

In many places along the route we found the water so strongly impregnated with an alkaline substance as to make it poisonous for both man and beast. Having reached a place of this description one Saturday night, we continued our journey, for the first time, on the Sabbath, and as we crept wearily along the dreary way not a stick, stone, bird or flower to break the monotony—the cattle poking along more slowly than usual on account of being deprived of their day of rest, we were suddenly surprised by seeing a great buffalo coming directly towards the train. Crossing the road in front of Harvey Hines' team, that was in the lead, Harvey seized his rifle with the intention of killing it. The wagons were simultaneously halted, as we waited for the shot; but before Mr. Hines could pull the trigger his wife reminded him that it was the "Sabbath," and he immediately returned the rifle to its place. Mr. Judson sarcastically remarked "He would not have hit it anyhow." Mr. Bryant's dog chased the buffalo out of sight, and we proceeded on our way, passing down into a grove of ash trees, appropriately named "Ash Hollow," where flowed a sparkling rivulet, from whose transparent waters we were delighted to drink.

How refreshed and comforted we were by our sojourn in this beautiful spot, for here we remained a whole day, while Mr. Hines reset his tire.

The dearth of timber along our route heightened our appreciation of this beautiful grove. I love the timber, and this beautiful wooded spot in a prairie country will never be effaced from my memory.

CHAPTER VII

Coming down again onto the river bottom, we passed a row of twenty graves. By the inscriptions on the rough head boards we learned that they died within a few days of each other of cholera. This dreadful scourge brought the journey of many poor emigrants to a sudden close, resulting in numerous pathetic incidents.

It was my privilege in after years to become acquainted with a refined lady who had buried her husband here, and she, besides caring for her two little children, drove her team through to the coast, and did as much, and more, than many of the men in helping to develop a new country.

A mother was also buried here, leaving five helpless children, the youngest only six weeks old. The father brought the little family safely through, and they lived to become useful citizens of this country. The sight of this little cemetery, so isolated and lonely, brought many gloomy reflections. Death to me was a shocking event, even at home, attended by all that love could devise to take away its gloom, and the thought of burying one of my dear ones here, or of myself being left by the wayside where only the savages and wild animals roamed, was awful to contemplate. I had yet to learn that the mystery which we call death is but a transition of the spiritual from the mortal, and it matters but little where the body lies; buried on the mountain top, in the briny deep, or consumed by fire, it is of no more account than the shell, or chrysalis, from which the bird or butterfly have flown; for we shall be clothed with a glorious spiritual body and be more ourselves than ever before. "I go away," said Jesus, "that I may come again," but the story of "the women was an idle tale."

And so we find it today, those who are immersed only in material things of this world are "slow to believe."

The next noted land mark to which we came was Chimney Rock, the tall chimney having been in view, and seemingly quite near, for several days, the peculiarity of the atmosphere causing distances to be quite deceptive. We camped within two miles of it, giving a number of our party the pleasure of paying a moonlight visit to this curious freak of nature, with its chimney-like shaft rising to a height of one hundred feet.

These land marks indicated our progress and helped to break the monotony—like the mile stones along the journey of life, there was one less to pass.

We were now nearing the territory of the Sioux Indians, and we shortly passed several of their villages, of more than a hundred lodges each. Many of the braves were parading around, fancifully arrayed in their Indian toggery, with an air of great independence—the buffalo, which constituted their wealth, being very plentiful at that time.

We camped over Sunday by a little creek on the suburbs of one of these little Indian cities. While our men and cattle were resting, some of the women improved the opportunity of making light bread, asserting that it was right to "do good on the Sabbath day." I baked my bread in a flat kettle, made expressly for the purpose, called a "Dutch oven," by heaping coals on the cover and underneath, replenishing when needed. Bread can be baked very nicely by this method. It was very light and I felt quite proud of my success. When done, I turned it out on the

grass to cool, while I attended to my housework in our
wagon home. Hearing the merry laughter of the children,
I glanced in that direction, and what was my dismay to
see little Annie standing on my precious loaf. I found
that she and little Alta Bryant had been having a most
enjoyable time rolling it on the grass.

The outcome of Mrs. Bryant's baking was even more
ludicrous. She set her sponge in the bread pan to rise and
left it in the wagon, where her little boy, less than two
years old, was sleeping, while she, with others, went for a
short stroll. When she returned to the wagon she found
her little boy in the bread pan, up to his knees in the dough.

Another incident transpired that day that I must not
forget to relate. While a party of Indians were pursuing a
band of buffalo, they surrounded them within plain view of
our encampment. The buffalo dashed around furiously
in a vain effort to get away, but to whatever point they
galloped they were met by the Indians, who were mounted
on active little ponies and armed with bows and arrows,
with which they slaughtered over thirty buffaloes. When
one would break through the circle it was quickly overtaken and brought down by the arrows of the dexterous
Sioux. This was a very exciting scene and greatly enjoyed,
especially by the men of our company.

The next river that we forded was the Laramie. This
river was narrow, but so deep that the water covered the
backs of the oxen. When across, we found ourselves at
Fort Laramie, another "landmark" on our journey, where
we remained two days and dried our goods. Here Mr.
Judson purchased a very fine buffalo robe, which added

much to our comfort in the cool region of the Rocky mountains.

After leaving Fort Laramie we began the ascent of the Black Hills. Our route over these hills was a perpetual succession of ups and downs, and the aspect of the country drearily barren. The soil was of a reddish clay, intermixed with fine, sharp stones. These stones cruelly crippled the feet of the oxen. Old Tom, one of our heavy wheel oxen, became quite lame for a time. The poor fellow was obliged to limp along, as it would not do to lay over among these barren hills.

Laramie Peak towered above the hills, and there patches of snow were visible.

CHAPTER VIII

We reached La Bonta Creek on Saturday, a little before sundown, and made our encampment on its banks, among the cottonwood trees, one of the most charming spots of the whole route, where we found good water, grass and wood—which was greatly appreciated.

The Sabbath dawned most serenely upon us, a bright, lovely morning, the twenty-sixth of June. I am certain of the date, for the day was made memorable to me by the birth of a son.

Monday morning our party were so considerate of my welfare, and that of the "new emigrant," that they proposed remaining in camp for a day or two. I assured them that we were both very comfortable, and, though reluctant to leave this most beautiful spot (the romantic birthplace of our baby boy) I urged them to proceed with the journey.

The next morning we found the name of Platt La Bonta inscribed on our wagon cover. The name was suggested by the captain in commemoration of the birthplace on La Bonta Creek, in the Platte valley.

The name did not exactly suit me, so we compromised by adopting half of it, adding his grandfather's name, Charles! so the little fellow took his place in the ranks of life under the name of Charles La Bonta Judson. Thirty years after his wife's sister, Miss Kathie Moore of York, Pennsylvania, wrote the following birthday verses for him.

A JUNE BIRTHDAY

One sweet and lovely summer-time in June,
One fair and tranquil day, near noon,
The great Creator thought a thought,
And lo! life's angel gladly brought
A baby boy on earth to dwell—
And thus it is the birthday fell
*   In June.*

Since then, in sweet array, the years
Have passed with far more smiles than tears;
But as some days are dark, some fair,
*   In June,*
So this life, too, held some of care;
Some rain-filled clouds have dimmed the sky—
But these drop blessings as they fly
*   In June.*

Still time goes swiftly on from June to June,
While blossoms grow and glad birds sing in tune;
And that the flow of future years
May bring thee nothing more of tears,
But that new joy may speed thy way—
Is my great wish for thy birthday
*   In June.*

Sunday evening who should come rolling into camp but the Missouri family who had left us on our first Sabbath encampment, because they feared to take the day for rest. We supposed they were at least one week in advance, but here they were, one day behind. Truly we had been favored by traveling with a company who believed in resting one day out of seven.

The captain decreed that our wagon should lead the train (although it was not our turn), saying if "our wagon was obliged to halt the rest would also."

It proved the roughest day's journey through the Black
Hills. The wind blew a perfect gale, and while going
down some of the rough sidling hills it seemed that the
wagon would capsize; but I had little to fear, for Mr. Judson had become an expert in handling his team. Some of
the ladies remarked that "he drove over the stones as carefully as though they were eggs."

When we halted for our noon lunch the ladies hurried
to our wagon with anxious inquiries. Are you alive? etc. I
quieted their fears by informing them that little "Bonta"
and I were doing finely—that Annie held on to her little
brother with both hands while going down the steepest hills,
for fear that he would roll out of bed among the pots and
kettles. Mr. Judson had buttoned and tied the wagon
covers down so closely that I could not get a peep out, and
I suffered but little inconvenience from the wind and dust.

During the week we crossed to the other side of the
Platte on a bridge owned by the Mormons, paying them
six dollars per wagon toll. Some of the trains refused to pay
so exhorbitant a price, but paid more dearly in the end,
by having their stock stolen from them by the Indians, who
no doubt were instigated by the owners of the bridge,
through a spirit of revenge.

The country over which we were passing was still a
succession of barren hills; but, as it was shut out from my
view I realized but little of its discomforts.

Saturday night found us at Willow Springs. Here a few
scattering willows were struggling for an existence in a
sandy desert, amid the gray sage and thorny cactus. The
name "Willow Springs" had a delightful sound, suggestive
of clear, purling water and grateful shade, but we were

greatly disappointed to find only a small amount of brakish water, compelling us to take up our onward march Sunday morning. Before night we came to the Sweet Water valley, and, turning to the right, we traveled about two miles from the road, where we found good grass for our stock and made our encampment by a stream of pure water, very close to the celebrated Independence Rock, where we proposed to remain over a day and celebrate the Fourth of July.

The morning broke brightly. The roaring of the cannon in our native country having failed to awaken us at the break of day, we had remained quietly, taking much needed rest. Awakening, greatly refreshed, we were now ready to enter upon the jollification of the day by a "picnic," the only method of celebrating that could be devised by our patriotic little band. We were isolated from all other trains, far from civilization, without the banner of our country to unfurl to the breeze, and there was no band of martial music to thrill us with its inspiring strains. But more loyal hearts never entered upon the festivities of the day with greater enthusiasm than did these pilgrim travelers through the wilderness. Each family contributed from their stores their very best.

I was able to sit in the little rocking chair my kind husband had thoughtfully purchased for my comfort the last thing before starting on our journey. An awning was attached to the side of our wagon to shelter the picnic party, and, with the curtains rolled up, seated in my little rocking chair, I gazed down upon the bountifully spread table and merry company surrounding it—heartily enjoying the delicacies constantly passed up to me.

The memory of the continual thoughtfulness of my fellow travelers to me glows with a brightness that can never be effaced. "Kind deeds can never die."

Our dinner was not so elaborate an affair as the customary Fourth of July dinners, but I doubt not was more keenly relished by all. As my readers may be curious as to our menu, I will give it: The crowning piece of the feast was a savory pie, made of sage hen and rabbit, with a rich gravy; the crust having been raised with yeast, was as light as a feather; cake of three varieties (fruit, pound and sponge), pickles, dried beef and preserves, rice pudding, beans and dried fruit. Beverages: tea, coffee, or pure cold water from the mountain stream, as we chose; while from the hearts glowed sparkling wit, in expressions of patriotic mirth well suited to the spirit of the day.

More than fifty of these national anniversaries have gone by since, but not one of them is so vividly portrayed upon my mind as the one celebrated by the little band of adventurers, so far from civilization. I imagine we must have been watched over and protected by an invisible army of the old Revolutionary soldiers, for "He giveth His angels charge over us to keep us in all our ways," or we could not have enjoyed ourselves with such a sense of safety in a barbarous country.

How remarkable that so many of the old patriots should have been translated from their worn out bodies on Independence day.

I stood by the bedside of my grandfather, William Goodell, a Revolutionary soldier, eighty-six years of age, as his spirit departed from the body, while the cannons were booming at sunrise, the morning of July fourth, 1842.

Thomas Jefferson, the author of the Declaration of Independence, expressed a desire "that he might live to see its fiftieth anniversary ushered in," and his prayer was granted. In company with John Adams, they took their light to the spiritual realms on that memorable day. "Independence forever," exclaimed President Adams, as he passed from mortal view amid the rejoicings and festivities of a whole nation.

In looking upon the map, I find Independence Rock located in the center of the state of Wyoming, very close to Rattlesnake Mountain. I little thought while camped by its side that I should ever be able to define its position in so enterprising a state as that of Wyoming.

Fremont, "the great pathfinder," described it in the report of his expedition of 1842 as "an isolated granite rock, 650 yards long and forty feet high." With the exception of a small depression at one place on the summit, where a little soil supports a scanty growth of shrubs, and one solitary dwarf pine, it is entirely bare. It is surrounded by level ground, from which it appears to have emerged, and everywhere within six or eight feet of the base, where the surface was sufficiently smooth, the rock is inscribed with the names of travelers, most of which were very legible.

He estimated the rock as being "one thousand miles from the Mississippi."

We had many reasons to rejoice that this distance had been accomplished without serious misfortune to any of our number.

CHAPTER IX

The fifth of July we reached another point of interest —the Devil's Gate, where the Sweetwater had cut its way through a spur of the mountain, rushing through a rocky gorge with perpendicular walls from three to four hundred feet high. Up these dangerous walls many foolhardy men had climbed, risking their lives for the mere pleasure, and supposed honor, of having their names inscribed upon these towering rocks. The larger portion of our party took time to inspect this place, so highly honored by the name of his satanic majesty. My curiosity was not at all excited, though I often concluded, when our way was rough and barren, that we must have traveled through his domain.

Passing over the ridge through which the river had cut its way, we again came into the valley of the Sweetwater, and had our first view of the Wind River mountains, whose snow-capped peaks glistened against the western sky in shining lengths, as though arranged by design. Humboldt estimates the tallest peak to be 13,567 feet high. It bears the name of "Fremont, the man of the empire."

We had many hills to pass over that bordered the river, which we forded twice, and found the water deep and cold. Ice formed in the camps, and banks of snow lay by the roadside, making the air so chilly that we were obliged to wear heavy wraps to keep from shivering. I managed to keep my baby warm by cuddling him closely to me in bed.

At noon, on the twelfth of July, we reached the highest altitude of the Rocky mountains. The ascent had been so gradual that it was difficult to distinguish the highest point.

From the beginning of our journey we had been wearily toiling on an upward grade, over vast prairies, up high hills, mounting higher and higher—not realizing the elevation to which we had attained, and now had nearly reached the region of the clouds, without being aware of the fact.

Many of the dangerous places which had loomed darkly before us were now things of the past. Safely upon this pinnacle, we could look down upon them as upon vanquished foes, with rejoicings, like those who have struggled for riches, fame and honor. When the pinnacle of success is reached, they look back upon the obstacles surmounted with a sense of pride and satisfaction.

But pride must take a fall, as we sadly realized, and all are sure to find the downhill grade is the hardest to travel.

The descent at first was so gradual as to be almost imperceptible, but became rougher and more precipitous as we proceeded on our journey. It was a satisfaction to know that we were now drinking from the waters that flowed to the Pacific. A number of great rivers have their source in this immediate vicinity—the Missouri, Colorado, Platte and Columbia.

Our first encampment on this side of the pass was made on the Dry Sandy, surely very appropriately named, for there was not a drop of water in the bed. We were obliged to dig down into the sand to obtain a little brackish water, and to drive our stock three or four miles up on the hillsides to find feed for them.

From the summit of the mountains to Green river our road led us through the most barren country of our experience, causing us much anxiety for our cattle. The nights were frosty, and the cold winds through the day made traveling very disagreeable. As we traveled along this barren ridge, Green river came frequently into view, flowing swiftly through the grassy plains. Cottonwoods waved their green branches by its silvery current. Our anticipation for the comfort of our cattle ran high. Already we could see them luxuriating on the succulent grass and slaking their thirst with the crystal waters.

Alas! for the poor cattle, when we reached the coveted spot, to our deep distress, the grassy plain proved to be but thorny cactus and bitter greasewood. Sadly we realized the truth set forth by the poet: "Distance lends enchantment to the view."

The river at this point was about three hundred feet wide and the swimming of the stock was only accomplished after many ineffectual efforts to drive the reluctant animals into the cold, rapid stream.

The great anxiety experienced by the emigrants at these river crossings can hardly be realized. The lives of our men were in constant danger, as they forded these perilous streams on horseback—swimming the stock.

The Mormons owned the ferry, and we were again compelled to pay six dollars per wagon for crossing. It was nearly night when all were safely across on the west side of the river and our oxen attached to the wagons, ready to move forward. Driving but a few miles, and then descending into a valley, it was our good fortune to come to a small stream called Slate creek, where we found an abundance of grass for our cattle, that had toiled hard all day without a mouthful to eat. And as our six days of labor had been faithfully performed, we encamped by the side of the rippling stream for a day of rest.

As I look back on the stream of time, the only places my memory recalls with pleasure while crossing the plains, are the ones where we found pure water and good grass for our cattle, and allowed them to rest over the Sabbath. When God made a day of rest for the welfare of man, I'm glad that He did not forget the poor, tired animals, and said, "Thou shalt not work thy ox." Had this commandment been observed, thousands of these poor creatures that were turned out by the roadside, in the sage brush and dust to die, would have been saved.

Memory vividly brings to view these patient servants of half a century ago. Our wheel oxen seemed more like rational beings than dumb brutes. The tears start as I see their great mild eyes, and think of the suffering they so patiently endured for our sake. It mattered not how tired, thirsty and hungry, when Mr. Judson lifted the yoke and said "come Tom and Jerry," they always came and obediently put their heads under the yoke. Buck and Berry were often found hidden away when it came yoking-up time, but they never shirked when pulling up the high hills and over the rough mountains. And as God was so merciful as to order a day of rest for them, He will surely reward them for their labor. Surely there is a heaven prepared for such faithful creatures, and I trust they are all on the "shining shore" where runs a pure stream of crystal water through a field of clover.

CHAPTER X

Monday morning we resumed our journey. The wind
blew so cold from off the bald mountains that all who
could walked, wrapped up in shawls and overcoats, in order
to keep warm.

Two days of travel brought us to Crow creek. As
we descended into the little valley a band of mounted Indians appeared in this distance, careening wildly across the
valley toward our train—hair and blankets streaming in
the wind. As they drew near at a terrific rate of speed,
their hideous faces covered with war paint, struck terror
to our hearts. It was a most terrifying spectacle, as they
galloped furiously around and around the train, endeavoring to peer into the wagons. I still feel the thrill of horror
that clutched my heart and curdled my blood as those
bloodthirsty faces circled about us. We did not understand
the cause of their threatening manifestations, and the only
thing we could do was to conceal our fears and proceed
quietly, as usual, to our encampment. Before we reached
our camping place the Indians left us to bestow their un-
welcome attentions upon other trains.

We were not long left in doubt as to the cause of these
exciting maneuvers. Two men appeared, before we were
fairly settled in camp, fleeing for their lives, seeking protection among us, feeling more assured of safety in the
"missionary train." These men, who were on their way
from Oregon to the states, got into trouble with the Indians and had killed one of the savages, as they claimed,
in self defense.

On hearing this startling statement, our captain explained to them that "we had but eight men in our com-

pany" and advised them to seek protection in a larger train, which they readily consented to do. We greatly feared an outbreak from the Indians before morning, and all of the trains in that vicinity prepared for a battle, by coming together and forming a large circle with their wagons. The mounted guard frequently fired their rifles and revolvers, in order to give the Indians to understand that we were prepared to give them a warm reception, should they venture to molest us, keeping up a vigilant watch all night for the enemy.

The fear of being scalped before morning drove all desire for slumber from my eyes, but I lay down by the side of our precious little ones and prayed God to protect us from the hands of the ruthless savage. He, who heareth in secret, answered our prayers, and we were saved from the awful fate that seemed to await us, and which had befallen many of the emigrants while crossing the plains in the early days to Oregon and California.

The Crow Indians followed us for a number of days, bent on revenge, but feared to make an attack unless they had the advantage of an ambuscade. Had they possessed a little of the bravery of old Tecumseh, "the king of the woods," or the spirit of King Phillip, the illustrious Indian war chief of New England, there would not have been an emigrant left alive in Crow valley.

When safely out of the Crow Indian country, the two men emerged from their hiding places, where they had been so effectually concealed that the avengers of blood failed to find them, although they had peered into the wagons of every train. They returned to Oregon, as they were afraid to continue their proposed journey to the states, and no doubt some innocent party paid the penalty for the death of this Indian.

Our road led up a high mountain covered with fir timber. The descent was so steep that we were obliged to "rough-lock" the wheels of our wagons, by winding heavy leg chains around the felloes and tires, allowing the chains to drag the ground. In this manner we made our descent into Bear River valley, where we turned our cattle loose to feed upon the luxuriant grass that carpeted the earth, filling the air with its fragrance. Here we experienced a delightful change from the frosty desert altitude to a lovely retreat, where the air was soft and balmy. A stream of pure water rippled through the valley, into which graceful willows dipped their drooping branches. Could foliage ever be more charming to the eye? It filled our souls with a spirit of perfect rest, inspiring us with the hope that the "ideal home" of which we were in search would be as sweetly enshrined by some mountain, or riverside, on the shores of Puget Sound.

How many delightful hours I passed, when but a child, building, re-building and furnishing the "ideal home" that should some day be mine—little dreaming that it would be located west of the Rocky mountains, and that to find it I would travel over two thousand miles in an emigrant wagon, through a country inhabited only by Indians and wild animals.

Traveling so far after the slow, plodding cattle nearly cured me of building "air castles," excepting those of a practical nature. I only hoped and prayed that we would live to get through with our little family, and now we press forward with all speed if we would escape being caught in the snow of the Cascade mountains.

We followed Bear river for a few days, finding good encampments all the way, until we reached the noted Soda and Steamboat Springs. These springs, lying about one mile apart, were natural phenomena—the water bubbling like a boiling pot. Steamboat Spring derived its name from the peculiar puffing discharge of its water. The waters were warm, with a bitter taste like some nauseous drug, being highly impregnated with mineral.

As we journeyed over a high ridge we had an extensive view of the surrounding country. The great panorama of nature presented a wide diversity of scenery. Mountains reared their lofty peaks, treeless and bare, far up into the sky; while others were capped with a soft mantle of snow, their broad sides clothed with timber.

As this constantly changing picture unrolled before us, in spite of our intense desire to reach the end of our pilgrimage, we were impelled to pause and contemplate this scene of wild and barren grandeur.

We crossed a few more small streams, usually finding good water and grass for our stock, but frequently a serious drawback to our comfort was a dearth of wood. Green willow, the size of a pipe stem, being the only substitute. Over this sizzling, smoky apology for a blaze we managed to heat water for our tea. I must say I preferred the willow to buffalo chips, which many emigrants used for fuel.

Fort Hall now lay before us in the near distance. To this point, located in Eastern Oregon, which we thought lay near the end of our journey, our longing eyes continually turned.

Arriving at Fort Hall, weary and worn with our long journey of more than a thousand miles, after the slow, plodding oxen, our hearts sank with dismay when we learned that eight hundred miles still stretched their toilsome lengths between us and the coveted goal of our ambition. Had we known of the desolation and barrenness of the route that lay before us, I fear we would have been tempted to give up in despair, for its proved by far the roughest and most trying part of our journey.

Looking back over the many conquered obstacles that lay behind us, we were inspired to press forward with renewed courage. We had passed through many rough and dangerous scenes, where the waters were deep, mountains high, and the Indians treacherous, and no serious accident had befallen us, and all were in good health. Surely we had reason to acknowledge Divine protection; and in a hopeful, trustful spirit we pushed forward, up and down, over more rough hills interspersed with springs of water, and soon after made our first encampment on Snake river, a name ominous of treachery and tribulations.

We were immediately beseiged by great clouds of mosquitoes, which annoyed us most unmercifully. By tying down our wagon covers as closely as possible and burning sugar to smoke them out, we managed to get a little sleep; and in the morning left this camp without one regret, like nearly all others from this one to the end of our journey.

Neither time nor space suffices to enter into certain details of each day's experience.

Following down this desolate valley, where scarcely a vestige of vegetable life appeared, we crossed several

streams where it was so rough with rocks that it seemed as
though our wagons would be broken to pieces.

On reaching Raft creek we filled our water kegs and
carried water with us, as our next encampment would be a
dry one.

For several days we traveled over a country that was
too dismal for description. The whole face of the country
was stamped with sterility. Nothing under the brassy
heavens presented itself to the eye but the gray sage brush
and the hot yellow sand and dust. Our men traveled by
the side of their teams, with the burning rays of the sun
pouring down upon them—the dust flying in such clouds
that often one sitting in the wagon could see neither team
nor the men who drove them. Camping at night where
water and grass were deficient both in quantity and quality.
There seemed but little life in anything but the rattle-
snakes and the Snake Indians.

The name was no misnomer, for these Indians were as
treacherous, and their poisoned arrows as venomous as the
reptiles whose cognomen they bore. Concealing themselves
behind rocks, or in holes dug in the ground for that purpose,
from which they assailed the emigrants and their stock
with poisoned arrows, and were more to be feared than
any tribe we had encountered.

CHAPTER XI

My father, J. W. Goodell, who crossed the plains in 1851, with his family, experienced much trouble with this tribe of Indians. They followed his train the whole length of the valley, killing and stealing their stock; and, while camped near Fort Boise, very early in the morning the Indians attacked them in great numbers from the opposite side of the river, suddenly appearing from behind the rocks, which concealed them, long enough to shoot their poisoned arrows and fire their flint lock guns. One Indian, bolder than the rest, stepped out upon a rock and shook his red blanket in defiance, as a signal for war. A young man in the train (who, by the way, was the betrothed to my twin sister) was a splendid marksman, and possessed of a fine rifle, took a careful aim and fired—the bullet did not miss its mark; the Indian tumbled off the rock into the river, frightening the others so badly that it put an end to the battle.

For protection during the engagement, the women and children remained in the wagons, with their feather beds arranged around their covers as a barrier against the bullets and arrows. Not one of the company were wounded or killed, but I have heard my mother relate "they were so terrified that their tremblings shook the wagons."

On a stretch of more than two hundred miles the country was nothing more than an arid waste; vegetation was so badly parched that our cattle could find but little subsistance. Tom and Jerry, our wheel oxen, became so thin and weak that they began to stagger in the yoke. In my great pity for the suffering creatures, whenever it was pos-

sible I walked ahead of the train and gathered into my
apron every spear of grass I could find and fed them as
we traveled. This, I doubt not, helped to save their lives.
When the close of the day's journey brought us good water
and grass both, we were rejoiced; and when so fortunate
as to find good water, grass and wood, all three, we felt
ourselves blessed indeed. No one can fully appreciate
these common blessings of life until they have been deprived of them in a hot desert country. The hot sunshine
and dust, with the constant disagreeable odor of the ever
abundant sage, or greasewood, as nearly resembling each
other as horehound and catnip in appearance, took away
my appetite, and for a time I became so ill that my life
hung in a balance. Mr. Judson managed to keep our poor
baby alive on sweetened water. All of the little delicacies
we brought with us from home were gone, and we had
nothing left but flour, bacon, beans, sugar and tea. And,
like the children of Israel, my soul loathed this food and
I longed for something fresh. The thought of a baked
"kidney" or "pink-eyed" potatoes caused the tears to roll
down my face.

The farther we traveled the more meager became our
fare. When we reached Salmon Falls, on Snake river, the
Indians brought some red-meated salmon to the camp.
They were the first ones that I had ever seen. Mr. Judson
traded some sugar for a fine, large one and as it was too
late to cook it that night, he dressed it and put it into the
water keg under our wagon, and then we retired for the
night.

Morning seemed a long way off. We were really so
delighted with the prospect of salmon for breakfast that we

could not sleep. Finally Morpheus stole in upon us un-
awares, with wandering dreams luring us away home to
Lake Erie's beach, where the fishermen were hauling in
their nets filled with fish of many varieties; there was the
muskelonge, pike, bass, cat, sturgeon and the ever abundant
white fish. Not one of them could compare with our red-
meated salmon, but, oh, despair! Just on the eve of successfully landing the net broke and let them all back into
the lake.

The shock of this disaster effectually dissipated the
vision. We awoke to the realities of our wagon home, with
the red-meated salmon in anticipation. Mr. Judson sprang
out quickly and hastened to build the fire and hang on
on the kettle, but, alas! our beautiful fish was missing, and
so was Mr. Bryant's dog. As we never saw him again, he
evidently indulged in too much salmon for breakfast, and
paid the penalty with his lfe. Consequently there was
much lamentaton that morning throughout the camp for
the loss of a good breakfast and a good dog.

We did not meet a team on the whole route, though we
passed numbers of them, all going in our direction.

One day we came upon a family who had left Missouri
in the spring, well fitted out, but who had unfortunately
lost all their oxen, the last yoke having just died. Truly,
they were in a desperate situation, having only two cows
to take the place of their oxen.

I can hardly conceive how they could have made the
journey, had not Captain Hines, moved with compassion,
offered them the use of a couple of yoke of their loose cattle,
which they thankfully accepted and went on their way rejoicing.

Our train was joined by an Irishman, with his family and team. I don't remember just when, or where, but have not forgotten that he nightly aroused the whole camp vociferating in his slumbers to his oxen to "Whoa, gee, and haw," and going for lazy Tom for not keeping "upp.'

We crossed Snake river a little above Salmon Falls, paying the usual exorbitant charge of six dollars per wagon. These ferries were a constant drain on our purses. This route was controlled by the Mormons, who built bridges where they were not needed—most unmercifully fleecing the poor emigrants.

By crossing to the north side of the river we were in hopes of finding a more fertile country. Driving over great boulders, we came to a small stream where we found food for our cattle and concluded to encamp a day, in order to give them a chance to recruit—Captain Hines being very thoughtful for the welfare of our dumb companions. It is Emerson who says: "Character is nature in the highest form.

Here on the plains each person was compartively free to act out human nature, and the quality of the character came to the surface. Our little train must have been a model one, for during all the hardships and trying scenes of our long journey I do not remember a harsh word or a murmur.

The oldest couple were good Jedediah Hines (who was called "Diah" for short), and his devoted wife, who was always by his side while he drove the team. When he got into the wagon to rest, she did also, but not before. The influence of these loving spirits was felt as a benediction by all in our little band.

Usually on the Sabbath Captain Hines or his youngest brother, Harvey Hines, preached us a short discourse, of a nature to cheer our drooping spirits. The three brothers took turns in leading our daily devotional exercises of the camp. This family altar in the solitude of the wilderness was very impressive.

Before leaving this camp, Mr. Judson lightened our load by removing the projection from our wagon. We would not be near so comfortable, but were willing to suffer any inconvenience to save our jaded cattle. And that they should not have an unnecessary pound to draw, I emptied one of our trunks and left it, with my little rocking chair.

Crossing the river did not better our condition and we deeply regretted making this divergence from our course. We were sixteen days sweltering slowly along under the scorching sun, through choking clouds of dust between the two crossings of Snake river. One could hardly conceive a more desolate country. I believe it was Bayard Taylor who said, "If I had any ambition, it was to enjoy as large a share of experience as this earth can furnish."

He should have crossed the plains in the early fifties in an ox wagon, and his ambition would certainly have been gratified.

Many of the experiences of this earth are of a nature that must be endured, instead of enjoyed.

The occasional little oases by which we rested and recruited our cattle were the only "enjoyable experiences" while traveling through this desert country.

Our route lay over high, sandy plains, then down a difficult gorge into Canyon creek, which we crossed, and again over more sandy plains, where we made another dry camp among the sage brush, and soon after reached Boise river.

We traveled slowly through this valley, frequently halting to give our stock the benefit of the pure water and good grass. It was on this river that the massacre of the Ward train (consisting of five families) by the Snake Indians occurred in 1854.

I have been permitted to make a few extracts from the journal of Mrs. Elizabeth Roeder, wife of Captain Roeder, of Whatcom, Washington, who was the dear friend of my childhood, as well as pioneer days.

"Thursday, Aug. 22, 1854. This morning we noticed four wagons approaching our encampment, and we waited for them to come up before resuming our journey. This sorrowful company imparted to us the distressing information that 'they had been attacked by the Indians, and two of their number killed and another wounded, and five of their horses stolen.' They traveled along in our company, and the next night the wounded man died.'

"Wednesday, the 24th. This afternoon an Indian brought us a message from Capt. Grant, informing us of the horrible massacre of the whole of Capt. Ward's train by the savages. We kept the friendly Indian who brought the message in our camp through the night. Only three miles travel the next morning brought us to the scene of the awful tragedy. Ten men, eight women, and all the children were killed, with the exception of one boy, who, although wounded, made his escape. We sadly assisted in performing the last mournful rites for our murdered fellow beings."

Mr. Judson's father, mother, sister, and my brother William, wife and child, and other friends were in the train with Mrs. Roeder, commanded by Captain Ebey, and witnessed the ghastly scene that she has described.

Captain Ebey was the distinguished Captain Jacob Ebey who served in the war of 1812 under General Harrison. He also commanded a company in the Black Hawk war, in the same battalion with Captain Abraham Lincoln, and was the father of the lamented Isaac N. Ebey, who was murdered at his own home on Whidby island by the Hadiah Indians in the summer of 1857.

CHAPTER XII

When we reached Fort Boise we found that our wagons must be ferried over the Snake river at the exorbitant price of eight dollars per wagon. The families were safely ferried over, and we made hasty preparations to have dinner ready by the time the swimming of the stock should be accomplished. Having replenished our stock of provisions at the fort, we were enabled to provide a better bill of fare than usual; and as this was the last crossing of this dreaded river we were all in the best of spirits, hoping soon to be out of the Snake river region.

Dinners were ready, and had been waiting for some time, when Mrs. Diah and Harvey Hines, becoming uneasy at the delay, and fearful that some accident had happened, started to go to the river and were met by a messenger with the shocking intelligence that one of our number was drowned.

From a fearful premonition, or spiritual perception, Mrs. Diah Hines cried, "Oh, it is my husband, I know it is Diah." Yes, her husband was drowned in the treacherous stream. His horse had thrown him, while helping to swim the stock, and he probably was hurt, as he did not come to the surface.

It was with much difficulty that the loving wife who was so suddenly overwhelmed with anguish was kept from throwing herself into the river. As I again recall this pathetic incident of our journey, I find myself again weeping in sympathy with the stricken ones.

Each felt his loss a personal loss, for he was not only a loving husband, affectionate father and brother, but possessed as social and genial a nature as ever animated the human form.

There was no food here for our stock, and, though our sorrowful hearts longed to linger a while near the watery resting place of our beloved friend, we were obliged to proceed on our journey, meditating on the mysteries of death, of which we only see the dark side. Could the veil, or shadow, of material nature be lifted we would witness the transition, and what appears so fearful would then be as glorious to us as to the angels in heaven.

Said John Elliott, the apostle to the Indians, "In the morning if we ask, where am I today? our souls must answer, in heaven. In the evening if we ask, where have I been today, our souls may answer, in heaven. If thou art a believer thou art no stranger to heaven while thou livest, and when thou diest heaven will be no strange place to thee. No, thou hast been there a thousand times before."

Our next Sabbath encampment was on the Malheur river. I greatly missed my little rocking chair. To sit in the camp, rock my baby, and sing some of the old church songs, made it seem quite "homelike." The hymn beginning:

> "Guide me, O thou great Jehovah,
>   Pilgrim through this barren land,
> I am weak, but Thou art mighty,
>   Hold me with Thy powerful hand"

seemed especially appropriate while traveling through the barren wilderness.

It was in this region of the country that another one of our company narrowly escaped a terrible death. While preparing for a noon lunch, Mrs. Capt. Hines' dress came in contact with the fire, and before discovered was a mass of flames. The captain, who was fortunately standing near by, saved her life by tearing off her dress, burning both hands severely.

After leaving Malheur river our road led us over alkaline deserts, up and down high hills, occasionally coming to a stagnant pool whose waters, like those of Marah, "were bitter to the taste."

We were two days traveling up Burnt river, continually enveloped in clouds of suffocating dust.

Making one dry camp, we descended into Powder river valley, and encamped for the Sabbath, where we were made happy by a pure stream of running water. Travelers on the Sahara could not have appreciated it more than these dusty, dirty emigrants, after traveling over high, barren hills, their imaginations haunted by visions of babbling brooks and bubbling springs.

"He sendeth the springs into the valleys, which run among the hills," making the name of "valley" suggestive of rest and comfort to the toiling emigrant. Traveling high above a beautiful stream, its cool waters in plain view, but utterly beyond our reach, was tantalizing in the extreme, and such was our frequent experience.

There is a living lesson in these scenes. Some souls seem as barren as these deserts, which at that time were too dismal a dwelling place for even bat or owl; but cultivation has made it to bear luscious fruit and to blossom like the rose, where the birds of the air build their nests and sing their songs. There is hope, therefore, for the most degenerate of God's children.

Crossing Powder river and several other streams, we

ascended a mountain. On reaching the summit, our captain
called a halt, that we might more fully view the magnificence of the grand Powder river valley, which lay unrolled
beneath us.

The beauty of this enchanting scene filled our souls
with delight—surrounded on all sides except the west by
blue mountains, covered with evergreen timber.

We rolled down the mountain into this picturesque valley. Crossing to the west side, we encamped near where
the city of La Grande is now located.

Many Indians were galloping over the prairies, sitting
as straight as so many cobs, on the little ponies which run
wild over the plains, and must have greatly degenerated
since Fernando Cortez first introduced their noble progeni-
tors into Mexico.

Among the Indians Captain Hines recognized "Red
Wolf," chief of the Nez Perces tribe, with whom he had
become acquainted while living in Oregon.

The next day, while ascending the Blue mountains,
"Red Wolf" overtook us for the purpose of letting us know
where we would find a spring of water and grass for our
stock.

Turning to the right and traveling a short distance we
came to the place this friendly Indian had described to us,
making our encampment under the fir trees, which rose like
stately columns, far above the earth—standing so closely
that their boughs interlaced. The ground had a lawn-like
appearance, covered with a carpet of grass and free from
undergrowth.

This great change from the desert sage plains, where
there was no verdure to refresh the soul, or to screen us

from the hot rays of the sun, made us feel we had come into a new world and among kind friends, for a tree comes as near being human as any inanimate thing that grows; and no wonder when "planted by the rivers of water" and made to bear good fruit that it is the type of a "good man."

As the smoke curled up among the fir trees, and our young ladies made the air melodious with the sweet strains of the "Silvery Light of the Moon," we felt nearer the longed for "home" than at any time since the beginning of our journey.

Having been without fuel for so long, except sage wood and willow, and often without even those poor substitutes, we were delighted to do our cooking one more over a good fire. We had tired of living on hard tack and crackers.

Magic yeast and baking powder were an "unknown quantity" in those days, and we did not relish sour dough bread as the "staff of life."

There was only the one kind—the old fashioned "salt rising" that "just filled the bill," as it retained the delicate flavor of the wheat.

As there are many girls and young wives who are not adepts in this simple art of the culinary department, I will give them my experience while journeying on the road over the plains. To one quart of water, one teaspoon of salt, thickened with flour until a stiff batter; I then set the little bucket containing the yeast into the camp kettle (covering it tightly to keep out the dust) and letting it remain in the front part of the wagon where the sun kept it warm. The secret in making it rise was the part the oxen and wagon performed—in keeping it well stirred, or in constant motion. When we came to a halt at noon it was sure to be light and foaming over into the kettle. I then poured it into the bread pan, adding as much more water and thickened flour; when it again became light I kneaded it into a large loaf while the wagon was jogging along; when we reached our camping place at night my bread was ready to put into the "Dutch oven" and bake.

By this method I never failed to bake as light and sweet bread as ever made by modern devices.

Many of the emigrants made their butter by allowing the jolting of the wagon to do the churning.

I did not like to see cows yoked to the wagons and made to haul the load, as was done in some of the trains. I know it was the custom of the Hebrews in the dark ages, when they sacrificed the males of their flocks and herds to atone for their sins, to commit greater ones by working their cows in the yoke. And in some countries even women are seen yoked to the plow and made to do the work of an ox.

When all the inhuman treatment and indignities that have been heaped upon the female sex are done away with, we may look for the millenium, and not before.

CHAPTER XIII

We crossed the Grande Ronde river and soon after bid good-bye to the beautiful pine forests and came out upon the summit of a bald mountain that overlooked the great Columbia river valley, and our captain again called a halt, that we might from Pisgah's heights view the promised land in all its magnificent beauty, which was fascinating beyond description.

In the rarified atmosphere of these upper regions this inspiring scene seemed but a short distance away. But we were too weary with our hard day's journey to indulge in any enthusiastic expressions of admiration. The one sentiment animating our souls was to reach Puget Sound as speedily as possible; and we fondly hoped that the remainder of our journey would not be as full of difficulties as that which lay behind.

Oh, vain, delusive hope! For we found the more sublime the scenery the more difficult became our progress. The descent from the mountain was steep and rocky. We made our encampment on the bank of the Umatilla, where we found good grass for our cattle.

This wild, picturesque valley was filled with Indians who were trading with the emigrants. We bought fresh beef from them at twenty-five cents per pound, and potatoes (no larger than walnuts) at one dollar a peck; but they were "potatoes," and we ate our supper and breakfast with more relish than any meal since we left home.

After crossing the Umatilla river our road led us over a desperate country—up and down steep hills and through rocky canyons, in which grew nothing but sage brush and thorny cactus, many times traveling all day under a scorching sun, without water, our eyes, ears, nose and mouth filled with dust. One night in particular, I shall never forget. We were obliged to make a day camp—the wind was blowing a hurricane so that we were unable to build even a sage brush fire. Locking the wheels of the wagons to keep the wind from running them down a chasm, we went thirsty, hungry and dusty to bed.

Strange to relate, while the wind was buffeting the wagons with such force that they seemed in imminent danger every moment of turning bottom side up, I fell asleep and dreamed we were living in our "ideal home" on Puget Sound, except that the ideal was lacking, for it was located on the wrong side of the river, and I was not at all pleased with the home of my vision. Glad was I to wake and find it only a dream.

These experiences of the old pioneers while crossing the plains in an emigrant wagon in the early days, to California and Oregon, for the purpose of digging gold and carving out homes for themselves on donation and pre-emption claims, will never be forgotten; and I doubt if a tract of land equal to that given to Fernando de Soto in Florida (which was ninety miles long and forty wide) would tempt them to again pass through those terrible experiences.

At John Day's river we stopped only long enough to fill our water kegs and then drove on up the canyon to a grassy plain and encamped for the night.

Indians often swarmed around the wagon while in camp, begging for food. One more hideous than I had yet seen came to our wagon while Mr. Judson was away with the stock, and begged for bread. As I had none to give him, I continued singing to my baby. He sat down on the wagon tongue and mocked me. It makes me smile now, when I think of the ugly faces he made, but when he began mocking my baby, it filled me with indignation. I paid no attention, though much afraid, and he soon tired of the performance.

Mt. Hood had been in view for several days, the transparent atmosphere, annihilating space, made it appear but a short distance away. We traveled towards it slowly and patiently, day after day, never seeming to diminish the distance between us, when finally, one Sunday morning, while searching for a good resting place for our stock, we suddenly came onto the banks of the great Columbia. At last, at last, at long last, we were surely near the end of our journey.

How our drooping spirits revived under the magical inspiration of the very name of "Columbia river." This name had long been associated with all that was desirable in the new country. And now we stood upon the bank of its mighty rushing waters. There was nothing attractive in the scene, not a tree, spear of grass, or vegetation of any kind to be seen, so we drove on down the river for a few miles and came to the Des Chutes river. Its bed was filled with great boulders, against which the rapid waters dashed and foamed as it sped on its way into the Columbia, making a hazardous fording place.

Here we met another of the Hines brothers, who was waiting to meet his out-coming relatives. We were obliged to continue our journey to find food for our stock, and after climbing several high hills came to a beautiful grassy valley, through which meandered a clear rippling stream called Fifteen Mile creek, and thankfully made our encampment for the night.

The next day our road led over high hills that bordered the Columbia, and, after descending its banks, we came to a little trading post called The Dalles, which at that time was composed of a few zinc cabins and tents occupied by Frenchmen, who lived with Indian women and trafficked with the emigrants and Indians.

We had decided, before reaching this place, instead of attempting to cross the Cascade mountains by the wagon road, to pass it by the way of the Columbia river.

Our captain hired an old Hudson Bay bateau, on which we loaded all our wagons and camping outfit. Just as we got it completely loaded, it seemed as though every seam opened, and the water rushed in and the old thing began to sink. Nothing remained for us to do but to wearily unload and go through the oft repeated process of drying our goods. We were in a great dilmena; how to proceed on our journey was an unsolved problem.

Our goods were dried, but still no signs of relief. But on the second day a nondescript craft made its appearance on the river. Its enterprising proprietor had placed a small engine in a discarded hull.

Thankfully we boarded this unique relief boat and were off on a ten-hour voyage to the Upper Cascades, where we made our encampment on the gravelly beach.

Our men drove the stock over a trail. The trip should have consumed one day, but they unfortunately missed their way among the many Indian trails, and it was three days before they rejoined us.

Although so near the settlements, I doubt that we spent three more uncomfortable nights during our long journey than these, passed on pebly couches, under cold, foggy skies. We greatly missed the comfort and protection of our wagons, as it had been necessary to take them apart for shipment.

Gladly we hailed the appearance of our cattle. Preparations were quickly completed, and we were off for the lower Cascades.

And oh, such a road! It was simply no road at all. Along the banks of the river we drove, bounding and bumping over large and small boulders. Fortunately for us, it was only a half's day travel, but the roughest of all our rough journey.

From this point a flatboat propelled by steam carried us to the mouth of the Candy. Again we were obliged to wait two days while our cattle were being driven around the trail. How my heart chafed at the delay, for only five miles separated me from my twin sister, Mary.

"It's a long lane that has no turning," but these long, seemingly endless days at last dragged to a close.

Here we parted from the little band with whom we had shared the pleasures and trials of our long journey. There had been no falling out by the way to mar the friendship that time has not broken, and will soon be renewed and perpetuated in the spiritual realms above.

Our captain had watched over us with a fatherly care. When our oxen became weak, he offered us the use of a yoke or two, just as we needed, and by observing the divine plan of resting one day out of seven our cattle were saved. Out of the fifty head belonging to the train, only two were left behind.

CHAPTER XIV

How could I wait the steps of the slow plodding oxen to carry me to my sister's home? The thought of being so near to her, while moving so slowly through the dense forests, drove me almost frantic. I felt I must fly. Leaving my baby asleep in the care of little Annie, I ran on ahead of the team and stopped at every clearing where stood a cabin and inquired the distance to her home; and was sadly disappointed, when within two miles of her home, I learned that she and her husband had gone to Portland for a day's shopping. As there was no reason now for haste, I sat down on a log by the roadside to rest. When the team came along, placing one hand on old Tom's hip, without halting the team, I mounted to my accustomed place in the wagon, where I sat sunk in pleasing reveries.

My sister would be greatly surprised at our appearance, as my father had directed us to Puget Sound by the Naches Pass, but we did not get his message in time, for which I was thankful. I could not endure the thought of settling down without first visiting this dear sister whom I loved as my own soul, and for whom I had often cried myself to sleep, when she had, three years before, with my father's family, emigrated to Oregon.

She was then a beautiful girl of eighteen summers; now, the wife of N. W. Meloy—he who shot the Snake River Indian from the rock, where he (the Indian) stood flourishing his red blanket in defiance of the emigrants.

But here we are at the door of her log cabin, which stood on a gentle rise in the dense forest of fir and cedar, in perfect solitude. All was as silent and solemn as the grave—not a sound to be heard but the familiar tinkling of our cow's bell. How constantly through our wanderings I had strained my ear to catch the tinkling of this bell to assure me that our cow was not lost.

Mr. Judson removed the yokes from the oxen and turned them loose into a little pasture, where stood the huge black stumps of the fir and cedar trees that had been felled and burned.

A vine-clad porch and shrubbery, with a few late flowers, betokened taste and refinement. We took possession of the house, and found everything within, as well as without, neat and cozy—an embodiment of home comfort.

Mr. Judson built a fire in the stove and dug some potatoes from the flourishing garden. They were perfect beauties. I had never seen finer ones. It did not take me long to get them ready for the oven. How strange it seemed to be in a house, cooking over a stove once more. I almost longed to wield the broom, but the perfect neatness of the little home offered not the slightest excuse for the indulgence of this desire.

Supper was nearly ready when I heard a shout, and ran out to the door just in time to see my sister and her husband ride up to the porch on their ponies, and soon Mary and Phoebe were clasped in each others arms, weeping for joy.

After introducing me to her husband, she said: "We heard you had come, and rode home as fast as our ponies could carry us." Mary was as beautiful as ever, with a complexion as lovely as a lily—while I had become so thin and tanned so black she jokingly remarked "she was half inclined not to own me as a twin sister." I replied "it would not take me long to get bleached out under the shade of such tall fir and cedar trees as those surrounding her home."

The first thing she did was to take little Bonta into her arms: "Poor little puny fellow," she exclaimed, "he hardly looks worth raising," and she dressed him in a robe that belonged to her little one who had been laid away.

Our visit must necessarily be short. The time had passed rapidly, but how much our twin souls lived in those few days. Hours were passed sitting on the porch, under the shade of the huge firs and cedars that were so dense as to hide all scenery from our view—or, for a change, on a mossy log by the spring, at the foot of the hill; living over some of the happy days we had passed on the shores of beautiful Lake Erie, in the good old "Buckeye" state of Ohio. I related to her all the interesting events that had transpired after she left the "old town"—of our brother William's marriage to a dear schoolmate we both loved, that took place a few days before our departure that we might be present at the wedding. They also intended emigrating to Washington Territory the following year.

She, in turn, related some of the hardships and adventures which had befallen them with the Indians, bears, cougars and wolves while crossing the plains, and while working to carve out a home on Uncle Sam's domain.

Their train was so late, she said, "that we were obliged to winter at Salt Lake City. In the spring we took a fresh start in a large company, but, ours being the first train over the road, we were obliged to fight our way through with the Indians. We lived in a tent until we had cleared a place large enough to set our cabin among the monster trees. One day, while getting dinner, I came here to the spring for a pail of water, and walking this log on which we are sitting was a great big black bear. You may be sure I was awfully frightened, and ran for my husband, who came and shot him. Since then I have practiced firing the gun myself, and have actually shot a whole family of polecats. The odoriferous little pests had made their home under the house, and nightly they came through a hole into the kitchen, tapping about as though their little feet were shod with wooden shoes—greatly to our discomfort. I placed some bait by the hole, watching my opportunity. When the little head appeared I took a careful aim and fired, repeating the operation until they were all destroyed."

I thought my sister quite brave, but wondered that she could content herself to live in the midst of so gloomy a forest. Such was not my "ideal home."

The time came, only too quickly, for us to continue our journey.

We had over one hundred miles farther to travel before reaching Puget Sound, and were anxious to reach our destination before the rainy season set in. How happy we had been living over the past and in building air castles for the future! and now we must separate, not knowing when we would meet again.

Once more, and for the last time on our long journey, the cattle were attached to the wagon, and taking our seats in the lumbering vehicle that had so long been our home, we were again enroute—hopeful, but with hearts aching from the pain of separation.

I can still see my sister standing on the vine-clad porch watching us out of sight through blinding tears. The slow cycles of fifteen years had revolved before my eyes were again gladdened with the sight of this dear, twin sister; and then she was a widow, for during that period she had lost her beloved and loving husband.

Mr. Meloy accompanied us as far as Portland, for the purpose of taking back the team, for we had concluded to leave the team and the cow with him until spring. To reach Portland, a distance of ten miles, we traveled through a timbered country where only here and there a small opening had been made.

Crossing the Willamette on a leaky ferryboat, rowed by two men and steered by another, we were landed amidst a cluster of small houses, surrounded by many tall trees, which long since have given place to the beautiful city of Portland.

The shades of evening were beginning to fall when we arrived, and the pale light from the standard tallow dip gleamed fitfully through the small paned windows of the modest hotel, which was a small framed building. The ceilings and walls were lined with muslin, and was quite a contrast to the city's modern "sky scrapers," with elevators and electric light, which at that time had not come into use; even coal oil had not been discovered.

As we knew nothing about these luxuries, we did not miss them, or the finger bowls at the table. We enjoyed the plain, wholesome meals that were served us for six bits a head, and the comfortable beds that were furnished at the same price. It took us some time to become accustomed to the monetary system of the country. The phrase of "bits," instead of shillings, sounded very odd to a "buckeye."

The people of the territory had no use for nickels or pennies at that time, and for more than twenty years after. When silver was divested of its monetary value, people became "picayunish,' and their nickels and pennies came into use.

We left Portland on a little steamer that carried the passengers and mail to Ranier. Here we crossed the Columbia in a skiff, to Monticello.. Monticello consisted of a hole in the woods, only large enough to contain one house, and the only one in a long distance.

We made our bed under a tree, spreading blankets over fir boughs, and found ourselves much more comfortable than upon the sandy beach of the cascades.

The next morning we began the ascent of the Cowlitz river in an Indian canoe, propelled by Indian muscle, making about the same speed against the strong current as did our oxen when pulling up a steep mountain. There were many portages, where jams of logs obstructed the river. Frequently the water was so shallow that the Indians pushed the canoe along more rapidly than they paddled through the deep water. For a time the novelty of the scene was quite interesting, but, as there was a lack of variation, it soon became monotonous—only varied by the mild excitement of the occasional salmon leaping from the water.

I amused myself learning some of the Chinook jargon used by the Indians in talking with the "Bostons," as they called all white people. This jargon is a conglomerate of French and Indian words compounded by the Hudson Bay Company when trading for furs during their expeditions in early days to the Coast.

The first word I learned to use was "hiak," meaning "hurry," which was frequently reiterated by the passengers when the Indians became slow or lazy.

Sitting in one position all day, in the bottom of a canoe, we found very wearisome; and we were only too glad when we landed at a stopping place with no name, only one building—a rude hotel kept by a "bach" who was known by the pioneers from one end of the Sound country to the other by the name of "old hard bread,' because of the hard bread he invariably served to his customers. We, however, fared sumptuously on salmon and potatoes.

At noon the next day we reached Cowlitz Landing, where, on the prairie, the Hudson Bay Company had a trading post, and here put up at a hotel kept by another "bach," but, from all appearances, it was run by the Indians. Here we learned that my brother had come every mail day for three weeks, in hopes of finding us here. 'Twas at little after dark that night when I was joyfully surprised by hearing some one exclaim, "Why, here is your brother now."

Sure enough, there stood my dear brother, Melancthan; he had grown so much in our three years' separation that I did not recognize him. He said they had not heard a word from us since we started on our journey; consequently he did not know when or where to look for us. I was greatly rejoiced to see my brother, and to find that he had come with the horses and wagon to take us home.

CHAPTER XV

I could hardly realize that we had only one more night to pass and one more day to travel before reaching the home of my parents.

We were up bright and early in the morning, having forty-five miles to travel in order to reach Grand Mound, where my father, J. W. Goodell, had taken up a donation claim.

It seemed like a long distance to make in one day, but then we were progressing more rapidly than when traveling after the tired, poky oxen. We enjoyed the change of locomotion, as well as the scenery of the Puget Sound country.

It was one of Washington's loveliest October days, brightened by the snow-capped peaks of the mountains glistening in the morning sunshine; and the gorgeous hues of the maple foliage on the low lands, with a background of the ever green fir and cedar, presenting a landscape that could hardly be surpassed for grandeur, or one more refreshing to the souls of the weary emigrants.

While admiring the various brilliant tints of the leaves we were reminded "that we all do fade like the leaf." A more perfect simile could hardly be given. For a time "we flourish like the green bay tree," and then comes adversity, trials and griefs that sear and beautify the soul, as the strong blasts and chilly frosts bring out the beautiful tints of the leaves, making "old age" as glorious as the autumn season of the year.

The first place of note, after leaving the French settlement on the Cowlitz was the home of John R. Jackson, who was one of the first pioneers to the Coast. He had a fine claim under cultivation, called "The Highlands." As we were passing by, the kind old gentleman came out to the road, shook hands, and gave us a hearty welcome to the country.

Passing over much unoccupied country, where only now and then a hardy frontiersman was clearing up a "ranch," we reached Saunders' Prairie, as it was called, but only a low, open country where for years, during the winter season, travelers were obliged to swim their horses through the swails.

The thriving little village of Chehalis is now located at this place, where at that time only the one family resided.

The next place we passed worthy of note was at the confluence of the Chehalis and Skookumchuck rivers. We forded the one with the long name (which is the Indian word for strong water). A more appropriately descriptive cognomen could not easily be found, as it was a very rapid stream. Although we had but little difficulty in fording it, shortly after the nephew of Governor Stevens, a very promising young man, lost his life while attempting to cross this same ford on horseback.

Here on the gravelly prairie, where four claims had been taken, those of Joseph Boyce, Cohorn, Holms and George Waunch, the flourishing city of Centralia now stands.

The next residence we passed was the home of Judge Ford, one of the earliest settlers on the Coast, who became one of our nearest and most genial neighbors. His home was situated on the bank of the Chehalis, in plain view of the road, where many weary travelers have been hospitably entertained on their way to and from Olympia. It was the home of the first American baby girl born in what is now the present state of Washington—Angeline Ford.

And here convened the first district court, where nearly every one in the county attended, in some capacity. It was at this court that "old Joe Meeks," the United States mashal, informed the jurymen and the witnesses, after the court adjourned, "that he could not pay them for their services, as there was barely enough left to pay the officers."

Driving through a dense forest of two miles or more, we came, just before dark, onto Grand Mound prairie, where my parents now resided, having recently moved from the Willamette valley.

We had cautioned the mail carrier who was carrying the mail from Cowlitz landing to Olympia, not to communicate the news of our arrival to our friends, for we wished to give them a surprise. But the news of the arrival of an emigrant in those days was too good to keep, for it was quite evident before reaching the house that he "had given us away," by the meeting of first a brother, then a sister, until we had met all, six of them; and last of all she who was not able to keep up with the others—*my dear mother.*

While embracing me with tears of joy streaming down her own face, she said: "Don't cry, Phoebe," the same words she repeated to me twenty-six years later, in my home in the Nooksack valley, when she bade adieu to the scene of life.

When she came to take little Annie, her namesake, from the wagon, she was greatly surprised to find a little grandson also.

My father was not at home to welcome us, having gone to do some surveying for a neighbor.

We went into the frame house, that was not quite finished, where we found the table spread and supper waiting for us. A more joyful gathering than the one encircling the table that night can scarcely be imagined, each expressing their joy in his or her own peculiar way. How they roared with laughter when I attempted to display my acquirements in the Chinook language.

Surely, we had much reason to rejoice, for we had come to the end of the long, perilous journey of seven weary months, and at last safely landed in our father's house, on the longed-for shores of Puget Sound.

To me, these family reunions are akin to the home coming above—Our Father's house. What radiant visions of perfect love, peace, joy and rest these words bring to the weary pilgrim on life's journey. In that blessed home we shall ever abide, freed from all the sorrow, pain and trials of this earthly life.

CHAPTER XVI

The next day after our arrival we tried to take in our surroundings and find "where we were at,' thinking we must be near the "jumping off place."

We found we were in Washington territory, Thurston county, on a gravelly prairie twenty miles from Olympia, at the head of Puget Sound.

When we left home the point of our destination was Puget Sound, "Oregon." We started the first day of March, and later in the same month Washington was created, by severing from Oregon all the country north of the Columbia. There was a slight sense of disappointment at the change of name, for the word "Oregon" had grown very dear to me as the name of the country wherein lay my "ideal home." But "a rose by any other name would smell as sweet," and I soon grew reconciled to the change. Washington is a name that is suggestive of all that is noble, grand and good.

The name of Thurston was adopted for our country, to perpetuate the memory of Oregon's first delegate to Congress, whose sad death occurred at sea, while returning home from the capital of the United States by the way of Cape Horn.

Grand Mound embraced an area of many square miles, a place of great natural beauty. A lone, bare mound, one hundred feet in height, rose in the center of the southwestern part. Little did we imagine that the future would see a railroad crossing this prairie, close to the mound (the North Pacific).

My father, who was appointed postmaster, called the prairie Grand Mound, to distinguish it from adjacent prairies that were covered with small mounds.

This prairie was abundantly covered with wild bunch grass, and was surrounded by stately evergreens. Mt. Rainier, with her white hood, in the background, overlooking all.

Here we located our claim of three hundred and twenty acres, adjoining my father's—making, all told, five claims located on Grand Mound, respectively: J. W. Goodell, L. D. Durgin, Josephus Axtel, Samuel James and H. A. Judson. Had the soil been more productive, it would have been a profitable investment, as well as a most delightful abiding place.

But what did we know about the nature of the soil, having no experience in agricultural lines. We selected our building place, close to the timber, by a spring of crystal water, making sure of one unfailing luxury should we be deprived of all others.

Mr. Judson began at once to fall the fir trees and hew them to build our habitation, the dimensions of which were sixteen by eighteen, surmounted by a shake roof, and the floors of the style called puncheon. The shakes, puncheon, doors, bedstead, table and stools were made from lumber split from a green cedar tree.

The fireplace he built of blue clay that was hauled from some distance, mixed with sand, and then pounded into a frame model. When it became dry, he burned the frame, which left the walls standing solid.

An old gun barrel, the ends embedded in either jamb, answered for a crane to attach the hooks to hang the pots and kettles. The chimney, built of sticks and mortar, ran up on the outside of the house.

When the crevices were chinked with moss we moved into our rudely built cabin, with scarcely an article to make it look attractive or homelike. Holes were sawed through the logs for windows, and over them I tacked white muslin to keep out the cold and let in the light. They were quite small, I remember, for while at the spring for a pail of water, Annie, the little mischief, pulled the "latch string" through and could not replace it. As she and the baby were both crying, there seemed no other alternative for me but to go down the stick chimney, or through one of the small windows. I chose the latter, as I was still quite slender, and barely managed to crawl through.

Mr. Judson put up a few three-corned shelves in the chimney corner, on which I arranged my china and glass ware, which consisted of three stone china plates, as many cups and saucers, and one glass tumbler that my thoughtful husband brought to me as we were about starting over the plains, thinking a tin cup would be distasteful to me. Bless her dear soul! Many a time on those hot, dusty deserts I would have been thankful to have drank from an old shoe for the sake of a draught of good water; and as a tin cup served me on all occasions, I put a cactus bulb into my glass, brought it through, and was that much ahead of my neighbors.

My glass was the source of, what was to us, quite an amusing incident. While stopping at my mother's two San Francisco gentlemen, who had heard of coal being discovered on Bellingham Bay, and were hurrying through to invest in the mine, stopped at her home and called for a glass of water. This simple form of a request for a drink of water, for a moment, quite nonplussed my mother, who had no such article as a glass tumbler in her housekeeping outfit. I came to her relief, saying "Use one of my glasses, mother," which was a happy thought, for her countenance immediately changed to one of mirth, while they never suspected that it was the only glass in the house—to say nothing of its being the only one on the prairie.

These articles, with our camping outfit of camp kettles, long-handled frying pan, and Dutch oven, comprised all our household effects, with the exception of a broom that I forgot to mention.

How often, while traveling through clouds of dust on the alkaline deserts, had I thought if I could only live to get into a cabin large enough to swing a broom, I would consider myself blest.

Now I was the happy possessor of both cabin and broom. Where the soil was too gravelly to raise a dust— though I did not regret the lack of dust.

We enjoyed the mild climate with its moist atmosphere —the average temperature making extremes of neither heat nor cold.

During the rainy season, when sky and the beautiful landscape were obscured by the fog and clouds for days together, everything wore a gloomy aspect, but we soon became accustomed to the pattering of the gentle rain drops, and when the fog cleared away the blue sky and mountain scenery in the pure atmosphere were a feast for the soul.

But for the unproductiveness of the gravelly soil, Grand Mount prairie would have filled my conception of an "ideal home."

CHAPTER XVII

Our provisions were all shipped around Cape Horn, requiring six months' time from New York to Puget Sound; consequently flour was twenty dollars per barrel—groceries and dried fruits in proportion, and as we were, like nearly all other emigrants, called "strapped," when their money was all gone, we possibly might have starved had not my father and nature generously provided.

The prairie abounded with deer, the forest with grouse and pheasants, and the streams were alive with salmon and trout.

The first night we slept in our little cabin Mr. Judson, while after a pail of water, managed to rustle up a lot of pheasants and came back to the house, unobserved, for his gun (he had a sly way of doing things to surprise me). When I heard the report of the gun I became greatly alarmed, fearing he had been attacked by the Indians; but I readily forgave him when he shortly returned with a half dozen pheasants—they were very fine, having fattened on crab apple. I thought the meat more delicate and sweeter than chicken.

The Washington crab apple is about the size of the eastern cranberry. We often made marmalade of them in early days. After straining out the seeds and skins they had a very fine flavor. These crab apples, with very few native berries, was all the fruit we had for a number of years.

One evening, a day or two after Mr. Judson killed the pheasants, he brought in a deer and laid it down by the door step, where I watched him dress it, by the light of the moon, and I began to think this country furnished a feast for the body, as well as for the soul.

Capturing deer became of frequent occurrence, and had bread come as spontaneously to us we would have fared sumptuously; but, as it was not rained down from heaven, some of the emigrants were obliged to go hungry for the "staff of life."

One of my neighbors, in giving her experience in those early pioneer days, relates the following amusing incident at the expense of her husband: "Our family was subsisting on bran, and were all sick, when my husband had the good fortune to find employment. I naturally expected that with his first day's wages he would bring home some nourishing food, but, what was my indignant disappointment, when in the place of food, he handed me a cook book."

This goes to show the "true inwardness" of some men's judgment; the good deacon (for such he was) no doubt expecting his wife from those receipts to manufacture a variety of delicacies out of "bran."

Six weeks after our arrival we were cheered by the accession to our settlement of five more families, who located their claims on the southern part of the prairie. They were the first party of Puget Sound emigrants that crossed the Cascade mountains by the Naches pass, having encountered many serious difficulties to retard their progress. Instead of the expected wagon road through the mountains, they found but a narrow pack trail, obstructed by fallen trees that had to be cleared away before their wagons could pass, requiring so much time that the rainy season had set in be-

fore they made their way into the settlements. They were
among our most useful and enterprising citizens.

These people were the Rev. Charles Biles and his
brother, James, Austin Young, Nelson Sergeant and James
Baker.

A black-eyed Kentucky girl, who came through with
the family of Rev. Charles Biles, was not one of the least
important among the newcomers. Mollie became the wife
of their son, David, the following year—this being the first
marriage on Grand Mound, where they located three hundred and twenty acres of land, to which he was now entitled as the head of a family.

We were now "all told," eleven families within a radius of six or eight miles, widely separated by our holdings
of three hundred and twenty acres of land to each family.
In those days anyone residing within twenty miles was
considered a neighbor; and we soon became united in love
and sympathy, for it was not riches, splendor, fame or
glory we were seeking, but happiness, peace and contentment, while each was bearing the privations incident to a
pioneer's life, and doing his part in helping to develop a
new country. Our wants and cares were few, for our simple style of living correspond with the primitive environments of the territory.

No churches or sectarian institutions of any kind, with
the exception of the Indian Catholic Mission at Olympia,
had as yet been established in the territory. Neither had
there been public worship held in any of the cabins on the
prairie.

When our good Presbyterian "deacon," who presented
his wife with the "cook book," came to the conclusion that

it was high time that religious services should be held on the Sabbath. Being remote from civilization and keeping no note of time, the first day of the week passed unnoticed by him. Accordingly, on Monday morning he donned his "boiled shirt" and Sunday-go-to-meeting clothes. With good intent, cane in hand, he crossed the prairies to the home of my father, who he had no doubt would join him in sanctifying the first day of the week; but what was his consternation to find a Christian brother busily engaged in finishing his new house.

On seeing the deacon in his ministerial garb and solemn face, my father at once took in the situation, and, after courteously receiving his guest, he applied himself more diligently to his work than ever. Now this was more than the good deacon cold endure. Filled with righteous indignation, the two brothers were soon by the ears, accusing each other of desecrating the Lord's Day."

At last the good deacon was set right, and he went home, feeling, no doubt, that he had committed the "unpardonable sin."

The little town of Olympia, at the head of Puget Sound, was the only one in the territory, and from this little trading post all the pioneers a half a century ago transported their supplies to all of the settled portions of the territory by the tedious and laborious process of plodding after a yoke of oxen, or paddling an Indian canoe.

A more rapid mode of transit was on the back of a "kiuse." These ponies were sure footed, making their way through the Indian trails, walking the foot logs across the sloughs, and small streams without stumbling. A gallop over the prairie on the back of a pony was as easy and enjoyable as swinging in a hammock, or riding the bicycle in modern times.

The citizens were anxiously awaiting the arrival of Isaac I. Stevens, who had been appointed governor and Indian superintendent for the new territory of Washington by President Pierce. He was also instructed to make a preliminary survey for the Northern Pacific railroad across the plains.

The little settlement at Olympia had been notified of the time set for the arrival of the governor and his surveying party, and a committee of arrangements was appointed to provide a suitable reception—when, about the last of November, he unexpectedly came over the trail, taking the little town in the forest by surprise, a few days in advance of the appointed time, and before the preparations for his reception were completed.

However, they did not lose any time in apologies. On learning that this diminutive man in the rough garb was really the governor, they welcomed him with the usual demonstration, firing a salute and unfurling the stars and stripes to the breeze.

The reception ceremonies were held at the Washington hotel, corner of Main and Second streets (the lone pine tree in front), kept by George W. Carliss and Lewis Ensign.

He delivered an eloquent address to the denizens of the territory, making his "debut" arrayed in a suit of clothes so much too large for him that his pants were turned up one-half foot at the bottom—as it had been found impossible to procure a suit to fit the body, so out of proportion to the large head that crowned it.

To these unimportant details of the toilet he paid but little attention, his mind being more usefully occupied with his executive duties.

He issued a proclamation organizing the government, fixing upon Olympia as the temporary capital of the territory.

Among many useful suggestions in his first message for the benefit of the country, he wisely recommended a special commission to report on a school system.

Our first legislative assembly was composed of only seventeen members in the house of representatives and nine in the council.

The most important law enacted at this legislature was the location of roads that would provide a system of communication between the isolated settlements, as they then existed. This was greatly appreciated, as our only thoroughfare (with the exception of the one road from the Cowlitz to Olympia) were the canoe and Indian trails.

The territorial seal that was adopted had on one side a log cabin and an emigrant wagon, with a fir forest in the background; on the other a sheet of water traversed by a steamer and sailing vessel; a city in prospective, the goddess of hope, and an anchor in the center, the figure pointing above to the significant Chinook word "Alki," meaning by and by, but interpreted by us, in our enthusiastic anticipations "very soon."

The letters written back to our eastern friends gave such glowing descriptions of our fair dwelling place that some of them were encouraged to make arrangements to cross the plains the following year.

CHAPTER XVIII

We were comfortable all winter without glass in the windows, and when gathered around our fir bark fires in the large clay fireplace, with the children, our cabin was bright and cheerful.

Our library consisted of the Bible and Webster's dictionary—the only two books we felt we could not do without, and to make sure of them we brought them all the way across the plains.

The Bible was the wedding gift from my father. On the fly leaf was written "The fear of the Lord is the beginning of wisdom." It was a very heavy, illustrated book, and had it not been the "Bible" to lighten the load for our poor, jaded cattle I would have discarded it away back on the plains with my little rocking chair and trunk, both of which I missed so much.

One can hardly conceive of a home without a Bible. From some of my early recollections, my fancy had pictured in my "ideal home" a library of the choicest books, that my soul might commune with the minds of the best authors; and a large Bible should adorn my center table.

Our dictionary did not take up much room, for the "unabridged" had not yet come into use.

During the long winter evenings, for amusement, as well as to be useful, I put out words from it by the firelight for Mr. Judson to spell, having a faint recollection, from a love letter or two, that his orthography might be improved.

The only paper published in the territory was a small sheet edited by T. F. McElroy in Olympia, called the Columbian, but soon merged into the Washington Pioneer, published by J. W. Wiley, which visited us weekly, helping to break the monotony of our solitary life, although it brought us but little news, as we had no telegraph, telephone, railroad or steamboat connection with the outside world.

The news of the great events that transpired on the other side of the world were not known to us for from six to eight weeks after they had transpired.

Our eastern mail came by the way of the Isthmus of Panama, and, later on, over the mountains by Ben Holiday's pony express—it frequently requiring three months to get returns from our letters.

I can never forget how eagerly we grasped these messengers which comforted our hungry, lonely hearts, informing us of the welfare of the dear ones in the far away home land.

God bless these paper bridges over which we can talk to our loved ones, though far severed by land and sea.

The marriage, or death, of some dear friend, or other important events that had transpired many weeks before, were fresh news to us—though not so exciting as when flashed across the wires in a few moments, as in modern times.

The report of Governor Stevens' survey over the mountains for a railroad was so favorable that a bright ray of hope beamed upon us, pointing to a more speedy transit across the continent in the near future.

But alas! How many long years passed, how many sad events transpired before our fond hopes were realized.

The country swarmed with savages, and the fear of

an Indian war repelled the tide of emigration. The census
was taken soon after our arrival by J. Patton Anderson.
The entire population of the territory did not exceed four
thousand; out of this number only one thousand six hundred
and eighty-two were voters.

It was owing to the sparsely settled condition of the
country that so little was accomplished by the early settlers
in developing its many rich resources.

The few pioneers were kept busy hewing down the mon-
arches of the forests, as they carved out homes in the wilderness; or, what was more difficult, striving to support
their families from the gravelly prairies that lay adjacent
to the Sound, before they had been fertilized.

Many thousands of acres of rich bottom land, through
which meandered beautiful brooks and rivers, sending
abroad through the land their life giving branches, as well
as many isolated vales, among the hills, were favorable lo-
cations, but lay dormant because they were so inaccessible;
neither were they safe for a home lying so remote from
settlements.

Before leaving Ohio, Mr. Judson had marked out on
the map of Grays Harbor as a desirable location for a home,
but, like nearly all the early pioneers, we settled where
we thought we would be least exposed to dangers from the
Indians.

We longed for spring, that we might make garden,
having been so long without vegetables or fresh fruit,
caused us to be exceedingly visionary in our plans for raising great crops the coming season; and our air castles,
within whose walls were stacked potatoes, onions, cabbages, beets, peas and beans, towered high.

Mr. Judson split out a fine lot of fir and cedar rails and fenced off a goodly portion of our preemption right of three hundred and twenty acres for a garden and orchard.

We never passed a more charming winter. It seemed more like a tropical, than a northern climate. A snowfall was of rare occurence, and then only remained on the ground for a few days. Surrounded by evergreen trees, shrubs and mosses, we did not notice the marked changes from winter to spring as we did in the east.

The hooting of the grouse in the fir trees that could be plainly heard while sitting in the house, was the first token of spring. There were not nearly so many song birds in the country as at the present time—indeed, I don't remember hearing any. We called the frogs our Irish canaries, as from their home in the swails they made the air resonant with their "singing." Soon the velvety pussy willows were all in bloom, and it required but a few warm sunshiny days after the winter rains to call forth buds and blossoms from many of our native flowers.

Among the first to make its appearance, decking the dismal swamps in gorgeous array, was the "beautiful golden lily,' as I have frequently heard them styled by newcomers, before they had made a close acquaintance with them. To these swamp lilies, however, the settlers applied the more appropriate cognomen of "skunk cabbage."

Although the golden gleam was charming to the eye, the noisome odor was a great drawback for the cows (having no fenced pasture) frequently added a dish of this spring beauty to their menu—much to the detriment of our butter, to which it imparted a very decided measure of unpleasant flavor.

The tall shrubs of the red currants, the lovely syringas, plumes of the tassel wood, with the low delicate trilliums, and violets, helped to dispel the gloom of the somber forests. While later in the season our eyes were charmed, and our senses delighted by the delicate coloring and delightful fragrance of the wild rose.

The rhododendron, that queen of the forests, one of the laurel family, with its glowing hues, reminding me of a large peony (which has since been adopted as our state flower) grew luxuriantly in the heavily timbered forests. Its place of honor, as the state flower, was warmly contested by Mrs. Ella Higginson in favor of the little white clover. This fragrant little rival was not without fair claims to the post of honor as the state flower, for it spread its blossoms prodigally throughout the land, following in the path of fire, wherever a little clearing is made—speedily covering the scorched ground with a fragrant carpet of snowy blossoms. Beautiful snowy blossoms, fit emblems of purity, and that loving mantle of charity which "covereth a multitude of sins."

Oh, how much need there is in this dark world of sin of this tender mantle of charity.

The fencing for the garden and orchard being finished, it was necessary for Mr. Judson to hasten off to Oregon for his cattle, leaving his family at my father's, as we were afraid of the Indians who were constantly roaming over the prairies on their ponies. Bands of them frequently crowded into our little cabin, where, squatted on their feet, they would sit for hours enjoying our open fire, as well as our "pire sublil" (bread), which, though so expensive, I always gave them on demand—because I was afraid to refuse them; while I, baby in arms, with Annie clinging to my side, stood near the door, which I kept wide open, in order to allow the odor from their filthy garments to escape, as well as an avenue of escape myself with the children, should they offer to molest us.

They were afraid of Mr. Judson, and usually kept one of their number on guard, watching for him, that they might get away before he returned from his work.

One day he took his turn "watching," and surprised them by appearing in "nick of time" with a tent pole in his hand with which he cleared the house in short order of the objectionable intruders, giving one of them a parting whack as he was mounting his pony. I did not quite approve of my husband's summary manner of teaching them good manners. It was their first lesson in civilization, and it seemed they had to be taught the "beginning of wisdom was to fear both God and man."

Not long after one of them came back with a pitiful tale of the treatment he had received at the hands of one of our neighbors. He said :"Boston man make siah mamaloose nika", (white man had nearly killed him).

To make one better understand his "la longe" (language) he threw off his blanket and laid face down on our rough puncheon floor and showed me his back. I inquired of him what he had done to deserve such an unmerciful punishment. He innocently replied "Nika cap swallowed peas" (I stole peas). With a serious countenance, I tried to impress upon his mind that he had done a very wicked deed, but did not succeed in making him look ashamed

However, when I offered him some bread and syrup he
readily understood that he had my sympathy, and ever
afterward considered me his "close tillicum" (good friend),
often visiting us and confiding to me his troubles.

I was much disappointed in not finding in these aborigines some of the noble traits with which Cooper character-
ized the red man of the forest. The evil and the good being
both set before them by the various settlers, how quickly
they fell under the vices which did not come to them by
inheritance—forcibly demonstrating the proneness of human nature to follow the evil example, instead of the good.

The most pitiful and sorrowful of these vices was the
liquor habit. The first English words they learned to
speak were profane ones, and they never failed to use them
when intoxicated.

While stopping at my father's, the hideous yells of
drunken Indians frequently greeted our ears. One day we
noticed coming from Olympia's trading post two drunken
Indians astride of a pony. The bridle hung loose over
the neck of the poor little "kiuse," which they were making
run at full speed. The cruel savages were beating the
poor beast, first on one side and then on the other, to in-
crease his speed, and, when just opposite my father's
house, the animal stumbled and threw both of them over
his head. We ran to see whether they were alive or dead,
and found "Kahora" (he who had stolen the peas) lying in-
sensible on the ground, while his comrade was blowing
water in his face in his vain efforts to restore him to con-
sciousness; he having filled his mouth several times for
that purpose from a small stream near the roadside. We
had him carried to the house and laid on the porch. When

he came to himself he looked quite bewildered and said: "Boston man's fire chuck hias masatehe, mamook nika hias pottelum." (Boston man's fire water very bad, made me awful drunk).

We agreed with him in pronouncing it very bad, but our condemnation rested more heavily upon the iniquitous one who enticed him to purchase the accursed poison than upon the poor, unenlightened Indian who was more to be pitied than censured.

CHAPTER XIX

I was anxiously looking for Mr. Judson's return with the stock. As the time drew nigh for his arrival—every hour seemed like a day, when hark! from away in the heavy forest came the faint tinkling of a familiar bell. Clearer and louder it sounded as it neared the prairie. Soon my eyes were delighted and my heart cheered by the sight of the old yellow cow, as she took the lead of the other stock according to her custom in our travels all the way across the plains. I noticed she carried her head a little higher than usual, but did not wonder when I saw a little red calf frisking along by her side. Oh, my! Weren't we proud of our cow and calf—the first ones we had ever owned, and I do not think we would have parted with them for their weight in gold.

Old Tom and Jerry soon put in an appearance, looking as meek and docile as ever after their hard drive over the Cowlitz trail. The dear, faithful creatures! I was so overjoyed that I could have kissed them in welcome, but contented myself by only putting my arms around their necks and telling them that they should never, never go to bed hungry or thirsty again, and they went right to feeding on the luxuriant bunch grass that covered the prairie.

Now that we had reached the "promised land" we had no more use for poor Buck and Berry, who had been our faithful leaders in the weary and dangerous pilgrimage all the way across the continent, so we were obliged to part with them.

Our earthly possessions now consisted of one yoke of oxen, wagon, cow and calf, and a squatters' right to three hundred and twenty acres of wild land, enriched with an unlimited supply of gravel—and we began to consider ourselves quite "plutocratic."

Had an aristocrat called upon us, we would have invited him to repose in the cozy depths of our fine upholstered, three-legged reception stools, by the side of the glowing flames in our mud tiled fireplace. But there were none of that class to call—God be praised for the dearth of them.

'Twas not the pretentious millionaire or magnate controlling the finances of the world who invaded these quiet domains, but the hospitable, whole-souled homeseekers were the first who ventured to penetrate the solitude of this wild, picturesque country of "never fading green," and they are the ones who lived the most happy, useful lives while toiling to develop its many resources.

A good cow at that time was worth one hundred dollars, but that sum appeared small in my eyes in comparison with the luxuries of butter and milk I anticipated she would furnish. Neither of us had learned to milk, and it makes me smile now when I think how little practical knowledge we had of farm life. However, I thought it would not take my husband long to learn. It seems so natural for a wife to think her husband smart and wise, but in this case I was doomed to disappointment, for he returned from the corral both morning and evening with less than a quart of milk in the pail. Sometimes the calf got it all, or he may have spilled it while dodging out of reach of old Bell's horns and tail. One morning, while standing at arm's length trying to milk, she kicked at him, and judging from the irate manifestations on his part, she did not miss him, and when I apologized for the old cow, by saying "the poor thing got

too much alkali on the plains," and suggested a little more
gentleness and patience, he waxed wroth and told me to
"milk her myself"—which I had intended doing all along.
As soon as they were both willing, and after a few persua-
sive efforts, I succeeded in getting six or eight quarts at a
milking, and have never regretted my experience, as I often
found the art of milking a very convenient acquirement.

Mr. Judson plowed the garden, turning the wild grass
under and the gravel on top, without fertilizing, for we had
nothing to fertilize with—planted the garden seeds we had
brought with us. He purchased a few seed potatoes, at
something like five dollars per bushel, which gave us a delicious foretaste of our harvest for we ate the heart of our
potatoes and planted the skins.

The nuts and seeds for fruits and ornamental trees he
planted in a small opening in the timber, where the soil
looked more promising.

After the gophers and squirrels had feasted upon them,
and our garden bid fair to produce a crop of sorrel, in the
place of vegetables, I began to fear this spot was not the
"ideal home" about which I had built so many "air castles."
For it must not rest upon a "sandy foundation.'

This gravelly prairie was well adapted to stock raising,
but it would take us a long time to stock our three hundred
and twenty acres from one cow and a calf of the masculine
gender.

To say the least, our prospects were not very flattering.
The misfortune of not being able to raise a garden was a
great disappointment to us, more especially as we were expecting our friends from the east in the fall. However, we
were far from starvation, for game was plentiful, although

I remember when a kind neighbor who had raised a good garden in the creek bottom gave me a few potatoes, I bedewed them with tears of joy as I carried them home in my apron.

Another kind friend gave me a fine "dominic" hen and rooster, and I raised a beautiful brood of "yellow-legged dominics." I was very proud of my fancy poultry.

Eggs at that time were worth one dollar a dozen, and had the gravel on our place been turned into grain we would have, in a short time, made our fortune.

The two pigs my father presented me met a deplorable fate. One of them died for the want of more milk, while the other, with all the milk, thrived vigorously and became as great a pet with the children as Mary's lamb, for "everywhere the children went the pig was sure to go." But alas! One day, while piggie was taking a nap by the doorway a great cougar stealthily crept out of the woods and nabbed him. I heard poor piggie's distressful cries and ran out just in time to see the monstrous animal making off with him—and that was the last that was seen of our little porker.

Mr. Judson was away, and as I was afraid to use the gun, I was helpless to rescue him (there came a time, however, when I was compelled to learn the use of firearms in self-defense), but now I could only be thankful that we had not been robbed of one of our children.

It was too late when Mr. Judson came home that night to hunt the animal, but early the next morning he and my brother Henry, with his two dogs, Cato and Nig, went in search of the marauder. It did not take the dogs long to scent his tracks and chase him up a tree, but he was such

an active climber, jumping from one branch to another, that
it was some time before the men succeeded in bringing him
to the ground. The dogs pounced upon him before he
was quite dead and were so badly mangled by the ferocious
beast that poor "Nig" had to be fed for a long time on
bread and milk before his wounds were healed.

This monstrous cougar measured, from the tip of his
nose to the tip of his tail, nine and one-half feet, resembling
the panthers I had seen on exhibition in the east. They
were a great annoyance to the early settlers, as they were
very destructive to sheep and calves. Though, of course,
this old fellow in his time had devoured many deer, no
doubt this was his first taste of pork.

We had been settled in our home but a short time,
when one day the little old Indian chief surprised us by appearing before our door with his dogs, and three other objects whom he called "Nika kloochmen" (his wives). On
their backs he had stacked, towering high above their
heads, all their worldly possessions, until, with the great
weight of their loads, the poor creatures bent double, and
nothing was visible but their legs and the walking stick
with which they helped themselves along.

We were somewhat dismayed, as well as indignant,
when he began removing his belonging from the backs of
his wives, and set them to building their wigwam close by
the spring—claiming the land as his "illihee."

We were much perplexed but, after talking the matter
over, concluded that it was no more than justice that they
should be allowed to build their homes wherever they
pleased, and we would not interfere with them, at least
before the government had treated for their lands.

How could they realize they were trespassing our rights, when no doubt this spring had been one of their favorite camping places and hunting grounds, as well as that of their forefathers for generations.

The earth with its haunts, and trails, had been as free for them to roam, hunt and fish as the air they breathed, and we, in reality, were the interlopers.

Mr. Judson, however, prevailed upon them to build their lodges below, instead of above, the spring.

The old chief was soon followed by his "tillicum" (friends) Kahorn, Ananatee and Yowanis, with their families. Only the chief, or a tyee of each tribe was allowed to practice polygamy—and the more wives he possessed the greater his wealth, as the wives were the bread winners of the family. When moving from one camp to another, as was their custom (before being settled on reservations or government claims), the head of the family, gun in hand, trotted along with his dogs by the side of his better half, who was always heavily loaded with their mats and other household effects.

A long lariat, or rope of woven cedar bark, wide enough in the center to fit the flat forehead, or her flat head, tapering at the ends to the size of a small cord, was used to secure the load on her head and back.

To this load frequently dangled a child, laced to a shoe-shaped board, and sometimes another one was perched on the top of the load.

The Indian woman was treated as a slave, her gallant lord and master compelling her to perform all the menial and laborious work, for it was beneath the dignity of a brave to do what he considered "squaw's" work, which, I

am sorry to say, is sadly true of some of his white brothers
in civilized countries.

The males wore blankets, buckskin leggings and mocca-
sins, but more often went barefooted in the coldest weather.
They wore nothing on their heads except nature's covering
—she being very liberal in bestowing upon them an abundant crop, which they seldom combed; they considered
attention to that part of their toilet superfluous, and very
distasteful, reminding me of a remark, attributed to an
Indian: "He could not see how a white man could stand
it to comb his hair every day, when he (the Indian) combed
his only once a year, and then it almost killed him."

I have never seen or heard of a bald-headed Indian. I
attribute that to the fact that they seldom wore a head covering. On rare occasions, they wore fur caps, decorated
with feathers. A belt and pouch for their ammunition, and
hunting knife completed the costume of a warrior.

The women also wore blankets, of red, white and blue,
for which they traded furs to the Hudson Bay Company.
Underneath they wore cotton chemise, which was about
the same color as their skins, as they usually smoked them
over the fire, instead of washing, to destroy the vermin.
They also wore short fringed petticoats, made from the
inner bark of young cedars, and which reached only to
their knees.

Their arms and ankles were ornamented with bracelets,
hammered from silver dollars and half dollars—often beautifully carved; they also wore rings on their fingers, in
their ears, and sometimes in their noses, all made from the
same material, or from shells. They usually went bare-
headed and barefooted, the same as the males; never cut-

ting their hair, excepting upon the death of a relative, which with them was a symbol of mourning—the greater their grief, the more disheveled their hair.

Their heads were infested with "ninapoos," which must have annoyed them, as I have frequently seen them performing the friendly office of relieving each other of the pests, by picking them off their heads. They had a very original and unique way of killing them. It is said that monkeys pick these insects off from each other, and dispose of them by the same process.

To do them justice, I must say they had one redeeming quality of cleanliness. It was no uncommon sight to see them sitting outside of their camps washing their bodies from a trough of cold water in the chill of the morning; or, to throw off their blankets on a frosty morning and plunge into the waters of a cold mountain stream.

One mother I knew, who lived on the banks of the Nooksack, punished her child by throwing it into the river, never fearing it would drown, as they were early taught the art of swimming.

CHAPTER XX

One old Indian, more noble in appearance than the others, whom I imagined resembled an old deacon in my father's church (reminding me so much of him by his grave, but friendly, manner, that I called him "Dean Clark") often spent the evening with us—sitting in one corner of the fireplace, trying to instruct us in his language by giving the names of different objects, while we, in turn, gave him the "Boston" names. As I became better acquainted with them my fears were, in a measure, dissipated.

As I listened to the legends and superstitions told in the limited Chinook jargon, of which I could understand only enough to make me long to know more, how I wished I could understand them in their native tongue, as it flowed so fluently and softly from their lips; but the jargon and signs were our only method of communication.

The women were usually loaded with clams and oysters from the bay, and it made by blood boil with indignation to see the males so aggravatingly slow in removing the heavy burdens from their shoulders. The poor wife never failed, when delivered from the weight she had carried for miles, to express her joy by a deep sigh of relief, that sometimes amounted to a groan.

When they were visited by friends that had lost a relative, the mournful wails of the bereaved ones could be heard while they were still miles away. These mournful cries were answered by the expectant friends in the same pathetic tones. These heartrending cries once heard can never be forgotten. As I write they still ring in my ears.

This interchange of lamentation was continued until

the mourners reached the camp, then, with grief stricken
faces and disheveled hair, together they sat on the ground,
and, like Job's three friends, in silent sympathy they "ut-
tered not a word." When again they would take up the refrain of woe, and "mommock tamanus" all night, and sometimes for a number of days, creating a hideous din by drumming on boards, or anything that would make a noise.

Their wigwams were made by setting poles in the
ground, converging at the top in order to make them oval
in shape. These poles were covered with bark and mats
made from flags and rushes, leaving an aperture at the
top for the smoke to escape from the fire beneath.

On opposite sides of the house two low openings were
left for doors, one or the other closed with mats, according
to the direction of the wind. These walls were also lined
with mats. The fire was built on the ground in the center
of the wigwam, while close to the walls lay the mats which
composed their beds.

Here the indolent braves could be found reposing almost
any hour of the day, game being so plentiful that it consumed but a small portion of their time to supply their
wants.

The "kloochmen" were more industrious. They gathered and dried the flags, wove the mats, picked the berries,
dug the camas, and shegawk (a wild root resembling the
carrot, only much smaller), dressed and dried the salmon,
dug the clams and oysters, and tended the fires and babies.

The camas root, a very nutritious, pear-shaped bulb,
about half the size of an onion, was their chief dependence.
It was to them what bread is to us, "the staff of life." After
steaming the bulbs in a hole in the ground, with hot rocks

covered with ferns, they were dried. This, with game, was their usual diet.

Their game was mostly roasted on sticks before the fire. Soups and stews were cooked in a waterproof basket; hot stones were thrown in quickly to set it to boiling. When the soup was done it was poured into a wooden trough and eaten with wooden spoons—one spoon frequently serving the whole family.

I have often seen them squatted in a circle around the trough, each waiting their turn to use the family spoon. This spoon was usually a very large one.

A most inhuman custom practiced by them was the flattening of the heads of their children. No child escaped this flattening process in its infancy. When the mothers were remonstrated with for the cruel practice, they usually replied: "Their child was not a cuetan or casmux" (horse or dog) and they did not want it "round, in the shape of a bullet, like the white man's latate." (head).

I have often watched the painful process as the mother laced them with cedar strings to a board, somewhat longer and wider than the child's body. Straightening the tender limbs, they began at the toes with two strings, crossing from one side of the board to the other, the same as in lacing a shoe, until they reached the little one's chin. A soft compress of deerskin was laid upon the forehead; over this was placed the board that was to do the cruel work.

A broad band, woven of cedar bark, fastened the bandaged head securely to the board. There were other methods of head flattening, but this is the only process that I have witnessed.

The constant pressure over the perceptive organs in their infancy no doubt is the cause of the "flat head" tribe of Indians being so inferior in mental caliber to most all other tribes of North American Indians.

Civilization, I am pleased to notice, has worked a great reform among them, this cruel custom having been entirely abolished, and we no more see young Indians with "flat heads."

One evening we heard an unusual "pow wow" in the wigwam of one of our neighbors. A young boy ran out of the camp, pursued by an irate old "kloochman" (the name usually applied to Indian women by the whites), cudgel in hand, beating him as he ran howling along—the old squaw meanwhile berating the boy in shrill tones of anger. He ran into our cabin for protection and related his sad story. He said: "Papa and mama were 'memaloosed,'" (dead); the Indians had driven him out of the camp, and he showed us the bruises the old kloochman had inflicted with her cudgel. We pitied the poor orphan boy and gave him permission to stop over night with us, giving him a blanket to sleep on, which he gladly accepted, spreading it on our rough floor. He laid himself down on his back as straight as an arrow and slept "like a log" all night.

The next morning we had a talk with the little old chief, which resulted in his giving us the boy, only adding to the boy's story that he was "cultus" (worthless) but we found that he had no more bad traits of character than are common to white boys of his age.

The Indians kept no record of the time, but we judged by his size that he was about ten years old, and unusually bright for an Indian boy, soon learning our "la longe"

(language) and making himself useful in many ways. As
he asked us to give him a "Boston" name, we called him
by the short one of Jack, in place of his long Indian cognomen of Skoqualamooch. He seemed quite pleased with his
new name, and also with his new home, living with us until
he was able to support himself by working for wages.

When a law was passed that Indians who had severed
their tribal relations could hold government land, Jack was
one of the first to avail himself of the privilege—filing and
proving up on his claim under the name of "Jack Judson,"
the only name by which he is known.

Not long since Jack surprised us by sending for our
pictures, "as he wanted to have them enlarged to hang in
his parlor." He married an Indian maiden, named Mary,
and they are blessed with a little family that is a decided
improvembent on the past generation of natives.

A lady who is acquainted with Jack and his family
writes me that "he is a Christian and as white as any one,"
meaning that he is a good citizen. Jack had a very happy
disposition—his merry laugh rang out quite frequently. I
can see him now, happily engaged in cooking the hot cakes
for breakfast, and I feel well repaid for taking the poor
motherless boy into our family.

CHAPTER XXI

Our friends in the east wrote that their preparations for their long journey over the plains were nearly completed, and if they were prospered they would be with us in the fall.

The company was composed of Mr. Judson's father, mother and sister, my brother William, his wife and child, Miss E. A. Austin, a very dear friend, and Charles Van Wormer and family. Mrs. Van Wormer was my husband's cousin. With glad hearts we began at once to make arrangements to build a more commodious dwelling for their reception.

The new house, a log one, of course, was to be a story and a half high, dimensions thirty by thirty-six; the logs were hewed square and the corners so closely dovetailed that it required but little chinking to make the house warm and comfortable. We bought glass for the windows, and when the partitions were in we had quite a respectable house, at least one we appreciated more thany many a millionaire of these modern times his costly mansion.

I cannot imagine a house, it matters not of what material or how pretentious the design, more comfortable than a well built log house. They are so compact that the wind, cold or heat does not affect them. Many of my happiest days have been passed in the "old log house," by the side of the open bark fire.

"Our box" that had been shipped around the "Horn" arrived soon after the house was completed—giving us a carpet to spread over the unpolished floor in the sitting room, and some crockery and silver spoons to take the place of the tin ones.

After we had stuffed a home-made lounge with moss and hung up the window curtains made of pink and blue lawn dresses of my girlhood days, we considered ourselves quite stylish, and felt much more at home than when living in the little low "shack," without windows.

We found glass a pleasant change from the cotton muslin that had before done service in our windows, depriving us of the refreshing pleasure of an occasional glimpse of the beauties of nature, so grateful to the busy housewife.

Our windows were quite a surprise to our Indian neighbors. One of them, seeing the cloth removed, attempted to expectorate through the window—his stoical face changing to one of amazement when he witnessed the disastrous result and saw how quickly the glass was restored to its original cleanness.

We were as much pleased with the temperature of the Washington summers as that of her winters; the Chinook winds prevailing the greater part of the time during the winter, and a sea breeze from off the ocean during the summer—that from the southwest warming the atmosphere, and the norther from the northwest cooling it, gave us a genial clime the year round. Taking it altogether, I think it would be difficult to find a more perfect climate.

The longest days were in June, when it was daylight from 3 o'clock A. M. until 9 o'clock P. M. The shortest ones were in December, when it was dark from half past four P. M. until half past seven, and even eight A. M., on a cloudy day.

The summer would have seemed very long, as it was our misfortune to have no crops to harvest, had not our time been fully occupied in building and preparing for the reception of our friends—keenly realizing the dangers and hardships they would have to encounter, we were in a state of constant anxiety and desired, as far as possible, to have everything in readiness for their comfort when they arrived.

As the time drew near for their arrival, the more anxious we became for their safety. Summer had passed. A few more weeks, at the most, before our loved ones would be with us when the dreadful tidings came over the mountains that on the twenty-fifth of August, near Fort Boise, a small train of emigrants, eighteen in number, besides the children, had been massacred by the Indians. And, as we could not learn the train's name, or any of its members, we were overcome with fearful apprehension for the safety of our friends, as we well knew they would travel in a small company; and if they had been prospered on their journey they would at that time, in all probability, have been in the vicinity where the tragedy occurred.

Days of fearful anxiety passed—a seemingly endless period of long drawn agony. All we could learn was that the women and children were tortured to death in the most atrocious manner. We could scarcely endure the heart sickening thought that "our dear ones" had met this horrible fate.

This fearful suspense continued for two weeks, then a messenger came over the mountains, bringing a correct report of the awful tragedy.

It was the "Ward train" that had been almost totally annihilated by the savages—only one 13-year-old boy escaping to tell the sad tale.

The same messenger brought us the joyful tidings that

our friends were in the Ebey train and were all alive and
well; that they had narrowly escaped the fate of the Ward
train, having been but three miles behind them, when the
dreadful scene of horror was enacted, and had assisted in
the sad rites of burying the dead. This news that caused
other hearts to mourn relieved ours, and we wept tears of
joy.

Mr. Judson and my father took their teams, with fresh
supplies of food, and started at once for the mountains to
meet them and to render any assistance needed.

On the eighth of October, 1854, while on watch, we
sighted the white covers of their prairie schooners as they
hove in sight off Point Axtell's, a mile away. No ships
from a foreign shore were ever hailed with greater delight
as they slowly tacked to leeward and entered the "home harbor," giving us time to spread the table with the best the
country afforded, while the weather beaten argonauts were
untackling the chains and casting anchor at the door of
our cabin home.

The joy of our hearts as we embraced first one and
then another of our loved ones, "who were dead, but live
again," cannot be described, but only realized by those
who have been separated under like circumstances.

It is needless to say that our friends did ample justice
to the bountiful dinner that my mother and I had provided.
Emigrants, after crossing the deserts, always came to the
country hungry.

Mother Judson was thought to be low with consumption when she left her home in Ohio. She began her journey on a bed, but by the time they reached the Rockies she
was able to begin to walk, and was so much improved by

the time they reached the Cascade mountains that she walked over them, and, although frail in appearance, she enjoyed good health after she reached Puget Sound; when, at nearly eighty years of age, she died of consumption at her home six miles south of Olympia, Father Judson following her a few years later at our home in the Nooksack valley, at the advanced age of eighty-seven years.

Our friends were in no hurry to locate claims until they had more thoroughly prospected the country, and for that purpose Mr. Judson and Charles Van Wormer made an extended journey down the Chehalis to Grays Harbor, following along the beach to Shoal Water bay.

On their return home they reported having explored a vast country of fertile land, but concluded it would not be safe or expedient to take their families into this wild region of country, so remote from any settlement, and so vanished our "air castles" of a home at Grays Harbor.

In after years Charles Van Wormer and his son were drowned while carrying the mail in an open boat from Shoal Water bay to Grays Harbor, leaving families to mourn their loss and to struggle alone in a new country.

My brother, William B. Goodell, located a claim on Grand Mound, but abandoned it during the Indian war, taking refuge with his family in Fort Hanness. After the war he sailed the "old General Harney" until he was appointed inspector of customs at Port Angeles, where he met his sad death by drowning in the catastrophe that overtook the town on the sixteenth of December, 1863; the custom house having been removed from Port Townsend to Port Angeles through the plotting of Victor Smith, in order to build up a rival town.

To show how he was frustrated in his plans, and the people who had gathered there disappointed in building a commercial city, I will give you an account published in a Victoria paper at the time of the calamity:

"The beautiful little American town of Port Angeles (or Angels' port) which is nestled at the foot of one of the loftiest spurs of the Cascade range of mountains, in a direction nearly opposite to our own city of Victoria, has been nearly swept away by a torrent of water which burst upon it suddenly through a gorge, or ravine, which opens into the rear of the town. The calamity occurred about six o'clock on Wednesday evening last. The first intimation which the inhabitants had of the danger was a rushing, roaring sound proceeding from the gorge, and on turning their eyes thitherward they saw a great body of water several feet in height bearing upon its surface, or sweeping before it, logs, trees and stumps, rushing down upon them. Before they could even realize their danger, the flood was upon and over the greater part of the town. The customs house, a fine two-story structure, stood exactly in the path of the vast torrent, and was overturned and swept away in a moment. Of the three occupants in the customs house at the time, Dr. Gun, the collector, who was fortunately standing near the door, was the only one who escaped. His deputy, Mr. J. W. Anderson, and Capt. Wm. B. Goodell, the inspector, who were engaged in singing church music at the time, were overwhelmed with the buildings and lost their lives. Their bodies were recovered from the ruins after the water had subsided. A person who visited the town on Saturday says that the picture of ruin and desolation presented is indescribable.

"The fragments of houses and hundreds of trees and stumps lie scattered in every direction, and in some places they are piled one upon another to the height of thirty feet. The face of the townsite for the breadth of at least one hundred yards by one mile long is completely changed.

"The accident is supposed to have been caused by the late rains and melting- snow and ice in the mountains causing avalanches into the lakes at the foothills. These lakes were then overflowed, and rushing down the gorge, carried everything before them. It is said the Indians told the whites when they were laying out their town that its site was subject to overflow, but no heed was paid to the information.

"By some it is thought the customs house will be returned to Port Townsend, while others believe the damage will be repaired, and that with proper care the recurrence of a calamity of the kind may be prevented."

The sudden and distressing death of my brother was a great shock to his relatives. His dear little family, wife and three small children, returned at once to her father's home in Vermillion, Ohio.

The parting with these loved ones, who were as dear to me as my own, caused many tears to flow.

In 1865 the customs house was returned to Port Townsend, and the same year Victor Smith, the proprietor and principal owner of the ill-fated Port Angeles townsite, was drowned while on his way to the Sound from San Francisco, on the Brother Jonathan, which struck an unknown sunken rock off Crescent City, California, and immediately began to sink. Nearly two hundred passengers, with Capt. De Wolf and most of the officers, were carried down to a watery grave, casting a gloom over the whole of the northwest coast, as many of our most influential citizens were among those who were lost.

CHAPTER XXII

Very soon after our friends arrived from the east, Capt. Roeder sailed from Bellingham Bay to Olympia in his little vessel, the H. C. Page. By the way, this little craft was the first sailing vessel built on Puget Sound. He left his boat at Olympia and completed his voyage over the prairies which laid between him and his destination, Grand Mound, on the "hurricane deck of a kiuse," to visit his Ohio friends. His real object, however, was to meet his fiance, Miss Elizabeth Austin, whom he had not seen since he parted with her three years before at the old home in Vermillion, Ohio.

His coming, though bringing joy to her, cast a shadow over the hearts of those who had learned to love her sweet and gentle character.

We reluctantly yielded her to his care, knowing that with her he would carry away much of the sunshine and joy of our isolated lifes; and when she sailed away from Olympia with him, as his bride, she was followed by the heartfelt prayers and blessings of the friends whom she left in tears.

But few have been more true to their betrothed than she—braving the dangers and hardships of a long and perilous journey across the plains with my brother's family in an emigrant train, for the purpose of uniting her fortunes with those of the man of her choice.

She was aunt to my brother's wife, so we called her "Aunt Libby," little dreaming that in after years our families would be more closely united by the marriage of her son, Victor A. Roeder, and my little Annie's daughter, Effie B. Ebey.

As she was one of the best known among the early pioneers, who gave her life and influence to the development of the country, it will not be out of place at this point to describe her personal appearance when she left us as a bride, with the bloom of youth still on her cheeks. Soft brown hair, in becoming ringlets, surrounded her sweet face; her clear gray eyes beamed with gentle mirth, and, possession of one of the sweetest and most sympathetic dispositions, she became the repository of all our joys and griefs.

It is not strange that one with so many attractions should have left more than one disconsolate bachelor friend who cherished hopes of winning her effections, not to mention the additional acres that would be added to his possessions, for at that time a wife enjoyed equal rights with her husband in respect of taking land—being entitled to one hundred and sixty acres of government land in her own right, a just and righteous law, to which it is a pity others have not been added, granting her rights to which she is equally entitled, but most unjustly deprived.

As the departure of the friend of her childhood, Elizabeth Austin, left Lucretia, Mr. Judson's sister, without a companion of her own age, she was naturally very lonesome. However, the friendship of U. S. Marshal Geo. W. Corliss, who frequently came from Olympia to visit her, in a measure alleviated her grief and loneliness, as they were congenial spirits, and he in every respect worthy of her affection. Lucretia was an only daughter, the idol of her parents and only brother. Our winter was greatly brightened by her presence, as she was attractive in person, charming in manner, sprightly and intelligent in conversation—having completed her education at Oberlin college, in Ohio.

In the spring she and Mr. Corliss were married, making their home at the Washington hotel, in Olympia, of which he was part owner and proprietor.

How little we dreamed that their life, beginning so auspiciously, should have such a tragic ending. (The sorrowful event will be recorded elsewhere in these pages).

Memory recalls several of our bachelor ranchers who were disappointed by not being relieved of washing dishes, sewing on buttons, darning socks, baking bread, etc.

I still see the tall form of a Norwegian "bach" who had many times crossed the prairie on a "kiuse," his head thrust through a hole in the center of his blanket that served as an overcoat, and hear his insistent voice as they sat by the open fireplace, pleading for her hand. It brings a smile as I recall her repeated answers that "she did not like him," which failed to cool his ardor in the least, pressing his suit by presenting as an inducement the number of his cows, and promising "to do all the churning," as she time and again told him "she knew nothing about the duties of a farmer's wife."

The poor fellow, not long after, was killed by the Indians during the Indian war, and had not a relative to mourn his loss or to inherit his "ranch," upon which the upper portion of the city of Centralia now stands.

Father and Mother Judson resided with us, as they did not consider it safe to live on a claim by themselves until a treaty had been made with the Indians for their land— father having had more or less experience with Indians in pioneer days in Ohio, when the British were striving for the

mastery of Lake Erie. We never tired of listening to his
stories of Perry's victory off Put-in-Bay and the exploits
of Tecumseh at the head of his warriors, while under command of the "red coated officers." These experiences led
him to apprehend trouble with our Indians.

Governor Stevens left the territory in the spring for
Washington City in the interest of the Pacific railroad survey. Before leaving he made a voyage down the Sound,
looking for the best point for the terminus of the Northern
Pacific, and he named Steilacoom, Seattle and Bellingham
Bay as impressing him favorably. Little he thought he
would not live to see the fruits of his labors, for ten years
later this grand man was killed in the battle of Chantilly,
while leading his command in a desperate charge—himself
carrying the flag which he had snatched from the hands
of the stricken color bearer.

History tells us by this last act of courage and devotion he saved the capital of our nation.

More than twenty years unrolled their slow lengths before
the first train passed over the road covered by his survey.

Previous to Governor Stevens leaving the territory, two
Indians on Lake Union killed a white man. These Indians were promptly arrested and hung by their own tribe.
To us this action on their part was a proof of their desire
to deal fairly with the whites, and led us to believe our relations with them were of the most friendly nature.

But shortly after this event James Burt murdered an
Indian near Olympia. He was tried and acquitted, but
fled the country to avoid the vengeance of the Indians. In
the estimation of the citizens, he should have met the fate of
the Indians who killed the white man.

CHAPTER XXIII

Goveror Stevens returned to Olympia in time to be present at the second session of the legislature. We did not doubt he felt the importance of treaties being made at once with the Indians, for in his message to the legislature he expressed the hope that the people would give him their support, and said, "I believe the time has now come for a final settlement with the Indians."

This message was delivered on the fifth of December, and by the last of the month he had completed treaties with all the tribes at the head of the Sound. The governor estimated the number of Indians in Western Washington at that time to be between seven and eight thousand.

Three small reservations were made, and under these treaties the Indians had the right to fish as usual, to pasture their herds on any unclaimed lands, and to gather food of berries and roots wherever they did not trespass upon enclosed ground, or to reside near the settlements—provided they did nothing to make their presence objectionable.

Between six and seven thousand of them signed the treaty.

This settlement with the Indians for their lands effectually quieted all fears, promoting a feeling of safety, as the different tribes in both eastern and western Washington had agreed not to go to war, unless in self-defense.

Many enterprises were promulgated for the benefit of the settlers, one of the most promising being a flour mill, built by Ward and Hays at Tumwater.

A Presbyterian church was organized at Olympia by Rev. George Whitworth, the first one of that denomina-

tion in the territory, but was soon followed by others in
the settlements by the zealous efforts of Mr. Whitworth,
who is still living, at an advanced age.

The first Methodist church in the territory was built
at Olympia by Rev. J. F. Devore, who, by his individual
effort, built a score more of churches throughout the
country.

In soliciting a subscription for his church at Olympia he
called upon the saw mill owner at Tumwater for lumber.
Judging the young minister by his ministerial suit of black
broadcloth and kid gloves, the millman sarcastically replied:
"Yes, I will give you all the lumber you can carry from
my mill down to the wharf between sun up and sun down."

According to contract, the young preacher was on hand
the next morning, dressed in blouse and overalls, waiting
for the sun to rise, when he began his day's work by
piling cedar lumber, which was the most valuable, at the
water's edge.

The mill owner, beginning to get uneasy, tried to divert
him from his work by entering into conversation and invit-
ing him to dinner, but he only had time to eat his lunch
from his "little tin pail." By sundown, being powerful
in stature, he had enough lumber piled to build a fine,
large church, with some left to sell. And as his day's
work was considered the greatest ever done in the Puget
Sound country, the estimation of the working qualities of
a preacher underwent a great change.

This church still stands, a monument of a great day's
work, accomplished by this stalwart young minister.

At this time religious services were instituted on the
prairie, but owing to the small dimensions of the pioneer's

home, and so widely scattered as they were, these gatherings were very inconvenient, consequently the Sabbaths were frequently passed under the shade of the evergreen trees that fringed the prairie, while we whiled away the almost immeasurably long summer days enjoying the beauties of nature.

On one of these Sabbaths of solitude, while wandering under the overhanging branches of the wide spreading cedars and lofty firs, listening to the drumming of the grouse perched on the highest boughs, next to the body of the tree, and so near its color they were very difficult to find, we suddenly startled a band of five deer from their haunts, near the spring, and not far from the house. They ran out onto the prairie, where they did not escape the keen eyes of old Youanis, who, having never been taught to keep any day "holy," sped forth from his "wigwam," gun in hand, and secured two fine deer for the replenishing of his larder.

We became more and more dissatisfied with our stony possessions, when we were fortunate to have an opportunity to exchange with a man who wanted a stock ranch. His claim lay twelve miles south of Grand Mound, on the bottom lands of the Chehalis, a fertile agricultural district in Lewis county, which derived its name from the Lewis and Clark expedition of a hundred years ago, which did more to prove the worth of this far western country than almost any other agency.

This county, when still a part of Oregon, was the first created, and therefore at that time was under better cultivation than any other county in Washington territory.

Once more packing our household goods in the old

wagon, with Tom and Jerry on our lead, and "the old bell cow" and baby calf bringing up the rear, we again set forth on the quest for an ideal home.

After leaving the gravelly prairie and crossing the Skookumchuck river, we entered the heavy timber. The road leading to our new possession had just been opened—indeed, it was no road at all, merely an opening chopped through the dense forest and the logs rolled out of the way. I don't know that it is any particular honor, and I must say it was no pleasure, that I was the first woman to pass over the road.

We met with no serious obstacles on our journey over this new road, but a very steep and long hill reminded me somewhat of the "hill difficulty" in Pilgrim's Progress—it seemed we would never get to the top. But "never is a long day," and at last we reached the summit and came out on a little rolling prairie where the little town of Claquato now stands. Passing through a narrow strip of timber brought us to our own domain. A hundred acres of its was low-lying bottom land, all prairie, and completely fenced.

This home was a great contrast to our former environments—not so soul inspiring, but of more material worth. The soil was a rich alluvial deposit, fourteen feet in depth, and like Pharaoh's "seven years of plenty," our land "brought forth by the hand fulls"—yielding fifty bushels of wheat, and from seventy-five to one hundred bushels of oats to the acre; and all kinds of vegetables of a phenomenal size, and of the finest quality.

But oh, the drudgery entailed by this marvelous yield, without the aid of modern machinery for harvesting and threshing the grain, which is such a saving of flesh—both human and brute.

The grain was cradled by hand and threshed by turning the head of the sheaves to the center of the threshing floor; then two or three yoke of oxen were driven upon them and kept going round and round until the grain was tramped out, and then separated from the chaff by a winnowing mill, turned by hand.

During the haying season the meadows resounded with the musical ring of whetting the scythes, as the toilers paused in their labors to sharpen them. The scythes were kept swinging from early morn 'til night by human machinery, with backs bent double, life Prof. Markham's "Man With the Hoe."

All work was performed by the "sweat of the brow." It was before the day of labor saving machines. Driving a span of horses, with a mowing machines to do the work, while sitting on a cushioned seat would have been considered by the old pioneers a "soft snap."

One of our enterprising citizens, having bought a horse power threshing machine, Mr. Judson was encouraged to put nearly a hundred acres of our rich soil into grain, and that season he harvested three thousand bushels of wheat, fifteen hundred bushels of oats, and an abundant supply of other produce, which nearly proved our ruin.

I have heard of people being "land poor," and I think I can most emphatically say we were "crop poor." The rainy season setting in before we could get it secured, the great unsheltered stacks of grain became covered with the verdure of a June meadow. We realized that our farm would yield a handsome income but for the lack of harvesting and transportation facilities.

The inconveniences of our environment and the constant drudgery effectually took all the romance and poetry out of our farm life. Had we remained on the gravelly prairie we would have found, as others did, that by fertilizing the loose, warm soil it produced a good crop of early vegetation, and with a few cows, sheep and chickens, we would have all required to supply our material wants, and have lived more happily than when troubled by so great an overplus of crops, which laid upon us a great burden of care and perplexity.

Truly this experience caused us to realize that "a man's life consisteth not in the abundance of the things which he possesseth."

CHAPTER XXIV

A heavy growth of alder, cottonwood, maple, poplar and willow obstructed our view of the snow-capped mountains, river and other scenery that would have lifted our thoughts from the sordid things of earth. The only object in nature during the dreariness of winter that presented any beauty, was the heavens that canopied us.

Here the sky was as blue, the clouds as fleecy, and the stars as bright (when it was not raining) as in any portion of the world. The comet which blazed in the autumn sky of that year proved an unfailing source of admiration and pleasure to both old and young of our little family as long as it favored us with its glowing presence.

Our meadows in the spring, summer and autumn were carpeted with the richest verdure of tall grass, wild roses and other fragrant flowers.

The annual inundation by the overflow of the river contributed greatly to the beauty and luxuriance of our flora. There was not a spot on the whole place but was submerged, as it was as level as the house floor. Many times husband and I had wandered over it searching in vain for a little hillock or a slight elevation, upon which to build our "ideal home" where the floods would not wash it away.

Three days and nights of continual rain, accompanied by a Chinook wind that melted the snow in the mountains, was sure to bring the river out of its banks; and, as we listened to the seemingly never ceasing pattering of the rain, watching the water spread over our place, carrying off the fences, rising higher and higher, until it reached the

high water mark, we began to make preparations to reach
a place of safety in our canoe, which we kept fastened to
the corner of the house, but fortunately never obliged to
paddle out, as many others did.

One poor woman, with a babe less than twenty-four
hours old, was carried on her bed to a place of safety, where
she remained until the water had abated.

One dark night, while the rain was descending (we can't
say "it pours" in this country) and the river booming, we
were alarmed by a dismal hallooing from the opposite side
of the river. Recognizing the shout as an appeal for aid,
Mr. Judson hastened to the relief. Taking his Indian boy,
Jack, and little perforated tin lantern, our only means of
illumination at that time being a tallow dip, he hitched our
old reliable Tom and Jerry to the canoe and hauled it a
half mile up the river, where they found the shouts proceeded from a party of government surveyors, who had
been creeping through the bushes and over logs in a dismal
swamp for a couple of days. Mr. Judson, with Jack's help,
ferried them over the river, and when they returned to the
house with the water soaked refugees, a bright fire was
blazing in the large clay fireplace, the tea kettle singing on
the hearth, the Dutch oven full of piping hot potatoes, and
it only required a few moments to set a warm supper on the
table. They greatly appreciated our hospitality, but no
more than we the privilege of welcoming them to our humble, but comfortable, home and ministering to their needs.

Now that they were "out of the woods," it was amusing
to see them so jolly as they dried themselves before the fire,
congratulating each other on their good fortune in finding
such comfortable quarters. "Well," exclaimed one, "this is

better than standing in the water above our knees in that cheerless swamp where we were last night." "Yes," replied another, "whenever I fell into a doze leaning against a tree, down I slipped into the water, which kept me sliding up and down the tree, and in and out of the water all night."

They were the Farnsworth and Smith deputy surveying party, the first sent by General Tilton, who held the first appointment to that office in the territory. It is not probable that there is one of this surveying party left on earth, but, whether in this world or in the one beyond, I imagine they will never forget that night's doleful experience.

As we looked upon our inundated home, covered by this broad expanse of water, it did not seem possible that in the summer season our river was but a mere brook.

I remember on one occasion Mr. Judson waded a rift in the small stream, carrying me on his back, that I might visit our good neighbor, Dr. Spinning and family, who lived on the opposite side.

Mr. Judson found that hauling his grain thirty miles to market and selling it for fifty cents per bushel was not a very profitable business. To say the least, we were not getting rich very fast, so he concluded to stock his ranch with hogs and fatten them on the grain.

But it soon became evident that he fattened as many bears with hogs at he did hogs with the grain. Had we not owned two faithful watch dogs (Lion and Tige) always on the alert when they heard a pig squeal, we would not have saved one. When Mr. Judson was not on hand with his gun, the dogs would chase the bear to the river, never leaving him until he was safely in the water headed for the opposite shore.

Often in the night we were aroused by the frantic barking of the dogs in pursuit of bears. Lying in the darkness,
we listened to the barking growing fainter and fainter, as
they neared the river. When all was silent, Mr. Judson
would say in a tone of great satisfaction, "Now they have
got him into the river."

We killed quite a number of these animals, and had
there been a bounty on them we would have been well repaid for the loss of the pigs.

Mr. Judson and our Indian boy contrived a trap that
caused one of these troublesome creatures to commit suicide. Taking a pig that had died from wounds inflicted by
a bear, they tied a strong cord around it; this they attached
to the trigger of a heavily loaded musket and fastened all
securely to a stake set in the ground. After getting all sat-
isfactorily arranged, they came to the house and waited results. We had scarcely fallen asleep when the loud report
of the gun, sounding in the darkness and silence of the night
like the roar of a cannon, aroused us from our slumbers.
Jack was greatly excited, and, boylike, could scarcely wait
for morning. As soon as it was light enough they went out
to reconnoiter, and they found bruin dead beside the pig.
He had just closed his jaws on the tempting bait when
the death-dealing missiles cut short his meal, as well as
his life.

After breakfast, taking Tom and Jerry, they soon had
bruin drawn into the yard, and I saw at once that this was
not the "little wee bear," nor "the middle sized bear," but
the "great, huge father bear" the children read about in
their story books, that lay shorn of his strength before us.

It was amusing to see Jack's delight as he gathered the yard full of his Indian friends to feast on "ichoot."

Bruin's noble proportions were in prime condition, being covered with two inches of fat. It was interesting to watch the Indians roasting the meat on sticks before the large camp fires, and devourig it with an appetite, needing no condiments on the side to add a relish to their food.

They were a jolly crowd, with no thought beyond the enjoyment of the present moment. There is no occasion where their predominant characteristics are more fully displayed than in such a scene as this. A plentiful supply of "ichoot" meat constituted their highest ideal of human enjoyment, and they had the faculty of distending their stomachs to contain an almost unlimited amount of food. When they had finished gormandizing there was nothing left of the animal but the hide, and I prevailed upon them to dress that for me. The fur was long and of the richest black. It made a most beautiful robe that served for a rug upon which little Annie and La Bonta rolled and played.

Jack also had his share of amusement in bruin's skin, frequently wrapping himself in it, playing "bear," which proved an unfailing source of delight to the little ones. But when a minister from California, who was traveling through the country for his health, visited us, he took so great a fancy to our rug that on his departure for home we presented him with the last relic of old bruin.

Bruin is very fond of all kinds of fruit. They almost ruined Father Judson's young orchard climbing the trees after the fruit and breaking the branches. He conceived a scheme to keep them out of his trees by tying a sharp scythe to an apple tree that stood nearest the gate. The next morning the blood on the tree and gate where the bear climbed over gave proof that the marauder had tested the sharpness of the scythe. That one lesson was enough; he never molested the orchard again.

We had many interesting, as well as laughable, experiences with various members of the bruin family. The salmon berry was his special favorite. The tall bushes in the river bottom were heavily laden with this luscious fruit—being as great a favorite with us as with the bears, a goodly portion of our leisure was spent in gathering them.

One lovely morning Grandma Judson and little Annie put on their sunbonnets, took their pails, and sallied forth in quest of salmon berries. When they had their pails about half full, they saw a dark object which they thought was an Indian picking berries on the other side of the bushes; having no fear of the Indians, they continued filling their pails. As they drew nearer their fellow picker Grandma said, "Klaw haw ya" (how do you do?) "kin clallies" (many berries). A muffled grunt, something like the tones of an Indian, seemed to answer the friendly salutation. A few steps farther, to their horror and dismay, brought them face to face with an immense black bear. Standing erect, master bruin was bending down the tops of the tall bushes with his fore paws and greedily filling his mouth with the luscious fruit, and so absorbed was he in this pleasant occupation that he did not notice his human companions until they came upon him. Down went pails and sunbonnets;

frightened Grandma and little Annie fled homeward, fear lending wings to their feet, while bruin dropped upon all fours and tore away through the bushes in the opposite direction. It would be difficult to decide which was the most frightened, Gradma, little Annie, or the bear.

CHAPTER XXV

Tribes of Indians often camped near by for the purpose of gathering the cammas roots. These nutritious bulbs were indigenous to the soil and grew abundantly in the river bottoms. So eager were they to gather these roots that we had to closely guard our enclosed fields to keep them from destroying the crops. It was hard for them to understand that the Boston man has any right to cut them off from their natural supplies of the spontaneous fruits of the earth that the Great Father had ordained for their support. During one of these cammas gathering expeditions one family was thrown into deep grief by the death of their only little girl. It was not their custom to bury their dead; they build a scaffold by driving crotched poles into the ground, laying on them a platform which they covered with mats; wrapping the child in blankets, they placed the little body upon their rude structure, with its little tin cup, beads and other trinkets, covering the whole with mats. To this sacred shrine the sorrowful mother often came, with a wailing cry that greeted my ears long before she reached the tomb of her child, mourning for her little ones in tones of pathetic grief. The weird intonation of this requiem "sin a mon-ah, ah," still sings in my ears when memory brings to mind the little scaffold that was reared in sight of my door.

The immortality of the soul is deeply implanted in all the Indian tribes. On the death of a chief, or brave who possessed slaves and ponies, the lives of all, or part, were sacrificed to bear him company to the happy hunting grounds.

Very early one morning a strong, young Indian of more than ordinary intelligence, who spoke many words in English, stopped at our house and told us that he was an "elita" (slave), that his master had died and he was fleeing from the relatives, who were seeking his life. His sad story at once enlisted our sympathy. We gave him a good breakfast of hot cakes and coffee, which proved to be his last meal. His lifeless body was found a few hours later in the road, where he had been overtaken and shot by his master's friends. The young man was trying to reach Shoal Water Bay, where he hoped to escape on a vessel to California.

One mile north of us lay a number of acres of high, rolling prairie, owned by Esq. Davis and son, who were blessed with fine families, and we with good neighbors. On this prairie a small schoolhouse was built of boards split with a frow from green cedar trees, and painted red. This was the first public building in the territory, in which we attended church—Rev. G. F. Whitworth, from Olympia, and my father, from Grand Mound, preaching alternately to us once a month, and good Deacon Stearns never allowing a Sunday to pass without holding religious services in the little red building, which services consisted mostly in singing the old spiritual songs, chanted so often by our sainted ancestors in the days of "auld lang syne," and to whom nearly all of that pioneer band are now gathered.

Ever since I can remember I had longed for a musical instrument of some kind, even an accordion would have satisfied me in my childhood days; and now in this far off corner of the world, buried in the wilderness, for the first time the desire of my life seemed to lie within my reach. As

Mr. Whitworth was about to send for an instrument for the Olympia church, I gave him my order for a Mason and Hamlin melodeon, the standard instrument of that time. They had to be brought around the "Horn," and it was nearly a year before I received mine. While waiting I improved the time by making myself thoroughly acquainted with instrumental music and practicing fingering on the table. At length the longed for treasure arrived. It was a beautiful rosewood instrument, and cost us, all expenses paid, one hundred dollars, but many hundreds would not be a costly price to pay for the joy this little instrument brought to me; it was an unusually sweet toned instrument. I could play a few chords and the whole family participated in my joy. In a short time I was able to play simple hymns. These two instruments were the first that came to the Coast.

Esq. Davis called his prairie Claquato, an Indian name for high land. A road was cut through the heavy timber by the settlers, from the prairie to the mouth of the Skookumchuck river, and other roads radiating from this point made Claquato a very pretty little town—nature having been lavish in her adornments, the scene was of picturesque beauty. For a number of years Claquato was the county seat of Lewis county. A half mile of heavy timber separated us from this little town. An overflow from the river caused the road, for a time, to become impassable. That I might enjoy the privilege of enjoying my neighbors, Mr. Judson thoughtfully cut a trail around through the timber of higher ground, and as the organ of locality was very poorly developed in my head, he "blazed" the trees for me to follow, that I should not get lost! but, in spite of the blazing, in crooking around the stumps and over and under the logs, I was sure to lose my way and be compelled to turn back for Mr. Judson to pilot me through, until he finally declared he "believed I would get lost in my own garden."

One day I was walking over this same trail, carefully looking for the trees that were "blazed," I was startled by the sudden appearance of a monster cougar leisurely crossing my path but a few feet in front of me. He was a fine specimen of his species and traveled along majestically, though switching the ground with his long tail detracted materially from his dignity. I should have been badly frightened had he deigned to look at me, but he turned his head neither to the right nor to the left— neither did I take another step forward, but turned and ran with all speed for Mr. Judson, who lost no time in securing his rifle, and together we hastened to the spot, but in spite of our haste his majesty had disappeared in the brush.

When Mr. Judson went to Olympia with old Tom and Jerry for supplies, I usually accompanied him for the purpose of visiting my friends on Grand Mound, and his sister Lucretia, the wife of U. S. Marshal George W. Corliss, of Olympia. The monotony of the tedius journey with the slow plodding oxen was frequently enlivened by the sight of wild animals, with which the country abounded; it being no uncommon sight to see a black bear cross the road ahead of the team, or a band of frightened deer, with their towering antlers and white tails, bounding away in the distance.

One fine morning, in the month of June, we got an earlier start than usual and had proceeded but a short dis-

tance before Jack, our Indian boy, spied three "mowich"
(deer) in the opening, near the timber. We always carried
the rifle with us on these expeditions. Leaving Jack in
charge of the team, Mr. Judson, gun in hand, crept cau-
tiously around the edge of the brush. I remained in the
wagon, as interested and amused in watching Jack as the
deer. He stood by the team, ox goad in hand, open mouthed
in his breathless interest, as Mr. Judson, creeping stealthily
out of their sight, drew near where the unsuspicious creatures were feeding. When we heard the report of the rifle
and saw the deer leap into the air, Jack excitedly shouted
"memaloose" (killed), and ran to help carry the game to
the wagon. We then jogged along over the road as fast
as the team, with their heavy grist of wheat, could travel,
in order to make up for lost time. On reaching the road
that had been lately cleared through from Claquato to
the Skookumchuck river, as it was very rough, I decided
to walk on ahead of the team, hoping by so doing to gain
time to call upon a friend who lived at the crossing of the
river. I was a good walker in those days, and the prospect
of soon meeting my dear friends filled my mind with happy
anticipations. I hastened over the rough way, my whole
being in unison with the sweet influences of my environments, drinking in the harmonious sights of beautiful nature, undispoiled by the hand of man. The majestic firs,
wide spreading cedars, the spruce with its spicy odor, the
graceful yew and hemlock combined to form a dense green
wall on either side. The varied hued mosses, with their
fairylike fronds, added greatly to the beauty of the scene.
The chirp of the lively little chipmunk was the only sound
that broke the deep silence of the forest. Occasionally a

saucy fellow, with his bushy tail, bounded chattering across my path, springing through the trees from branch to branch without any evidence of fear.

The snowy syringa and the graceful blossoms of the tassel wood with their beauty and fragrance charmed the senses into that dreamy state that brings one close to the divine, through His wonderful works of nature.

Surrounded by these sweet influences, I walked blissfully along, without any doubt that I'd reach the river before the team arrived. As I plunged more deeply into the heart of the timber, its solitude became oppressive; the tall trees, forming a lofty arch overhead, shut out the sunshine throwing a somber twilight over my pathway. I began to feel a sense of fear and realized the loneliness of my situation. So far from human sight or sound, and the thought of the wild animals that made their lairs in the depths of the forest, impelled me to hasten my footsteps, and when I came to where the "big bend" had been cut off to straighten the road, instead of going straight ahead as I should have done, I followed the old road which led around the bend, and while circling around and around it gradually dawned upon me that I was lost. Mr. Judson passed along on the new road, thinking I was in advance; and no doubt I would have continued these revolutions until exhausted, as I was greatly bewildered, had he not providentially met a party of surveyors, and learning from them that they had not seen me pass, he at once took in the situation. Leaving the team in the care of Jack, he came back to where the "big bend" had been cut off, and, after making one trip around the circle, finding only my track, and concluding that he could not overtake me, he very wisely sat down on a log and calmly awaited results. Great was my relief when rounding a clump of trees, I suddenly came upon him; fatigue, fear and anxiety vanished in a moment. Mr. Judson looked up with a familiar twinkle in his eye and coolly said, "Where are you going, Phoebe?" I answered by saying, "How long have you been sitting on that log, Holden?" Mr. Judson enjoyed the joke, and I profited by the lesson "that to progress through life, one should leave the crooked paths and travel the straight ones, that will carry us out of the wilderness."

My experience in traveling "the circuit" was always a standing joke with Mr. Judson; he never tired of repeating it, and many a hearty laugh we have both enjoyed, at my expense.

In consequence of this adventure, it was too late to even exchange greetings with my friends when we reached the river.

CHAPTER XXVI

Grand Mound prairie never looked more beautiful to me than at this time, after coming out of the forest. Mount Rainier, the highest mountain on the coast, rearing its lofty head 14,444 feet heavenward, was an ever fresh and unfailing source of joy and inspiration. Where there were no intervening objects to obstruct our view, we beheld her magnificent grandeur, glowing in purity and pristine splendor, in all the beauty of her shining height, from base to summit. Words but feebly describe the glorious sight.

This was the most delightful season of the year to visit our old home and that of my parents. The prairie was covered with such an abundance of wild strawberries that a white pony rolling on it was transformed into a bay, changing its appearance so completely that its owner would not recognize it by the color.

My old Indian neighbors, Yowanis, Cahorn, Ananates, "Deacon Clark," and their families, always greeted me with a hearty "Klaw-how-ya" (ho do you do).

I was quite elated over my prospective visit to Olympia, only wishing we had a span of spirited horses that would put on a little style going into town. I would have gotten out and walked as we neared the Corliss hotel, had I not been afraid of getting lost among the many high stumps and black logs that covered the townsite. I ought not to have been ashamed of Tom and Jerry, after having profited by their willing service in our long journey across the continent, though they were not quite so stylish as horses.

At length, however, my ambition was gratified. Mr.

Judson purchased a fine span of horses. I shall never forget our first experience with them, after Tom and Jerry
had been retired from service.

We were fording the river called Skookumchuck (the
unmusical name for swift water); all went well until we
reached the middle of the river, and then, to our great disgust, our fancy team balked. In spite of all persuasions
they could not be made to budge an inch. We must have
sat in the middle of the river a full hour, and began to
fear we might be forced to spend the night in this pre-
carious situation. Fortunately, however, a man on the
other shore spied us, and comprehending our predicament,
shouted, "Tie their tails to the whiffletrees," and, surprising to relate, that simple expedient seemed to take all the
balk out of them. They meekly went forward drawing us
safely to the shore.

Tom and Jerry never served us such a trick, nor left
us in the lurch in any emergency.

Pride assumes many forms to bring us into trouble—
often making us a laughing stock to our friends.

A lady of my acquaintance, who crossed the plains the
same year that we did, helped to defray her expenses by
performing camp duties—yoking and unyoking oxen, etc.
Soon after her arrival in the territory she married a man
of good position, and, upon entering society, her pride impelled her to claim that she "came around the Horn;" of
course, she referred to the "horn of the oxen."

The meeting with Lucretia was a happy reunion. We
were rejoiced to find her happy and contented in her new
home.

Before our return to Grand Mound we were prevailed

upon to remain until after the Fourth, and help to celebrate the anniversary of the great national day of freedom
that would take place in a few days, giving us an opportunity to visit our old neighbors that with us, were the first
settlers on the prairie. The future prospects for our country never looked brighter than at this time, and with hearts
inspired with love for our country, we loyally entered into
the preparation for celebrating the day, little realizing
while so happily engaged that an outbreak from the Indians
would soon enforce us to abandon our peaceful homes and
fly to the forts for safety.

CHAPTER XXVII

The ground chosen for the picnic was across the little creek opposite my father's home. There, under the grand old forest trees, we spread the tables, loading them with the best the country afforded. Here all the settlers within a radius of ten to twenty miles had gathered. The company was not so large but I could count them all, for I have not forgotten their names or faces, but we found a good time did not depend upon numbers; for never was festal day spent more joyously than this, our first Fourth of July celebration in the territory—showing our patriotism by unfurling the Stars and Stripes to the breeze and saluting it by hearty cheers that made the sunlit air ring with the music of peace and joy—a more fitting tribute than the deafening roar of the cannon, which speaks of carnage, and the awful desolation and woe that follow in the train of war.

After doing justice to the various dainties spread before us, patriotic songs were sung and an address delivered by my father, J. W. Goodell, with as much enthusiasm as though in a large assembly.

As it was one of the first Independence Day orations delivered in the territory, I will give a brief synopsis of it to my readers.

After congratulating the citizens that an all wise Providence had brought them together as one family to celebrate this glorious natal day, he said: "Love of country is a virtue; he that loves not his country loves not his God. Man is a social being; he was made for society, and from necessity he associated with his fellowmen for mutual help and protection, this being the spontaneous impulse of his being —to meet this demand governments have been divinely instituted, and only through these divine instrumentalities can our country be preserved and the blessings of society secured and enjoyed.

"The spirit of emigration did not die with the pilgrim emigrants who settled the Atlantic states. Believing there was a country away over on the other side of the Rocky mountains, on the shores of the Pacific two thousand miles beyond where the searchers of the west had gone, we gathered up what little of our effects that would bear transportation, and with our wives and little ones we undertook the long, tedious and dangerous journey.

"Through a kind Providence we were safely guided to this goodly land, and we have found what so many before sought but never found, the 'Far West,' we can truly say that our lives have fallen in pleasant places."

So happily closed this day, the first that we, as a community had celebrated in the territory. We returned to our homes refreshed and invigorated with our happy intercourse with friends, and bright anticipations for the future. But alas! Their speedy fulfilment were suddenly blasted by an Indian war, which broke upon us like a thunderbolt from a clear sky—that had so disastrous an effect that only a few of the "advance guard" of pioneers lived to enjoy an advanced state of civilization, crowned with a "paradise of blessings." After weary years of "hope deferred" one by one they exchanged the home for which they had left civilization, home and friends many a weary mile behind, for one already prepared for them. My father, with faith undaunted in the future greatness of the country, and in perfect submission to the will of his Heavenly Father was one of the first to "pass over."

CHAPTER XXVIII

During the summer of 1855 gold was discovered east of the mountains, in the vicinity of Fort Colville. Several prospecting parties, allured by the hope of gain, left the Sound country for the new gold fields, which to reach they were obliged to pass through a country infested by hostile Indians, with whom treaties had not been perfected. Governor Stevens, apprehending trouble with these tribes, had proceeded with an escort to negotiate with them for their lands—leaving Hon. C. H. Mason, territorial secretary, acting governor during his absence. But the Indians were not satisfied with their treaty, nor with the influx of white men into the country. Many of the prospecting parties were waylaid and massacred by the Yakima tribes. Maj. G. O. Haller, of the regular army, who had been sent out on the plains with a small detachment of troops to protect the emigrants and, if needed, to co-operate with Governor Stevens, was attacked by these same tribes, and retired with the loss of one-fourth of his men and a large amount of government stores.

Agent Boland was also massacred. This startling intelligence was conveyed to Olympia about the first of October, by pony express, over the trail of the mountain, by Messenger William Tidd.

Acting Governor Mason immediately organized a company of mounted volunteers at Olympia, with Gilmore Hays, captain; James Hurd, first lieutenant, and William Martin, second lieutenant; Henry Cook, Joseph White, Thomas Prather and Joseph Gibson, sergeants; John Scott, Whitfield Hirlly, T. Wheelock and Joseph Taylor, corporals.

Colonel Casey, who was in command of the regulars at Fort Steilacoom, ordered nearly the whole force stationed at this post, under command of Captain Pickett.

These combined armies started at once to go over the mountains by the Naches pass, expecting to be reinforced by the regulars and volunteers from The Dalles at the foot of the mountains, to go with them into the hostile country to quell the disturbance.

We were living on the most friendly terms with our Indians west of the mountains, not entertaining any fears from them while pursuing our usual vocations in promised security.

The sun of prosperity never shone more brightly upon us, when suddenly the black cloud of the Indian war rolled up in darkening volumes, obscuring our sky and checking our prosperity.

While we were equipping our two hundred volunteers with all the available firearms in the country, never giving a thought for our own safety, messengers were passing and repassing from tribe to tribe between British Columbia to the California line among these wily savages, who were secretly conspiring to rise enmasse and exterminate all the white settlers in the territory, which they would no doubt have accomplished had it not been for the too hasty work of some of the more desperate tribes giving the citizens warning in time to frustrate their plans.

No sooner had the soldiers departed from the settlements, and entered the deep defiles of the mountains, than our Indians, in whom we had placed the utmost confidence, began to put into execution their nearly matured plans of "exterminating the whites."

The work of death in the Sound country began by mas-
sacring Lieutenant McAllister and Mr. Connell by the Nisqually and Puyallup tribes, headed by Leschi, who was the
chief and leader of the hostile Indians west of the mountains. These men, ignorant of any dissatisfaction among
them, went with a party of rangers to interview and counsel
them not to be influenced against the settlers by the hos-
tiles east of the mountains, and to show them the confidence
that they placed in their professed friendship, they were un-
armed—which resulted in their being assassinated by the
well laid snare of the enemy.

Soon after they attacked the unsuspecting citizens of
White river, ruthlessly slaughtering men, women and children in the most revolting and cruel manner. The members
of three families were all massacred, while others escaped,
some of them wounded; alarming their neighbors, they fled
to Seattle, a distance of twenty-five miles.

General alarm and consternation prevailed upon all the
inhabitants of our once happy, but now distracted, country.
Stockades were built as speedily as possible and their families gathered into them. The larger portion of our forces
were gone, leaving us without means of defense, and to in-
tensify our fears, the news came to us that, for some un-
explained reason, the troops from The Dalles would not
probably leave for several days. Our small volunteer forces,
therefore, moving through the mountain passes, must
meet the combined strategy of the hostile tribes single
handed. Recognizing the nature of the ground through
which they would be obliged to pass—the deep and narrow
canyons, where they could be surrounded and destroyed
without seeing an enemy, the mountains back of them cut-

ting off all chance for retreat, we could see no way for
their escape. They were undoubtedly now within two or
three days' march of where two thousand hostile Indians
were lying in wait for them. The road between the settlements and the foot of the mountains were ambushed, and
those savages whose hands were reeking with the blood of
innocent families, were camped at the fording of White
river, where an express would be compelled to pass.

Our fathers, brothers, husbands and sons composed that
little band of volunteers whom we looked upon as about to
be sacrificed. It was a time of deepest anxiety and agoniz-
ing suspense. They must be recalled; and William Tidd
was again dispatched with preemptory orders from the governor at Olympia and Colonel Casey at Fort Steilacoom,
to Captain Pickett and Hays in command of the troops, to
return at once.

Messenger Tidd volunteered that "live or die" he
would carry the express; and, in less than two hours after
reaching Fort Steilacoom, he was flying with the utmost
speed for the mountains.

In vain he was warned by the defeated rangers "that
death lay in his path." Neither did the pale light of the
moon reveal to him the ghastly forms of the citizens of
White river. A deep slumber had fallen upon the savages
after their work of butchery and plunder, and they heard
not the clatter of the pony's hoofs as he flew along the road
or plunged into the foaming waters of White river.

The first dangerous ford is passed; there are others, but
he presses on, and in less than forty-eight hours from the
time he left Fort Steilacoom he entered the camp of our
"soldier boys," just beyond the summit of the mountains.

He has accomplished his mission, and now to relieve the anxious settlements, he hastens to return.

Five of the volunteer soldiers obtained permission to come ahead of the main company with him, and as they retraced their steps they are ambushed by the way, and A. B. Moses, sheriff of Thurston county, and Joseph Miles, an Olympia lawyer, were both killed. Messenger Tidd was struck by a bullet in the back of the head, but not seriously wounded. He, with the others of the survivors, abandoned their horses and took to the woods and brush, where they crawled by night and hid by day—reaching the settlements the third day in a deplorable condition, having thrown away their shoes to make less noise while traveling.

When the joyful tidings swept over the settlemets that our volunteers and soldiers were safe on this side of the mountains, there was great rejoicing, as there was scarcely a family but had a loved one in that devoted band.

Days and nights had passed in the deepest anxiety, and now that all doubt was removed as to their safety, their pent up hearts could be restrained no longer, and tears of joy streamed from many eyes.

We looked upon Messenger "Bill" Tidd as a hero, and consider his name as honorable in the annals of history as that of Dewey, Hobson, or other of our modern heroes, for by his daring exploits the lives of the commands of Captain Pickett and Hays, as well as the citizens of the whole Sound country, were saved.

The battle on White river, a few days after the return of our soldiers, in which the Indians were defeated and completely routed, with a loss of between twenty-five and thirty killed and wounded, struck terror into the hearts of the Indians among us—preventing any more joining the hostile bands. Still the war was continued and a large portion of our able-bodied men were kept constantly braving the dangers and enduring the hardships of a savage war.

Twenty-two forts were built in the Sound country. The one in which we were forted was situated at Claquato, was built of heavy timbers and enclosed by a palisade of fir and cedar posts, twelve feet in height, driven firmly into the ground. Port holes were made in the walls of the block houses, through which we might defend ourselves from the enemy.

But we did not propose to leave our homes unless forced to go. We noticed each day that our Indians were becoming more and more insolent, while at the same time professing friendship by asking with a well feigned solicitude, "Mica quas mesachie Siwash?" (were we afraid of the bad Indians), and "What would we do if they should come on this side of the mountains?"

CHAPTER XXIX

Although living in fear, we never acknowledged the fact, but gave them to understand that we would fight should they come. They frequently came to the house, appearing unusually interested in all of our belongings, peering into everything that was open to their inspection.

On one occasion, when Mr. Judson was absent, they took down the rifle, examining it critically, meanwhile talking earnestly among thesemlves.

We afterwards learned through the native wives of some of the white settlers that they had taken an inventory of the property of every white settler, and had allotted to each one his share, to be appropriated as soon as they had disposed of the rightful owner.

One day a number of them were bent on going into our wheat fields to dig camas. When Mr. Judson remonstrated, one of them, much more repulsive in appearance than the others, whom we called "Pug Ugly," made an impertinent speech, claiming the land as his own. When Mr. Judson picked up a stick with which to knock him down, they all rose to their feet, and with their camas diggers threateningly raised, were ready for battle. Mr. Judson ran to the house for his revolver, but I had anticipated him, and with the help of loyal Jack, who never joined the disaffected Indians, with much difficulty prevailed upon him not to use it. Mr. Judson was followed into the house by two of the Indian women, who stood visibly shaking with fear as they witnessed his determination to use his revolver. They, however, were not more terror stricken than was I, fully realizing the disastrous result had an Indian been wounded or met death at his hands.

Our neighbors had many similar experiences, convincing us that our Indians were only waiting for an acession to their numbers before exterminating us and dividing the spoils.

It was an exciting time when an expressman rode through the settlements warning "all who were not already in the forts to hasten there at once," for, said he, "the hostile Indians are on this side of the mountains."

It was nine o'clock A. M. when we received this alarming message. Father and Mother Judson were with us, and we all began at once to pack our bedding, cooking utensils and provisions. Such crockery and various useful articles that we need not take with us, mother and I carried into the woods and hid under a large cedar log, where it remained over a year. I brought my clothes from the line where they were hanging in the rain, pulled off some dry cedar boards with which our house was lined, made a blazing fire in the fireplace, and soon had them dry.

I shall never forget, while in the midst of our excitement, of seeing little Bonta, with his red cheeks and sparkling black eyes, dragging the loaded rifle from the sleeping room as he cried with all the courage and assurance of a little child, "Me'l shoot the Indians."

We had carelessly left it standing at the head of the bed, where Mr. Judson placed it, with the axe, every night, ready for use, before retiring—keeping the revolver under his pillow. We were all packed before night, and, with hearts filled with forebodings for the future, we sadly departed from the home where hope had filled the bright hours with gladness, holding before us such glowing promises for the future. Our bright dreams lay shattered. With

tear dimmed eyes we bade farewell to the dear abode that
we might never again behold.

Old Tom and Jerry were again pressed into service,
and, as we slowly wended our way to the fort in the dusk
of the evening, we were somewhat startled by seeing an Indian standing by the roadside under a tree. He stealthily
sneaked off into the brush out of sight, like some wild animal, but we recognized him as one of our friendly Indians,
whom we called "Squatty." That he did not come and
speak to us in his usual manner looked rather suspicious.
No doubt he was a spy and would report our movements
to the other members of the tribe.

It was dark when we reached the fort, where we found
the people of the settlements had already gathered. One
man, through fear and excitement, had become insane
and was confined in the lower part of the block houses.
He was raving furiously when we entered the fort, and as
his maniacal screams greeted our ears, Father Judson
drily remarked, "We are safe now." We had nothing to
fear, however, from the poor demented creature, for he
was so violent that they were compelled to keep him in
chains.

Taking possession of our apportioned quarters, we found
ourselves comfortably domiciled. Our accommodations
were commodious—only a half dozen families, and as many
bachelors, comprising our small settlement. Our strong,
but rude, tower standing on the crest of a gently sloping
hill, in the center of a small prairie, we commanded a
fine view of the surrounding country, where an Indian
could not attempt to secrete himself without being discovered.

How sweet and restful were our slumbers under the protection of our stronghold. We only realized the terrible strain under which we continually dwelt in our unprotected homes as we rested in the security of the fort. However, during the day there was still cause for great anxiety, for our men were exposed while cultivating their land to "keep the wolf from the door."

When Mr. Judson and his father went to work on the "ranch" I went with them, leaving Annie and La Bonta with their grandma for safety. While the men were engaged in planting and harvesting the crops, I stood guard, keeping a sharp outlook for the enemy.

On one occasion, while we were busily engaged in threshing wheat with the flail in the barn, I was greatly frightened by seeing two Indians creeping along in the edge of the brush in a skulking manner, very near the barn, but when I gave the alarm they quickly disappeared from sight.

One day while on duty I heard the doleful cries of a pig in the claws of a bear. The dogs were with me. Climbing the fence, I ran with them down into the hollow, from whence the sounds proceeded. The dogs speedily outstripped me and before I arrived upon the scene of action they had succeeded in liberating the pig; but old bruin, nothing daunted, still held his ground—standing on his haunches, eying me defiantly, but his temerity cost him his life, for Mr. Judson, taking in the situation, followed quickly in my footsteps, and assuming the leading role in the play, planted a bullet between the eyes of the daring monster. Poor piggy, I had met him as I followed the dogs into the hollow, torn and bleeding, running with speed from the scene of his disaster; but piggy had received his death wound—breathing his last breath a few minutes later.

I helped roll bruin onto a sled. The accomplishment of this feat taxed our strength to the utmost. Old Tom and Jerry did their part in drawing him to the fort. As I followed the sled, I could not help wishing it had been Leschi (the wily old leader of the hostile Indians) we had captured.

The quartermaster general of the Claquato stockade was good Esq. Davis, who did not object to "women's rights" (in times of danger). He gave me a musket to carry and I practiced loading and firing at a mark, and, had it become necessary, would have used it in defense of my home and country, as did the heroic Mrs. King, of White river, whom, it was said, shot and killed two Indians while fighting to save her husband's life, but was overpowered at last and ruthlessly murdered. Her little son managed to make his escape and told the mournful story.

The King family crossed the plains in the year 1854 in the Ebey and Judson train, when Mrs. King was heard to say that "if George (her husband) was killed by the Indians, she would fight them the rest of her life." Their little daughter died on the way, and her casket was a trunk, decorated with wild roses. Her fate was not so sad as though she had lived, to suffer the death of her parents.

Many other deeds of bravery, stimulated by affection, might be related.

It was bedtime when Indians were heard prowling around the premises of the home of Mr. Kincaid. Quickly all lights were extinguished, and the family fled for the Stuck river. Miss Susan seized her young brother, Joseph, to whom since her mother's death she had been a mother, and on that dark October night carried him in safety across a small alder log spanning the river, to a place of conceal-ment where they, with the rest of the family, lay hidden during the night, and upon the next day they safely reached Steilacoom.

Lieutenant Slaughter and his regiment, while camped at the forks of White and Green rivers, unwisely allowed themselves a fire to dry their clothing. The Indians, guided by the light, shot and killed the lieutenant, also two non-commissioned officers, and wounded several others.

An Indian servant boy, who had been employed by the lieutenant, turned traitor and pointed him out to the sav-age, who took deadly aim, the bullet piercing his heart and causing instant death. His body was carried to his friends at Steilacoom. His death was greatly lamented, because of his high character and fine abilities. He was a man of great promise. The scene of his death bears the name of Slaughter, in honor of the brave lieutenant.

Mr. Northcraft, while driving a wagon loaded with provisions on the Yelm road, was waylaid and assassinated by these stealthy miscreants, and his team and provisions taken into the mountains.

Mr. White, with his wife and a neighbor woman, left the fort on Chambers prairie to attend church. The two women rode in a one-horse cart and Mr. White walked by the side. While returning home, a number of Indians on their ponies suddenly sprang out from a point of timber near the road and attempted to surround the cart; but the horse became frightened and outran the Indians to the fort, saving the lives of the women. When the frightened horse

reached the fort, only one board was left on the cart bed
to which they clung. One of them, through all that fearful
ride, held a small child in her arms, and had one foot badly
mangled by the wheel. Mr. White was murdered and
scalped and left by the roadside, in sight of the fort.

Mrs. Dr. Spinning, the sister of Mrs. White, was forted
with us when the sad news was brought.

Reports often reached us of our friends being waylaid
by these lurking foes, and the settlers were afraid to leave
the protection of the forts as long as these depredations
continued.

There were thirty families confined in Fort Henness,
on Grand Mound, including my father. This being a cen-
tral fort, all the families from the surrounding country
flocked into it, and here they lived for sixteen months, as
thick as bees in a hive, and in perfect harmony, nothwith-
standing the fact that only a thin partition separated the
families.

Mrs. Biles, a dear friend who is still living, to "tell the
story," recently writing about "those times," said, in re-
ferring to the wonderful harmony which reigned throughout the fort, "that they were afraid the Indians would kill
them and they wanted to die in peace with all mankind." A
common danger levels all differences and brings humanity
into that condition of mutual love where the dove of peace
reigns supreme "and pity 'tis, 'tis true" that in this beautiful world we find that fear is most frequently the chief
factor in subduing the human heart.

When I visited the fort and saw the number of children,
of all ages, sizes and conditions, truly I marveled that such
a reign of peace was possible.

A number of notable events transpired in our fort—the marriage of Mr. Ben Spinning to Miss Mary Castor, and the birth of a son to the wife of Dr. Spinning; also a son to the wife of Edwin Davis. The saddest event was the death of little Mamie Spinning. We all loved the bright little prattler, with the dark, expressive eyes, and the sweet, innocent face, and we followed, as one family, with the sorrowing parents, the precious form from which the bright jewel had fled, to the little grave on the hillside near a small grove of evergreen trees and sang "Sister Thou Wast Mild and Lovely." being a very impressive scene, and the first burial any one of us had attended in the country.

CHAPTER XXX

When the Yakima and Klickitat warriors learned that the Oregon volunteers were entering their country, on the east side of the Cascades, they returned to their homes east of the mountains, leaving the Indians on the west side to take care of themselves—which they did by seeking refuge in the dense forests and canyons of the foothills, from which they would occasionally sally forth and commit some horrible depredation.

Governor Stevens finally offered to protect and feed them if they would come in and give themselves up, and many of them were only too glad to accept his offer. A price was set upon Leschi's head, which subsequently led to his capture by the treachery of two of his own people, Sluggia and Elikukah. They went to the place where Leschi was hiding, and, having decoyed him to the spot where their horses were concealed, suddenly seized, bound and carried him to Sydney S. Ford, captain of the Chehalis company of scouts, who delivered him to Governor Stevens at Olympia.

Much sympathy was expressed for the poor outlawed Indian by all lovers of justice. His own tribe, that had been subdued by the government, were induced to turn against their chief, not permitting him to remain in his own country, except as a slave.

Leschi, deservedly, had many friends. Those who had been well acquainted with him before the war considered him a good Indian. It was well known that he had been deceived by unscrupulous traders, who, to serve their own interests, had caused him to believe that the govern-

ment, to make room for the white people, would banish the
Indians to a dark island, where the sun would never more
shine upon them. He was also assured that there were but
a few white people in the world, and that if the Indians
would kill those in the territory, no more would come.

Filled with dismay at the dismal prospect set before
him, what could the poor Indian do but to exert all his pow-
ers to save himself and people from such an unhappy fate?

Leschi was tried by a special term of court, but not
convicted, the jury failing to agree. But at his second trial,
in March, 1857, he was convicted and sentenced to be
hanged on the tenth of June. His counsel at once instituted
proceedings to carry the case up to the supreme court in
December. Chief Justice McFadden sustained the action
of the district court, and the verdict of the jury.

Leschi's execution was fixed, the second time, to take
place upon the twenty-second day of January, 1858.

In the meantime Governor Stevens had resigned, and
Governor McMullen had arrived, to whom a strong appeal
was made by the counsel and friends of Leschi, but to no
effect—seven hundred settlers protesting against a pardon.

When the day of execution arrived a large concourse of
people assembled at Steilacoom to witness the death of so
celebrated a character. But the friends of the doomed man
had prepared a surprise for them. The sheriff of Pierce
county and his deputy were arrested upon a charge of selling liquor to the Indians. An attempt was made by Secretary Mason to obtain the death warrant, in possession of the
sheriff, which was frustrated until after the hour fixed for
the execution had passed, during which time the sheriff remained in custody with no attempt to procure his freedom.

This plot, executed between the prisoner's counsel and the military authorities at Fort Steilacoom, aroused a lively indignation on the part of the majority of the people. Public meetings were held and all persons concerned in the frustration of the sentence of the courts were condemned, and the legislature requested to take cognizance of it. The legislature passed an act requiring the judges of the supreme court to hold a special session on or before the first of February, at the seat of government, repealing all laws in conflict with this act. The case was remanded to the court of the second judicial district on a writ of error, and an order issued for a special session of the district court, before which Leschi was again brought, when his counsel entered a demurrer to its jurisdiction, which was overruled, and Leschi was, for the third time, sentenced to be hanged on the nineteenth day of February.

After enduring the long drawn agony of suspense in prison, the emaciated form of the poor savage, with hands pinioned, paid the penalty exacted by law for taking human life. It was proven that he killed A. B. Moses before war was declared.

I would not controvert the justice of the sentence, according to the old law, "An eye for an eye, and a tooth for a tooth," but this merciless law obtains with the educated white man, as well as with the ignorant savage.

What a pitiful spectacle such a scene presents of the hardness of the human heart. I could fight to save life, but to witness the deliberate strangling of a helpless, ignorant human being, after having been so many times encouraged to hope that his life would be spared, fills my soul with horror—reminding me of the pitiful scene of a captured mouse in the custody of a cat, who allows her victim, now and then, a little deceptive freedom, as she pats it with her velvet paw, ere she strangles out its life.

Capital punishment is a relic of barbarism and a disgrace to every civilized nation that upholds it. "Thou shalt not kill" applies to rulers and governments, as well as individuals. It gives me great satisfaction to know that some of our states repudiate this inhuman practice.

Soon after Leschi's capture and arrest, three others, leaders of the hostile bands of Indians, trusting in Governor Stevens' "promise of protection," came out of their concealment, going to a white friend, requested him to accompany them to Olympia and deliver them to Governor Stevens to be tried. Every precaution was taken to convey them secretly to Olympia. Their arrival was under cover of darkness, but in vain was every effort for their safety. All three of them were assassinated by white men. Two were shot while landing from their canoe by Joe Brannon, in a spirit of revenge for the massacre of his sister and her child on White river—their bodies having been found, mutilated, in a well. The other Indian was shot in Governor Stevens' office, where several people had gained access through the back door among whom was James Bunton, son-in-law of McAlister, who had been killed by some of Leschi's people. Governor Stevens, who had in all of his dealings with the Indians, been actuated by a high sense of justice and sympathy for them, was greatly incensed. He had perfected every arrangement to convey the Indians to Steilacoom before daylight, where they were to be imprisoned while awaiting their trial. Bunton was arrested, but for lack of evidence was not convicted.

The assassination of these poor Indians, after they had surrendered themselves for trial, makes one feel like reversing the application of the old saying, "There is no good Indian but a dead one"—for the Indian could not do a more treacherous deed than this committed by the civilized (?) white men.

What a contrast to the forgiving spirit of President McKinley, who, in the midst of his sufferings, pleaded with the incensed crowd that was ready to tear his assassin to pieces, "Don't hurt him." Would that the world held more such men.

Few of the Indian leaders of the war on the Sound survived it. A number were hanged at Fort Steilacoom—three were assassinated out of revenge, Kitsap was killed by his own people, and Sluggia (who betrayed Leschi) was killed by Leschi's friends.

After the war was over, and depredations had ceased, we left the fort for our home, thankful that our settlement had not had any actual encounters with the Indians. But it was a long time before we felt perfectly safe. Mr. Judson made double doors and windows out of heavy plank, which we set up every night before retiring, and when aroused from our slumbers by the barking of our dogs, with hearts palpitating with fear, we tiptoed around the house listening for the stealthy tread of the Indians.

The misfortune of the war had blighted our prospects. Fences were down, fields that had waved with luxuriant crops were lying waste and desolate. Many families had left the country, leaving but a few straggling settlements for many years. Still we did not yield to despair, but went forward, trusting that the clouds would disappear from our sky and the sun of prosperity shine again upon us.

However, our troubles were not entirely over. The following summer Mr. Judson's sister narrowly escaped the fate met by so many of our lamented pioneers.

CHAPTER XXXI

The war of 1855-6 with the Indians east and west of the mountains had hardly come to a close, when the Northern Indians, who were in the habit of making annual raids to Puget Sound for the purpose of plunder, began murdering, as well as robbing, the white people living in isolated settlements along the Sound. On the twenty-fourth of February, 1856, the U. S. Steamer Massachusetts arrived in the Sound, and the commander, Swartout, pursued several large canoe loads of these prowling tribes, overtaking them at Port Gamble, where they were encamped in the woods. After making many overtures, to induce them to return peaceably to their homes, and all had failed, he opened fire upon their wigwams, killing and wounding a large number of them, and destroyed their canoes. The survivors were taken on board of the Massachusetts, where they were treated kindly by the officers. When they reached Victoria, a passage was secured for them to their own country.

The citizens naturally flattered themselves that this severe chastisement would put an end to their turbulent spirits. But an Indian chief had been killed by a ball from the war ship, and to avenge his death the life of an innocent man had to be sacrificed.

The following summer, on the eleventh day of August, 1857, one of their large canoes, carrying seventy warriors, glided along the shores of Whidby island, in quest of the white man's "tyee," or chief. No ordinary man would answer their purpose. Col. I. N. Ebey was a representative of the government, having been for a number of years collector of customs, and to offset the death of their chieftain, he was doomed to pay the penalty of their old heathen law "An eye for an eye, and a tooth for a tooth." They stealthily moved along the shores of the island until they reached what is known as Ebey's landing. This was the landing place for all the boats from Port Townsend. 'Twas here that a number of officials from Olympia were landed to attend court at Penn's Cove, Whidby Island, but a few days before the awful tragedy, which I am about to relate, occurred. Among them were Col. William Wallace, who later became representative to Congress, and governor of the territory, and George W. Corliss, U. S. marshal, both accompanied by their wives, who were improving the opportunity to visit their friends, Mrs. Corliss having crossed the plains three years before in the Ebey train, in which were Colonel Ebey's father, mother, brother and two sisters. They settled on claims adjoining their son and brother, Col. Isaac N. Ebey, who came to the territory in 1850— his wife being the first white woman on Whidby island.

Court at Penn's cove had adjourned on that fatal night. Colonel Wallace and his wife were the guests of Father Ebey, while Marshal Corliss and wife were entertained at the hospitable home of Colonel Ebey—they all intending to cross over to Port Townsend in the morning. Mr. and Mrs. Corliss, in speaking of the last hours spent in Colonel Ebey's company, said they had passed a very enjoyable evening, the colonel entertaining them in his usually happy manner, appearing even to be in exceptionally high spirits, speaking with glowing enthusiasm of the bright prospects that lay in the near future for this new country. Mrs. Corliss, always a delicate, timid woman, was more nervous than usual, on account of having noticed during the day

Indians on the beach, with war paint on their faces, and she had scarcely closed her eyes in sleep when, a little past midnight, they were aroused by the furious barking of Colonel Ebey's dog. Thinking that the crew had come for the U. S. officials, Colonel Ebey got up and went outside, when the Indians immediately opened fire, and the poor colonel was heard by the inmates of the house to fall on the porch. Mr. Corliss sprang to the front door, and, while attempting to fasten it securely, advised his wife, Mrs. Ebey and the children to escape through the back window. Mrs. Corliss was the first one out. An Indian who was stationed there fired at her. She jumped a high picket fence and fell in the tall grass. The Indian, no doubt thinking he had killed her, went around to the front of the house and joined his comrades. She then ran to a bachelor's ranch where a party of five men were stopping, and gave the alarm by knocking on the door and exclaiming, with broken sobs, "The Northern Indians have killed them all." The men at once sent friendly Indians that were camped near by to carry the shocking news to the settlers. They quickly loaded their guns, giving Mrs. Corliss a wrap, as she was in her night clothes, and also a pair of socks to cover her feet. Although crippled by jumping the high picket fence, she accompanied them back to the home of Colonel Ebey, where they were reinforced by many of the settlers whom the friendly Indians had aroused from their slumbers.

As they drew near the house, they heard the Indians paddling off in their canoes, singing their war songs. In the yard they found the headless body of the brave colonel, lying in his night clothes, the Indians having carried off the head as a trophy. They had used the axe (that the colonel had that day sharpened) to execute their bloody deed. All was silent as the grave. Even the faithful watch dog was so cowed by the murder of his master that he made no demonstration at their approach.

Entering the silent house, with anxious forebodings, they began the search for the missing ones. No trace of them could be found. Sadly they were forced to the dread conclusion that Mr. Corliss and the two boys, Eason and Ellison Ebey, had been killed, and Mrs. Ebey and her little daughter carried away captives. But at early dawn their anxious hearts were relieved by hearing one of the boys shout from the woods, where they had been hidden, "that they were safe." They escaped through the window while the Indians were battering down the door with their hatchets; pulling a few pickets from the back fence they hurriedly fled to the woods. They owed their escape from detection to the tall grass between the house and the woods, which effectually concealed them.

The house was thoroughly plundered—all of the supplies taken from the storeroom, blankets and even the feather beds emptied, and the ticking taken, as well as all of their clothes. Only one thing of value escaped their notice. In their hurry to get away, they overlooked a purse of money that Mr. Corliss had left in the bed, and it was found among the feathers that the Indians had emptied from the bed tick.

The tragic death of Mr. Ebey created a wild excitement throughout the whole country, as he was one of the most prominent citizens of Washington territory, having faithfully filled many offices of honor, and had largely assisted, while a member of the Oregon legislature of March,

1853, in securing the separation of its northern portion, and the organization of Washington territory.

Colonel Ebey's family have all passed to the immortal side of life, with the exception of one niece, Mrs. Enos, of San Francisco, California, who was at the home of Colonel Ebey's father, on Whidby island, at the time of the tragedy; and five grandchildren, one, Harold H., the son of Ellison Ebey, and four children of Eason Ebey—two daughters and two sons—who are also our grandchildren. Eason Ebey, some years subsequent to the death of his father, entered our family by claiming the hand of our daughter, Annie.

CHAPTER XXXII

In 1858 Mr. Judson was elected to the legislature on the Democratic ticket, and I accompanied him to the capital.

The legislature convening the first of December and adjourning the last of February, gave me a very pleasant three months' visit with Lucretia. She was still on crutches and in an exceedingly nervous condition—the effect of her terrible experience on Whidby island at the time of the Ebey tragedy. She lived in a state of continual terror, and so great was her fear that she kept her windows fastened day and night.

Among the many who frequently visited Lucretia's pleasant home was Miss Mary Wood, an old friend who crossed the plains the same year we did. Here she first met and became acquainted with Fayette McMullen, who superseded Stevens as governor.

Mary was deservedly much admired, and when the governor left the territory, the following year, he bore away our sweet friend, a bride, to his Virginia home.

It was at this time that we became acquainted with John A. Tenant, a member of the legislature from Whatcom county. In after years Mr. Tenant became closely associated with us, as a friend and neighbor. At this time he was a member of the bar, and a rising lawyer.

A beautiful young lady, the daughter of Judge ———, had taken captive his heart, but evidently she did not give him hers in exchange, at least her hand was given to General————, a man of much wealth and position.

Poor Mr. Tenant never recovered from the disappointment. He returned to Whatcom county, took up a claim on the Nooksack river, and, following the example of many other bachelors, lived with a "kloochman."

When the country began to be settled a law was passed compelling those who were living with Indian women to either marry them, or put them away. Mr. Tenant honorably married Clara, his kloochman, thus making their boy their heir.

The only exciting events of our three months' sojourn in Olympia were the final execution of the poor Indian, Leschi, after the many ineffectual struggles for his life— and the memorable Fraser river excitement. When it was learned that the Hudson Bay Company had for three years been receiving gold dust from the Fraser River Indians in exchange for lead, ounce for ounce, the wildest excitement reigned.

And when the steamers began coming into Bellingham Bay once, and sometimes twice, a day, fairly black was passengers, our hopes for the speedy development of the country were raised to the highest pitch.

Mr. Corliss and Mr. Judson invested in Whatcom lots, and contributed liberally to the fund for opening the trail to the Fraser.

On account of the difficulties of the route, very few of the thousands of adventurers reached the mines. Many of the disappointed ones, not having the means to carry them home, took up government land in the territory—probably proving a greater benefit, both to themselves and the country, than if they had reached the mines.

The winter passed swiftly away, brightened by the congenial intercourse of which we had been so long deprived, and I dreaded the return to the lonely "ranch" life.

Mr. Judson had a canoe made to order, large enough to carry fifty bushels of grain. It was now completed, and he intended taking it home on a wagon, but fortunately, much to my comfort and pleasure, we were surprised by a snow storm. Seeing the ground covered with snow, a bright inspiration came to Mr. Judson, and he invited me to "take a sleigh ride."

Attaching old Tom and Jerry to the canoe, much to the delight of the children, we had our first sleigh ride in Washington territory, slipping over the gravelly prairie very smoothly, until we reached my father's home on Grand Mound, where we remained over night. The next day, the snow having disappeared, we finished our journey in a wagon, and once more settled down to the monotony and drudgery of "ranch life."

During the summer Mr. Judson was re-elected to the legislature, and I looked forward with much pleasure to another visit with Lucretia and other dear friends.

When November rolled around again, we climbed into the wagon, our only mode of transportation, with never a thought we were bidding a last farewell to this home. Before the legislature had adjourned, Mr. Judson sold the farm for four thousand dollars, taking groceries and dry goods in part payment.

However, instead of accompanying him to Olympia, I spent the first part of the winter with my parents on Grand Mound. Annie and La Bonta were visiting Father and Mother Judson, near Olympia.

Annie was now a rosy cheeked girl of ten, and La Bonta a sprightly little mischief of seven summers.

I arrived at my parents' home about the middle of November, and on the seventeenth of December a letter was sent to Annie and Bonta, announcing the arrival of a baby brother. The following Saturday Mr. Judson brought the happy children to see the new baby.

Mr. Judson was passionately fond of babies, and a more delighted trio than this papa and brother and sister it would be hard to find.

When baby George (named for Mr. Corliss) was six weeks old we went to Lucretia's home, and when the legislature adjourned we began our home life in Olympia, in a frame house—the first one we had occupied since coming to the Coast.

Mr. Judson, having placed all his capital in the business, a dry goods and grocery store, our "ideal home" still lay in the future, and we contented ourselves for the present in a rented house.

The change in our environment was great—surrounded by friends and neighbors, with school and church privileges, after living so long with our nearest neighbor a mile away, made us feel that we were again within the bounds of civilization.

CHAPTER XXXIII

To Isaac N. Ebey belongs the honor of christening this town, a name suggested while admiring the snow-capped peaks of the Olympic range of mountains, which rose abruptly to the north, and repeating the following lines:

> *"After their crystal summits rise,*
> *Like gems against the sunset skies,*
> *While far below the shadowy mist,*
> *In waves of pearl and amethyst,*
> *Round stately fir, and somber pines,*
> *Its dewy jeweled fingers twined,*
> *Olympia's gods might view with grace*
> *Nor scorn so fair a dwelling place."*

Olympia wore an air of dignity that may be attributed to the location, at head of Puget Sound, and her political station as Capital City, and also to her superior class of citizens. Added to this, Olympia had many natural advantages which augured fair for her future greatness.

The beautiful body of water which lay in placid loveliness before the town forcibly reminded us of our beloved Lake Erie, though the shores were not so prominent, nor the beaches so beautiful with pebbles and shells, and the waters were salt, instead of fresh.

The absence of the numerous steamers and sailing vessels which majestically floated over the bosom of Lake Erie, adding life and beauty to the scene, greatly detracted from our enjoyment.

However, in her later years, on these waters there was no lack of vessels loaded with passengers and freight, to enliven the scene.

We exceedingly enjoyed the intellectual and social privileges of this progressive little town.

Olympia was incorporated in 1859, shortly after we
were numbered as its citizens. It was the first incorporated
town in Washington territory. The citizens celebrated the
event by ornamenting the wide streets with the beautiful
broad leafed maple that grows so luxuriantly in Washington. In due season their spreading branches added greatly
to the attaction of the city.

Prominent among the most enterprising citizens, these
names stand out clearly in my memory.

Perhaps Edmund Sylvester's name should come first,
made important as the owner of the donation claim upon
which this embryo city was built.

Gholson succeeded Fayette McMullen as governor—
neither of them tarrying long with us.

McGill was the next to hold the office of governor;
also honorably filling many other important positions. In
1860 he issued the first Thanksgiving proclamation of the
territory. The following amusing incident is illustrative
of his native wit.

Olympia was visited by Prof. ————, a talented lec-
turer on the various "reforms" of the day, "free love" being
a favorite subject. The beautiful Widow ———— was
fully converted to his views, which they forthwith enthusias-
tically put into practice—much to the disgust of the uncon-
verted citizens. For these unlawful proceedings Prof.
———— was arrested and thrown into jail. They were
brought before Lawyer McGill for trial. Quizzically eyeing the accused, he put the following questions: "Do you,
professor, look upon this woman as your wife?" "I do,"

replied the professor. Turning to the beautiful widow he asked, "Do you, madam, look upon this man as your husband?" "I do," she answered. Then, said Judge Mc-Gill, with a comical twinkle in his eye, "if there is no one here to object, in the name of the law, I pronounce you man and wife."

Deafening was the sound of clapping and cheers that greeted the ears of the twain, thus unwillingly made one, by law.

I must say here that Mrs. ———— was a woman of good character, much admired by a large circle of friends until she fell under the hypnotic influence of the "professor," who persuaded her that a contract marriage was sufficiently binding.

She and her first husband were among the early pioneers to this Coast her husband was killed by accident in the early years of their married life.

Elwood Evans, a talented lawyer, crossed the plains in 1853 as private secretary to Governor Stevens, in his surveying expedition. Although there is nothing of special note to relate of Mr. Evans, he filled many important offices in the territory, and was deeply interested in all things pertaining to the development of the country.

Salucious Garfiend, the "silver tongued orator," T. M. Reed, George Barnes, David Phillips, G. W. Dunlap, Edward Giddings, T. F. McElroy, Williams, Dr. Williard, Rev. G. F. Whitworth, John Murphy, all these, with their noble "helpmeets," in connection with many others, did effective work in developing the resources of the country.

Before we settled in town, Mr. Corliss sold his interest in the hotel and purchased a residence in what was then

called Swantown, a suburb of Olympia, situated on rising
ground on the opposite side of a small creek, or arm, of the
bay, and connected with the city proper by a bridge—just
a short and pleasant walk from the business portion of the
city.

The lovely walks across that bridge to Lucretia's home
are treasured pictures on memory's walls. The bay, the
sky, the beauties of the surrounding landscape, with dear
Lucretia waiting at the door to greet me with smiles
of welcome, are sweet memories never to be forgotten.

Lucretia had no children, and when our little baby girl,
Mary, was added to the household band, she devoted herself to the care of my little ones as though they were her
own. How greatly I appreciated the ministry of this loving sister she can never know. With the care of the little
ones I would have been closely tied at home, had not Lucretia constantly planned outings—a picnic, a clam bake
on the beach, or a trip to Father and Mother Judson's—
always making the children her special care.

Father and Mother Judson had selected their preemption claim six miles south of Olympia, in the depths of the
great dense forest. It seemed a hopeless task for two old
people to undertake to build a home amid such unpromising
surroundings; but they were full of courage and went to
work boring, burning and chopping down the giant trees.
It was necessary to fell every tree that would endanger
the house. At last a space large enough for the little cottage was cleared among the great black logs, and the house
went up, while still many of these fallen giants of the forest lay piled criss-cross in every direction around it, nearly
as high as the house.

Whenever we visited the new home I would think however can they get all those logs cleared away? But their courage never failed. Continually the fires were kept burning, until the last log was consumed, and beautiful shrubs and flowers now bloomed around the vine embowered cottage, where erstwhile the lords of the forest stretched their pointed heads skyward.

One night, while the logs were still piled high, they heard a calf bawling in distress. Mother, who was a plucky little woman, could not endure the thought of remaining inactive while the helpless creature might be saved. Hastily dressing, she took the lantern and walked over the high piled logs in the direction of the pitiful cries, and there beneath her feet, down among the fallen logs, she beheld an immense cougar devouring her favorite calf.

She saw at once there was nothing to be done but to go to the house and wait for daylight. The next morning La Bonta, who was visiting his grandparents, sent for some neighbor boys, who came with their guns and dogs. The cougar had buried the remnants of the calf just where he had killed it, and was found concealed in a tree a short distance away, where he was watching his buried treasure. The boys, with their guns, soon brought it to the ground, and the dogs, pouncing upon him, did their share to bring his cruel, thieving life to an end.

As little Mary grew older, the summer visits to Father and Mother Judson's were her chief delight. How she loved mother's beautiful flowers. She had been taught not to pick them. As soon as we were in the gate, with a scream of delight, she flew to the flower beds, crying, as her tiny feet scampered up the walk, "Mozzer's posies, mozzer's

posies." So tenderly the small fingers bent down the blossoms, that she might inhale their fragrance and lay them
lovingly against her cheek, and when mother would pick
a few of the much-loved "posies" and place them in her
little hands, her blue eyes would fill with tears of joy.

While on a prolonged visit in the springtime, little Mary
watched the process of potato planting with much interest.
She was told that when put into the ground they would
grow more potatoes. One day the combs were missing;
high and low we searched for them. The loss of the combs
was quite a catastrophe, as we were so far from a store. At
last mother said, "Mary, have you seen the combs?" How
the blue eyes sparkled, and every tendril of her golden hair
quivered with joyful excitement as she answered, "Yes, I
planted them to grow some new ones." The little sprite
had noticed that the combs were wearing out, and no doubt
wondered in her baby mind why the big folks did not plant
them to grow new ones. Taking mother by the hand, the
baby farmer triumphantly led her out to view her first efforts in the agricultural line.

We had many delightful visits with Father and Mother
Judson, but New Years day was the crowning event of
each year, when the table fairly groaned under its load of
appetizing viands. Holden and Lucretia were their only
children, and separated from all early associations, the
chief happiness of their lonely lives lay in their family gatherings, and mother spared no pains to prepare the best the
country afforded to set before her loved ones. Not that
she considered the creature comforts of this world of para-
mount importance, for she was preeminently of a spiritual
nature.

I well remember a remark made to me by a neighbor and intimate friend of mother's. Gazing upon the tiny mound that covered her mortal remains, this friend said: "How could so small a grave contain so geat a soul?"

During our residence in Olympia peace reigned throughout the territory. The Indians were finally subjugated. Many of them lived in Olympia, making their living by peddling "clallies" (berries), "lagoon pitch," as they called pitch pine cut into kindling lengths, and shell and other fish of various kinds.

The organs of imitation is largely developed in the Indian—especially noticeable in the women. They greatly delighted in copying the dress of the whites. Large hoops were in vogue, and it was amusing to see a "kloochman" on the promenade, arrayed in hooped skirts, sometimes carrying a parasol to protect her brown complexion from the sunshine.

The women learned to wash, clean house and do garden work. They made very useful servants for the white settlers, and were usually the only help obtainable in those days.

CHAPTER XXXIV

In 1861 the eastern mail brought us the news of the dreadful Civil war, where brother faced brother, and father met son in deadly combat. Though so far removed from the seat of war, most intense was our interest in the terrible conflict raging in the home land.

In our great anxiety for news, the lagging wheels of time moved slowly between our once a week mail, carried by Captain Finch on the steamer Anderson.

With the most intense interest we followed the events of the war, from the bombardment of Fort Sumpter in 1861 to the fall of Richmond and the surrender of Lee, in 1865.

We were still rejoicing over the end of the long struggle for the preservation of the Union, when the sad tidings of the assassination of President Lincoln reached us, casting a gloom over the whole country, and our rejoicing was turned into mourning.

Lucretia had fully recovered from the lameness, caused by leaping over the high picket fence as she made her escape at the time of the murder of Colonel Ebey by the Indians on Whidby island, but her nerves had never recovered from the shock of that night's terrible experience.

In the spring of 1864 Mr. Corliss, having resigned his office of U. S. marshal, disposed of his property and invested in a sheep farm at Las Cruces, Santa Barbara county, California.

This change was made almost, if not entirely, for Lucretia's benefit, for she was very frail, and still lived under a continual fear of the Indians.

Great was our grief when it was decided that we must

be separated from this loved one. As for myself, I felt that my loss would be irreparable. Our lives were interwoven from childhood days, and it seemed as though I could not live without her. Yet even could I have kept her by my side, I would not, for I knew she was haunted by the torturing fear of being murdered by the Indians.

But where could I find another who would so love and care for my children? They would never again be so beautifully dressed, for Lucretia relieved me of nearly all the burden of planning and making their clothes, and I lacked the skill and taste that she possessed.

All too soon the sad morning dawned when we must say our last farewell. Mother Judson had come in the night before. We accompanied them to the wharf, and through blinding tears watched the steamer out of sight.

Among those who took passage on the steamer with Lucretia and her husband were a number of our fellow townsmen, who never came back, Dr. Henry, Mr. Heffron, and others whose names I have forgotten.

Though they did not meet the terrible fate of our dear ones, the steamer on which they were returning carried them down to a watery grave.

Mr. and Mrs. Corliss had a prosperous journey to their new home in California. Lucretia's health began to improve at once—her weekly letters were filled with the beauties of the country and climate. She was perfectly free from the haunting fear that made her life a burden in this country. Her letters repeatedly referred to the feeling of safety she enjoyed in her new home. They owned a large tract of land, well stocked with sheep. They had built a cozy home, and now Lucretia was earnestly urging us to

close up our business and come down there. Father and
Mother Judson were willing to go, for they sadly missed
their only daughter.

As business was dull in Olympia, we were seriously de-
bating the question whether or not to go to California.
Lucretia's glowing description of their new home inspired
us with the hope that on California's golden shores the
"ideal home" of our dreams would at last be realized. Mr.
Judson and I, with the children, were spending a few days
with Father and Mother Judson. We occupied a front bed
room. One night, shortly after retiring, we were startled
by hearing a carriage drive up to the house. My husband
answered the knock. A low murmur of voices followed. As
I listened in the darkness of the night, my heart sank with
a premonition of evil.

Soon Mr. Judson returned and whispered to me the
awful tidings: "Lucretia and George are both murdered."

My blood froze with horror. Poor mother and father!
How could we break the horrible truth to them? My husband first called father from the room and imparted to him
the sad truth, then kindled a fire in the sitting room. By
this time mother had joined us.

Mr. Burr, who had brought the sad intelligence from
Olympia, remained with us, and we all gathered around the
fire, which blazed and crackled merrily in the large open
fireplace.

Dear mother! I can see her diminutive form and sweet
face, as she sat in the firelight, waiting in placid expect-
ancy an explanation of these unusual proceedings.

There we sat around the fire, none of us having the
courage to break the awful tidings to the loving mother. At

length I felt that I must be the one to tell her. How I shrank from laying this burden of pain upon that loving heart, but it must be done, and I said:

"Mother, Mr. Burr has brought us more sad news." (It was just four weeks since he had brought us the sad intelligence of my brother Williams' sudden death by drowning). "George and Lucretia are both gone."

Calmly and bravely this loving heart bore the terrible blow. I looked at her in astonishment, for I could not understand it. Now I know "she had found the secret place of the Most High." She "rested in the everlasting arms."

Mr. Burr had the paper containing the account of the tragedy, and he read to the sad group of mourners the meager details. "When the stage that ran between Santa Barbara and San Luis Obispo made its daily call at the Corliss farm, on the 16th of January, 1864, the home lay in ashes. The charred bodies of Mr. and Mrs. Corliss, with their shepherd boy, were found in the ruins."

It was evident, from the blood stains under the window, that Mrs. Corliss had attempted to save herself by escaping through the window, as she did on Whidby island. Traces plainly indicated that her body had been dragged from its position under the window and thrown with the other bodies into the burning building.

How thankful we were that we had been brought together to comfort each other in this time of deep affliction. Long we sat before the fire. There was a mournful comfort in being together.

In the morning I was surprised to see mother calmly attending to her household duties. What an object lesson of perfect submission and faith in the love of our Heavenly

Father. Not a murmur escaped her lips. Well I remember one remark she made: "I am growing old," she said, "and I may see Lucretia sooner than if she had lived."

A few days later a letter came to me, written by Lucretia just two days before her death. She was in fine spirits—her health was so good, her house finished, they had brought their winter supples from San Francisco, and were expecting a dear Olympia friend, Miss Dorcas Phillips, to visit them for a few weeks. "You know how afraid I always was in Olympia," she wrote. "I have gotten all over that now.'"

Poor Lucretia! Miss Dorcas Phillips was on her way to make the "promised visit," and was in San Francisco when the sad news reached her.

My husband went at once to Santa Barabara. The perpetrators of the dreadful deed were never discovered, but it was supposed to have been done by Mexicans, plunder being the incentive.

We did not remain long in Olympia after Lucretia's death.

CHAPTER XXXV

The Indian war had checked the tide of emigration, causing great financial depression. Trade was at a standstill for a number of years, our business suffering with the rest. The Civil war coming on did not improve matters.

In the excitement and distress which ensued in the States, we seemed totally forgotten, or set aside. Even the Indian war claims were not paid. The settlers had contributed liberally, both means and time, besides the suffering many of them had endured all through the Indian war.

Uncle Sam had invited us here to subdue this wild country, and while engaged in the perilous undertaking we naturally expected to be sustained and protected by the strong arm of the federal government. But our appeals were all unheeded.

Mr. Judson was always willing to give his customers long credit, especially when he knew they were in financial difficulties. When he did succeed in collecting a bill it was always in "greenbacks," worth fifty cents on the dollar.

He trusted an Indian agency with goods to the amount of fifteen hundred dollars, and I don't remember that he ever collected a penny.

We began to sigh for the "old ranch." Our ideal home still lay in the dim and misty future. We realized that if we must have a home, we must again take up a piece of land. We had used our right to a donation claim, but we still had a preemption right to one hundred and sixty acres. We could not for a moment think of settling on any of the gravelly, sandy prairies bordering the Sound.

A short time before Mr. Judson closed out his business we became acquainted with Colonel Patterson. He was an educated Tennesseean, about sixty years of age, of distinguished birth. Two of his brothers were senators, and a niece presided lady of the White House, as the wife of President Johnson. This noble lady was greatly instrumental in fitting her husband to occupy the nation's most exalted position. Andrew Johnson was born of poor, but respectable parents; his father died when he was but five years old. Andrew ran the streets, a ragged, barefooted urchin, supported by the meager earnings of his poor mother until he was ten years of age. It was then necessary for him to help support his mother, so he was apprenticed to a tailor. Here he learned to read, through the assistance of a journeyman tailor.

When his apprenticeship expired, he faced the world with only his trade and the ability to read. He comfortably supported himself and mother.

His marriage to Miss Patterson, a lady of education, was the turning point in his life. She instructed him in writing, arithmetic and other branches. Being an ardent student, he soon obtained a good practical education, and she was rewarded for her love and devotion by sharing with him the honors of the White House.

The colonel was dealing in cattle, and deposited his money in the Judson safe. He became a frequent visitor at our home, and talked continually of his two little motherless girls, for whom he was trying to find a home. Their mother had left them, and he was not satisfied with their present situation, and was urging me to receive them into my home.

The colonel had taken a claim on a piece of unsurveyed land in the Nooksack valley, Whatcom county, and, like many another bachelor, he had taken an Indian wife. He was much attached to his two little daughters, Dollie and Nellie, and he never ceased to regret the part he bore in bringing upon their innocent lives the sorrow which is the sure result of such mixed marriages.

How many a bright young life has been blighted by this cause. Alas! that it should be so. Truly does the poet cry "Man's inhumanity to man makes countless thousands mourn."

It seems that the more refined and educated the father, the greater the sufferings of the children—especially if the children are educated.

I have heard intelligent young people of this class say "they would have been happier if left to grow up in ignorance with the Indians."

There seemed no place for them; they were looked down upon by the whites, and their training and education unfitted them for a life among the Indians.

I was acquainted with a senator in Oregon who sent his two sons to college, but the more highly they were educated, the more bitterly they realized the so-called blot upon their birth.

When one considers the utter loneliness of these men, old and young, toiling in the howling wilderness month after month, year in and year out—though far from approving their course, we cannot utterly condemn them for seeking the only human companionship within their reach.

Many of these men had true fatherly affection for their offspring, sparing no pains and expense to place them in homes where they would enjoy the advantages of good training and education.

Gaining our consent to care for his little girls, Colonel Patterson brought them to our home. Dollie was six years old, with large dark eyes and soft black hair. Little three-year-old Nellie, with her keen brown eyes and abundant hair of the same color, greatly resembled the colonel. Colonel Patterson's enthusiastic description of the Nooksack valley decided us to try our fortune in that part of the country.

Another incentive lay in the fact that the dear friend, Elizabeth, of childhood days, and the later experiences on Grand Mound, was living in Whatcom, where I would have the joy of an occasional visit.

Once again we were envoyage for the "ideal home"— however, this time not in the old ox wagon, with Tom and Jerry for steeds. Nor did we have little Annie with us. No longer "little Annie," for she had become the bride of Eason Ebey, a valued fried, eldest son of the lamented Colonel Ebey of Whidby island.

We left our little Mary on Whidby island with her sister to attend school.

It was the first of March, 1871, with Bonta, George and little Dollie and Nellie, we took passage on the once-a-week boat, the "Mary Woodruff," a small steamer plying between Seattle and Whatcom, carrying the mail, passengers and freight, to all intervening settlements.

There had been no wharves built along the route in those early days, and the landings were made with a canoe, or low boat, and it was no unusual occurrence to be detained hours for favorable wind and tide before a landing could be effected.

The next day, after having wandered among the many beautiful islands, leaving the mail—now and then a passenger, with a small amount of freight, we reached the place we are now proud to call the City of Bellingham, presenting at that time a most forlorn and dilapidated appearance—containing but a few primitive cabins in a doubtful state of repair, amid many Indian wigwams.

However, there was one lone brick building, erected by a wealthy gentleman from New York during the Fraser river gold excitement. After the mines played out he returned to his home in the east, leaving a native woman so disconsolate over his unfaithfulness to his family, that she committed suicide by hanging herself to a tree. She belonged to the Nooksack tribes, and her two little red-headed orphans, Johnnie and Annie, were raised in the camp of Indian Seclamatum, the chief of the tribe. Johnnie was sent east and educated by the ladies of the Home Missionary Society. Annie married an Indian named Louie, and is now living near Lynden.

I have never known of another case of suicide among the Indians.

The old brick building was used for a number of years for a court house, and is still standing.

We were the only passengers for this point. When we reached Whatcom the tide was out, and, in attempting to make a landing in a canoe, we were stranded on the mud flats, and were in a dilemma whether to wade ashore or wait for the tide, when Siwash Joe politely offered me a ride to shore on his back, and although he was short in stature, and I weighed something less than two hundred pounds, I gladly accepted his offer.

Anything was better than sitting there, waiting for the tide on the dismal tide flats, with dear Elizabeth "so near, and yet so far."

Once mounted on the shoulders of my willing bearer, there was little left visible of poor Joe. As he plodded through the deep mud, I was in constant fear that he might stumble and pitch me over his head, or weaken and let me down into the mud and water. But he proved equal to the emergency, and, with a few of those gutteral exclamations peculiar to the race, he landed me all in a heap, high and dry, on the beach. I imagine he was as much relieved as "Sinbad, the Sailor," when he got rid of the "old man of the sea," and I, I am sure, was quite as much, if not more so.

We wended our way over the old telegraph road, around the black stumps and over logs (that have now given way to the handsome residences of Broadway) to the Roeder homestead, where stand, towering high above the wide spreading elms, the two Lombardy poplars, like sentinels, before the gate; always reminding; me of the two heroic characters who lived so many years under their shade, bearing the trials incident to a pioneer's life, while the country was a wilderness, swarming with savages and wild animals, and, like these grand trees, are the best known landmarks in Whatcom county.

Here, with the dear Ohio friends of our childhood and pioneer days, we have passed many of the happiest hours of life.

Their hospitable home ever stood open for the cordial reception of friend or stranger.

CHAPTER XXXVI

Mr. Judson procured three large "salt chuck" canoes, with two Indians apiece, to paddle and pole us to our destination, the head of navigation on the Nooksack river.

While crossing the bay to the mouth of the river, we were caught in a storm. The waves rolled so high I greatly feared our canoes, so heavily loaded, would be swamped by the huge breakers. As I watched the two canoes ahead of us disappearing from sight between the waves, I held my breath each time, fearing they would never rise again.

How thankful we were to safely reach the mouth of the river, at the Lummi Indian reservation, under the auspices of the Catholic church. Here we found a good sized Indian village, composed of board cabins, a neat little church, and a flourishing school. The Indians were taught to cultivate the land, and many of them now have fine orchards.

As the salt water canoes were too large to run up the river, our goods were here transferred to smaller ones, "shovel nosed," they are called. In these days of good roads and fine bridges, the "shovel nosed" canoe, with the Indians, have almost become extinct.

While our goods were being transferred to the small canoes, we built a fire on the beach, and had just begun to prepare our noon lunch, when Mr. Finkboner, the Indian agent, invited us to his residence, where we had the privilege of preparing our dinner on his cook stove. His Indian woman welcomed us very kindly, and seemed pleased to entertain us in her home.

It was our lot to travel in the canoe manned by old "Sally" and "Joe" advisedly, for she was decidedly the leading spirit in that family. Sally was one of the tallest of her tribe, and of unusual strength of character for an Indian woman; and Joe (the same Joe who packed me over the mud flats on his back) was slightly smaller in stature, and much inferior in character.

I soon found that Joe, for some reason, stood in much awe of his better half, who did not hesitate to use the paddle on him when she deemed occasion required.

With spirits much invigorated by the rest and refreshment, we proceeded on our journey up the Nooksack.

The scenery was wild and picturesque. Bowers of willow, maple, cottonwood, alder and crab apple beautifully fringed the banks of this winding river. On account of the heavy foliage and serpentine course, our glimpses of the valley were rare and brief.

Sitting in one position in a toppling canoe, with so little diversity of scenery, soon became exceedingly wearisome, and I was not sorry when we reached the "big jam," where we got out of the canoe and walked around the jam by the Indian trail.

The Indians packed the goods across the jam and then dragged the canoes over. This was no small task, consuming about three hours. That "jam"—how shall I describe it? It was three-quarters of a mile long; great logs and huge trees, in every conceivable position, piled high across a bend of the river, reaching from shore to shore. It was evident, by the large trees growing in the midst of it, that this "jam" had been accumulating for many years, and was still enlarging, as every freshet carried on its current a new supply of logs and uprooted trees.

The scene in this place of gloomy solitude, where white women's foot never before trod, was inexpressibly dreary and saddening. A scene more utterly desolate could hardly be imagined.

As I looked upon these fallen monarchs of the forest, denuded of leaves and branches—so mighty, yet so helplessly piled upon each other in the wildest confusion, seemingly immovably locked in a deathlike embrace, a sense of depression crept over my heart. They seemed almost like human wrecks; and underneath, silent and unseen, flowed the strong current that had built up this seemingly impregnable barrier to navigation.

I asked myself, does it lie in human power to remove this immense mass of compact timbers? Echo seemed to answer "No." With a sigh of despondency, I gladly turned my back upon the depressing scene.

Following the trail for about two miles, it was growing dark when we reached the ranch of Reuben Bisor, situated about a mile from where the thriving little town of Ferndale now stands. We expected to camp out that night, but Mr. Bisor kindly invited us to his house, where we were hospitably entertained by his wife, a large, pleasant mannered Indian woman, with whom I at once felt at home.

Mrs. Bisor soon had a huge kettle of potatoes ("wapatoes," she called them) over the open fire; with rich milk and keen appetites we fared sumptuously. At that time only five ranchers had located claims in this vicinity—John Tennant, our Olympia friend, Thomas Winn, Teddy

Crogan, John Plaster and Reuben Bisor—all with Indian wives excepting Teddy Crogan.

After we were settled, twelve miles above, we considered these ranchmen our neighbors.

These early settlers have all departed this earthly life, most of them leaving large families that have become useful citizens.

We left Mr. Bisor's hospitable home very early in the morning, as we were anxious to reach our destination before dark. The river was high, the current strong, and our canoes heavily loaded, so our progress was necessarily very slow.

Old Sally was in command of our canoe, which took the lead. Standing, Amazonlike, in the head of the canoe, pole in hand, her long, black hair streaming down her back, she gave her orders to Joe.

As we ascended, the river became more winding and narrow—consequently the current more swift and strong. To avoid the swift current caused by these many windings, the Indians kept the canoe zigzagging across from point to point, or "nose to nose," as they called the points. Occasionally an immense tree lay athwart the stream, leaving a narrow place through which the water rushed with the velocity of a mill race and the roar of a young cataract. In some places, the space between the log and the banks were so narrow that the canoe could barely wedge through. At times we could hear and feel the rasping and grating of the canoes against the rough logs as we were slowly forced along.

I suppose my countenance must have expressed some of the anxiety and fear that held me during these experi-

ences, for old Sally would encouragingly say, just before
entering one of these seemingly dangerous places, "halo
quass mica" (don't be afraid). Many times the Indians,
standing up in their canoes, grasped the overhanging
branches of the trees and pulled the canoe through these
narrow passages—a much easier method of progress than
poling or paddling.

Our canoes seemed to be the only ones bound up stream.
We met many going down—some of them well filled with
braves and their families. One pecularity I noticed:
when two canoes met, not a word was spoken by the occupants of either till they had well passed each other, then
the spell of silence was broken, and they continued to exchange salutations as long as their canoes were within
hearing distance. I never could gain any information on
the subject of this peculiarity, except that it was Indian
etiquette.

It was out of salmon season, but mountain trout
abounded in these water. La Bonta was a skillful angler,
and his luck did not fail him on this trip; he succeeded in
securing an abundant supply of the speckled beauties.

In these early days, before the country was taken by
the white man, beaver and otter were very numerous along
this stream. Sometimes while gliding along in still water,
Sally and Joe would stop their canoe and assumed a listening attitude. Presently we would come to a little trail
leading down into the water. Sally managed to make us
understand that it was a "beaver slide," and the sound to
which they had been listening was the pounding of the
beavers' tails as they built their homes.

At these places we saw scattered along the bank trees

and branches, some of these one foot in diameter, which the beavers had gnawed off with their sharp incisors, in lengths suitable for their houses, which, with their powerful little paws and mouths they carry through the water, using their broad tails as sculls, to the place selected for a lodge, or dam.

The flesh of these little animals, and beaver tail soup is esteemed very highly by the Indians, and the pelts were a source of great revenue to them.

It was noon when we reached the 'little jam," a miniature of the big one. While the goods and canoes were being transported across the jam, we prepared dinner.

Here, on the bank of the river, dwelt old Lockkanum, Sally's "tillicum" (friend), with his family and many dogs. Old Sally was at home among the Indians wherever she went. Entering Lockkanum's wigwam, she soon reappeared with a quantity of "wapatoes" (potatoes), that her "tillicum" had "potlatched" (given her) for our dinner.

Soon a blazing fire was built near the wigwam; the Indian women all took a hand in washing the potatoes. I noticed that old Sally took particular pains to wash the kettles clean. In short order three huge kettles of potatoes hung over the blazing fire. I made the coffee, and by the time the portage was completed, the potatoes were done.

We enjoyed our "picnic" on the river bank. It brought to memory many similar experiences while crossing the plains, only now we were traveling in a canoe instead of a "prairie schooner," and we had no fear of the Indians.

This was our last portage, to my great relief. Again taking our places in the tottering canoes, we continued our zigzag course and soon reached what the Indians called the "hias nose" (big nose) and what the whites termed the "Devil's bend."

This great bend in the river formed a circle a mile in circumference. The passage through it was appalling. Angry waters rushed, roared and boiled in mad fury around the many fallen trees with which the bend was filled.

In these dangerous passages, where the roar of the water drowned old Sally's voice, Joe kept his eye on her to catch the slightest motion of her paddle, by which she directed his movements, for well he knew a misdirected stroke would send us headlong into the seething torrent.

The deftness with which they managed these light craft, crooking around the sharp points of land, darting through the rushing current, was truly marvelous. I soon learned that I had nothing to fear while an Indian was guiding the canoe. Many times, in going down the river, I have made my bed in the bottom of the canoe and laid myself down to sleep, with a feeling of perfect safety.

It was a common saying among the old settlers, when our journeying was mostly by canoe, that one was perfectly safe anywhere on the water in the hands of an Indian. But occasionally a white man came along who, thinking he knew more than the natives, would insist on assuming control—sometimes with very disastrous results.

The case of Captain Barstow and G. N. McConnaha is a sad illustration of this truth. While returning from the legislature in 1854, the Indians knowing it was not safe to start out at that time, strongly objected, but being helpless in the hands of the white men, who thought they knew best, they were forced to go, and as a result all were drowned.

After we were released from "Devil's bend" the river became comparatively free from obstructions, and we moved along more rapidly. An occasional log, fast at one end, and kept constantly rising and falling with the action of the water, reminded me of the problem of perpetual motion.

Old Sally sought to cheer us by frequenty saying "Wake siad copa mica illahee" (not far to your home); and Mount Baker (Kulshan in the Indian tongue) in pure white mantle, towering 10,500 feet, seemed to beckon us on with the promise of a restful home, beneath his mighty shadow.

Before dark we were safely landed on the north bank of the Nooksack, and our feet one more pressed the soil upon which we hoped at last to build our "ideal home."

CHAPTER XXXVII

Crossing a short stretch of bottom land and ascending a gentle rise, we reached Colonel Patterson's little cabin— the old home of little Dollie and Nellie. The children were delighted to be again at home. Little Nellie, though but three years of age, expressed her pleasure in a marked manner. In spite of the confusion and bustle consequent upon advent in these small quarters, with all our household goods, I could not help noticing, with much amusement, this little one, as, with sparkling brown eyes and glowing cheeks, she stepped about the cabin with an air of great importance.

From the first moment of our arrival, I was greatly pleased with the location for my prospective home.

This gentle eminence was an ideal building spot. A narrow stretch of low prairie lay between it and the river; in the background rose the great fir forest, lifting their kingly heads skyward; the silvery windings of the river lay open to view.

A fringe of poplar, cottonwood, crab apple, alder and vine maple bordered the opposite bank; beyond, to the southeast, the blue foothills nestled at the feet of majestic Mount Baker, and the three beautiful peaks of the twin sisters, their snowy coverings gleaming in vivid contrast with the dark green garb of the foothills. Almost due east lay a smaller mountain, somewhat resembling an immense grave, with a headstone. The children gave it the name of the "Chief's Tomb."

Surely I never had seen a spot whose environments more perfectly fulfilled my dreams of an "ideal home."

As the lands were unsurveyed, Colonel Patterson held only a "squatter's right." Being of a restless disposition, he chaffed under the long delay and uncertainty of the government survey. Leaving his little girls with us, he relinquished all rights in our favor. Six years passed before the land was surveyed. We then filed a preemption right to one hundred and sixty acres, and again possessed a home that we could call our own.

The colonel had set out a small orchard and made other improvements. The cabin was very small and rough, but there was a fine milk house, built with double walls filled in with earth, which kept it very cool. It was lined with white muslin, and revolving shelves held the milk pans. In time wild roses, taking root in the earth between the crevices of the outer walls, so covered the milk house with their fragrant pink blossoms and green leaves that it became a veritable bower of beauty.

Mr. Judson and Ned Barnes, a man we had brought with us for that purpose, set to work at once to build a hewed log house. The old part, in which was a large clay fireplace (the stick chimney running up on the outside) we used for a dining room and kitchen. We sent to the head of the Sound and procured brick for a fireplace in the new part, and soon found ourselves comfortably domiciled.

Here we passed many quiet, uneventful years, remote from the world, surrounded by the beauties and bounties of nature. The snow-capped mountains were an unceasing joy and inspiration. The joyous sparkling Nooksack rolled at our feet. The forests teemed with game, the marshes with wild fowl, and the rivers and small streams abounded with salmon and trout.

I said we passed uneventful years—yet there were many stirring and exciting experiences with wild animals.

Our first callers, among the four-footed denizens of the forest, were a pack of wolves.

For the safety of the stock, the corral was built near the house, with fences almost as high as the eaves. At our Chehalis home we had known more than one cougar to scale just such high fences as these with a sheep in its mouth.

One winter night there was a sudden commotion among the stock, La Bonta, only half awake, without stopping to dress, rushed out to the corral. In the darkness he saw what he thought was a large dog endeavoring to climb the high fence. When he came near it the creature gave utterance to a blood-curdling howl, which was re-echoed by myriad howls from all directions, till it seemed as if the country was literally alive with wolves. He did not tarry to parley with the intruders, but precipitately turned and fled to the house.

The wolves were successfully balked in their efforts to capture any of our "tid bits." For a few nights these carniverous musicians treated us to howling serenades, without venturing near enough to molest us, but soon departed to regions unknown, and, to our great satisfaction, they never favored us with another visit.

Lizzie, the mother of little Dollie and Nellie, was still living. Colonel Patterson had purchased her from the chief of the Snohomish Indians, and, though she was a princess, the colonel being raised in a slave state, considered her only a piece of property. He was a severe tackmaster and left her alone much of the time with only Ned, a young Indian, to carry on the work of the ranch. On an average, there were twenty cows to milk, with the contingent daily work.

Lizzie was young and pretty, and Ned a bright young man, handsome above the ordinary Indian. The burden of life under the colonel's stern sway became unbearable, and, yielding to Ned's pleadings, one night while the colonel was at home to look after the little girls, she crept out in the darkness, and joining Ned, who was waiting for her, together they fled to the Sumas country.

Morning dawned, and vainly the colonel listened for the willing footsteps building the fire and performing the usual early morning household tasks. "Lizzie, Lizzie," he called, but no answer. The little girls were alone in their bed, and, waking, they called loudly for "Mama."

Ned, too, was gone. The colonel began to realize that his willing slave had at last rebelled and left him. His grief and dismay were great.

He loved his little girls, and now who would do all this work and care for them as Lizzie had done; but she was beyond his reach and safe from his power.

He sent pleading messages to her, trying to persuade her to return, telling how the little ones cried for her, but the bitterness of the bondage was too great for even her mother love to draw her back again.

When the colonel found that his persuasions were of no avail, he grew angry and declared, in his wrath, that she should never see her little girls again.

They greatly mourned the loss of their mother. One day, while playing in one of their favorite haunts among the hazel, they found some pieces of her dresses fastened to the bushes. The poor mother had placed them there as remembrances, knowing that her children would find them.

Dollie, who was six years old, told me much about her mother—how hard she worked, and how happy she made them. Their father had said they should never see her again, and they mourned as one without hope. But the Indians had carried to Lizzie the tidings of her children's return to their old home, and of the colonel's absence. Immediately she, too, returned, stopping at the Indian camp on the opposite side of the river. She sent a messenger to me, asking permission to "visit her children in the morning."

The little girls were wild with delight at the prospect of once more seeing their dear mother. Bright and early the next morning they took their positions by the window, commanding a view of the river path. For fully an hour they sat there as quiet as mice, their eyes eagerly searching the distance to catch the first glimpse of their mother. At last the silence was broken by the joyous exclamation, "Oh, I see her. I know it's mamma, she has on her red shawl." Going to the window I saw a lone figure coming slowly, oh, so slowly, along the river path. The dew drops glistened in the beams of the morning sun; the air was clear and fragrant; nature seemed to be chanting a song of rejoicing, but the children had eyes for nothing but the scarlet robed figure so clearly outlined against the dark green of the river bottom foliage.

Slowly she came. Perhaps she expected to see the children come to meet her. They seemed possessed of a spirit of shyness and never moved from their position at the window until their mother entered the house. For a few moments they gazed into each other's eyes in silence, then Lizzie gathered her little ones in her arms, murmuring words of endearment in her own soft musical language. It was an affecting scene. Dollie, in her quiet joy, snuggled close to her mother's side, nestling her head in her lap, a picture of perfect happiness, while little Nellie was all bustle and excitement, expressing her joy in various ways—now dancing around and laughing in the exuberance of her joy, again climbing up behind her mother, arranging and rearranging the hair which hung in loose braids down her back. Seeming to realize that her stay would be short, they clung closely to her side all day. When the time came for her departure, Lizzie's face grew sad. As she gave the little girls her parting words in her native tongue, that she hoped they would never forget, their tears flowed freely.

We did not think it would be Lizzie's last visit with her children, but it proved so, for she died soon after.

The little girls never forget their mother. Her memory is a living fragrance in their hearts and can never die. Though little Nellie was only three years old when she last saw her mother, her loss seemed to make her heart tender towards all young creatures. She could not bear to hear a lamb bleat, a calf bawl, a pig squeal, or a chicken peep, without running to see what was the matter.

I remember what a stew she was in with an old hen that was weaning her chickens. Night after night she would stay out after bed time holding the mother hen on her nest, that the chickens might cuddle under her wings; and at last come in filled with wrath and tears, scolding the old hen because she would not care for her babies.

Nellie now has a beautiful home of her own. Her husband, Mr. McDonald, is a mill owner. When their only child, Ivan, was five years old, the wife of one of Mr. McDonald's employees died, leaving a tiny, puny baby and several other small children. When Nellie saw that the motherless babe was not properly cared for, her tender heart prompted her to take it into her own home. Under her fostering care it soon grew plump and rosy. When I visited their home, it seemed as dear to them as their own little boy.

CHAPTER XXXVIII

We had been six months in our Nooksack home; it was in the midst of harvest. One day I had just got dinner on the table, when two strange Indians from Whatcom entered the kitchen door, bearing a telegram which read, "Mary is dangerously ill. Come at once."

As old Joe and Sally were camped right in our yard, there was no time lost. As soon as we could get our things together, with La Bonta, I hastened to the canoe, manned by Joe and another Indian. Old Sally, fully understanding the cause of our hasty departure, followed us to the river landing, expressing her sympathy in the mournful tones of their native requiem.

The river was high, caused from the melting snows in the mountains, and we glided swiftly along with the strong current until we reached the "jams." Oh, those terrible "jams," how their ugly lengths stretched like a forbidden prison wall between me and my little sick daughter. At length the last jam was crossed, and it was night when we reached the bay. The once-a-week steamer had left on her regular trip up the Sound, and there was no alternative but to continue our journey in the canoe. All night long, without resting, the Indians plied their paddles.

At midnight we reached Swinomish Slough, where many Indians were camped along the beach. All were wrapped in slumber. Presently we noticed our Indians began paddling very softly towards the shore; scarcely a ripple did they make in the water. We glided silently up to one of the canoes that was fastened on the beach, and old Joe stealthily lifted a sail from the bottom of the canoe, and without

making a sound transferred it to our own. Then how softly
and quietly we moved away. Not a sound broke the silence
of the night. The paddles dipped the water as silently as
muffled oars.

Now that we had left the sleeping camp at a safe distance behind us, the Indians sent the canoe along more
swiftly. We could not use the sail in the slough, and they
were anxious to get out in the open waters of the ocean,
that they might lay down their paddles and rest their tired
arms.

Suddenly a sound breaks through the somber stillness
of the night. Over the water comes the hurried sound of
many paddles; presently a large salt water canoe appeared
in our wake. It soon became evident that the pursuing Indians were the owners of the borrowed sail, for, swiftly
gliding to the side of our canoe, without exchanging a word,
they calmly laid hold of the sail, and turning about, rapidly
paddled away. When the distance required by Indian etiquette lay between the two canoes, they began calling back
and forth in friendly tones. I have since learned that the
Indians never quarrel over stolen property. Would that the
same peaceful policy held sway among their white brothers.

Oh, how the hours dragged—it seemed as though we
would never get through the Swinomish Slough. When we
reached the open water we found a stiff breeze blowing. It
was exceedingly rough, and I doubt if we could have used a
sail. Indeed, Captain Coupe, an experienced old sea captain, expressed surprise when we reached shore that our
small craft lived through so strong a wind.

It was six o'clock A. M. when we reached the landing
on Whidby island. We hastened to the home of Colonel

Haller, the nearest residence. Here we found breakfast awaiting us, and, to my great relief, learned that my little daughter was much better.

Mrs. Haller was the first white woman I had seen in six months and, as the anxiety for my little girl was relieved, I could enjoy the privilege of once more conversing with a woman of my own kind.

As soon as the breakfast was over, we were carried across the island to Annie's home, and were rejoiced to find Mary improving—in fact her physician said I was the sickest of the two. The long exposure and anxiety had completely prostrated me.

Our Indians had returned at once to the Nooksack, carrying to Mr. Judson and George the glad tidings of Mary's improvement.

By the time the "once-a-week" steamer was due we were both well enough to take the passage for home. Bidding a reluctant farewell to Eason, Annie and their sweet babies, Effie and Hettie, we were on the way to our Nooksack home.

When we reached Whatcom we found a canoe waiting for us, manned by three Indians. To insure our making the trip in one day, Mr. Judson had procured an extra hand —one of them (called "Skookum George") on account of his being the largest and most powerful Indian on the river.

Leaving La Bonta in Whatcom for a visit, early the next morning, as soon as it was light enough to see, Mary and I were gliding over the blue waters of Bellingham bay, headed for the mouth of the Nooksack. Under the powerful strokes of "Skookum George" and his two co-workers we made rapid progress.

It was salmon time; the bay was all aglitter and agleam
with the shining beauties that were constantly springing
from the waters in every direction, their silvery sides sparkling in the sunlight. Scarcely a breath of wind ruffled the
peaceful waters; only the leaping of the salmon broke its
mirrorlike surface.

Glorious paradise-like sheet of water, beautifully
studded with islands, covered with evergreen trees; a more
lovely scene I had never beheld; even my beautiful Lake
Erie did not surpass it. The wooded hills, the graceful
curvings of the shores, fringed by the pointing firs and
wide spreading cedars, rising gradually from the pebbly
beaches, formed a scene of wild beauty, around which memory loves to linger.

At the mouth of the Nooksack we exchanged our salt
water canoe for the "shovel nose," and soon again we were
stemming the strong current of the winding river. With our
stalwart crew, and no load to pack over the jams, our progress was rapid.

When within two or three miles of our home, a strange
sound came floating through the air. What can it be, asked
Mary. After listening in puzzled surprise for a few moments, I recognized the familiar toot of the old dinner
horn. As we drew nearer the sound grew louder, and when
the Indians began answering with shouts, the toots came to
our ears with redoubled force, and when, rounding a little
point, we came in sight of the landing, there was Mr. Judson standing on the bank, and George parading up and down
the beach with the old ox horn blowing our welcome with
all his little might.

Such a jubilee of rejoicing there was when the canoe

reached the landing. The long suspense was over. Mr.
Judson gathered Mary in his arms and carried her to the
house.

Oh, how good it seemed to be home again. A sense of
satisfaction came over me that I had never before experienced in any of my former homes. Surely, this must be the
spot for which we had been searching for so many years,
where we should build our "ideal home."

Everything seemed to smile a welcome home. Mount
Baker's frosted dome, the mighty fir forests, the shining
river, and last, but not least, my flourishing kitchen garden. How the cabbages, beets, turnips, tomatoes, and all
the rest of the toothsome array seemed to put on broad
smiles of greeting. Truly, I thought, this is a goodly land.

But there was one dark blot on the fair horizon of our
"ideal home." Those terrible "jams." Night and day their
ugly shapes haunted me like a spectre, barring our only
avenue of intercourse with the outer world. If it were a
possible achievement, they must be removed, and we determined to spare no effort for the accomplishment of that
end.

An energetic German, Mr. Klockie, settled on a claim
a couple of miles north of us. After thoroughly canvassing
the project, Mr. Judson and Mr. Klockie came to the conclusion that, with the help of the Indians, who were equally
interested, they could cut an opening through the little
"jam" that lay nearest our home; so they went to work.
Early every morning Mr. Judson sounded the bugle call on
the old "ox horn" and the Indians came flocking over the
river in their canoes. I always put up a lunch for them, and
sometimes gave them their breakfast.

This work continued, off and on, for three months, and one night, when they returned, very tired after an unusually long day's work, Mr. Klockie explained to me with an air of triumph, "I'll never have to work on that old 'yam' again—she's gone out."

Now that the "little jam" was out of the way, we turned our attention to devising a scheme for the removel of the "big jam."

While on a visit to Captain Roeder, he advised me to circulate a petition to raise subscriptions for its removal. Following his advice, I energetically circulated a petition, headed by Mr. Judson with a fifty-dollar subscription. At that time the coal mines at old Sehome were in active oper-ation. Here was quite a settlement, and between Sehome, Whatcom, and the settlers on the river the sum of fifteen hundred dollars was raised. Judge Plaster of Ferndale took the contract for its removal, and great was our rejoic-ing when the big "yam" went out, and the beautiful Nook-sack, our only thoroughfare, was at last freed from the terrible incubus that had so long rested on its bosom. And now, no more camping out on our trips up the river.

These "out nights" were not always pleasant. When the weather was pleasant, we sometimes made our bed in the canoe, but more often by the cheerful blaze of a camp fire, which greatly relieved the dreariness of the situation.

In all my experiences with the Indians, I have never known of an offensive word or act offered to a white wom-an. They were so respectful and solicitous of my comfort, appearing more like innocent children than adults, that I was never afraid to travel alone with them.

On one occasion, while camping up the river alone,

night overtook us at one of their camps. It is not Indian
etiquette to invite anyone into their homes, so I did not
wait for ceremony, but walked right into the wigwam, and
was made very welcome. They gave me some new mats,
made of rushes. I had my own blankets, and, except from
the ever present odor of smoked salmon, I passed a very
comfortable night.

There is nothing in their primitive huts to suggest
home comforts. The rude walls, the bare earth, with a
smoking fire in the center, the rough platforms covered
with mats for beds, the baskets and kettles in which they
cooked their food, comprised all their household effects,
and filled every want.

CHAPTER XXXIV

No one but those who have spent years isolated from the outside world, debarred from frequent mail privileges, can understand the peculiar excitement produced by the arrival of long delayed mail.

When an Indian made his appearance with the much coveted treasure, some one would wind the old "ox horn," and soon I would see Mr. Judson come tumbling over the fence, for no matter how pressing the work, when the mail signal reached his ears, it was dropped right then and there. Everything else was forgotten in the intellectual enjoyment, from which we could scarcely tear ourselves away to attend to pressing duties, or to secure necessary repose.

Mr. Judson and I were great readers, and we had subscribed for the leading periodicals of the times. Being the only white woman north of Bellingham Bay, and deprived of all companionship, the over crowding of fresh thought from letters and literature produced such a state of mental excitement that frequently drove sleep from my eyes for several nights after the arrival of our mail.

When living in our Chehalis home, I thought a mile a long distance to be separated from my nearest neighbor; but now I was twenty miles away from any white woman. I never could have endured the wearing loneliness without the diversion of our good literature. My dreams were filled with visions of old friends and visits to familiar scenes.

One night, in my dreams, I was with a dear companion of my younger days. She wandered with me on Lake Erie's beach; a soft south wind was blowing; the little ripples came creeping over the shells and pebbles; my hungry

heart was feeding on the joys of bygone days; a passion
of love filled my being; stooping, I extended my hands
over the clear waters as though I would caress them, and
exclaimed, "Beautiful, beautiful Lake Erie." I awoke
with my hands outspread, my pillow wet with tears, and
my heart aching with a lonely longing for the scenes and
friends of the "days of yore." I wrote this dream to the
dear friend of this vision; she expressed her love and sympathy by sending me some perriwinkles and a large shell,
on which was painted a lovely little water scene and a sail
boat. Underneath the words of my dream were written,
"Beautiful, beautiful Lake Erie."

One afternoon Mr. Judson and I set out on an ex-
ploring expedition. We had been told there was a fine creek
on our place, north of us, and such a time we had climbing
over and under logs and forcing our way through the almost impenetrable undergrowth of elder, salmon, thimble-
berry bushes, the thorny war club, and the prickly leaves
of the wild grape; but we found the creek—the thick brush
runnng to the water's edge.

After resting awhile and listening to the soft flow of
the waters, we set out on our return. We walked, climbed
and crept until we were tired out, and still no familiar landmarks appeared. At length a dim suspicion began to creep
into my mind that Mr. Judson was not the infallible guide
I had always considered him. It was rapidly growing
dark. I did not suggest we were lost, and he made no remark, but plodded on in silence. I was just beginning to
wonder what would be the outcome, when lo, the old familiar
sound of the "ox horn" greeted my ear—more welcome
than the sweetest music.

La Bonta and George had grown anxious at our prolonged absence and had come in search of us, and now all we had to do was to follow the familiar sound.

Mr. Judson never acknowledged that he had lost his bearings, but I noticed that he went right to work and opened a trail to the little creek, where we often resorted, both for the pleasure of the walk, and to catch the little speckled trout that at certain season of the year abounded in its waters.

A large fallen tree spanned the creek, which we used as a bridge after neighbors had settled on the other side.

About a half mile above this foot log the Indians had constructed a large fish trap and an immense dry house, where they dried the thousands of salmon that ran up the little creek from the river every fall, during the rainy season.

Their mission up the river is to deposit their eggs— running up the small streams as far as possible, leaping over many obstacles in order to reach the head of the creek, from which the majority of them never return to salt water.

The Indians carefully removed the spinal column, hanging them high in the dry house for safe keeping, as they have a superstition that the spirit of the fish dwells in the backbone and returns to the salt waters to lure other salmon to their traps. I have seen innumerable quantities of these backbones hanging in the dry houses, for they never destroy them.

Often thousands of these "hooked nose" salmon (the Indians' favorite fish) were to be seen lying in heaps on the banks near their traps.

This trap was community property, each Indian helping

himself to fish, as he desired, and when the white settlers began to come in the Indians freely gave them the privilege of choosing what suited them best, and all they wanted.

The little stream derived its name from this trap, and bears the name on the map of "Fish Trap Creek."

Now, the poor old chief comes to me with the pitiful tale that "his people are starving for salmon, because the Bostons stretch their nets across the mouth of the river and keep the fish from running up."

It is sad that the prosperity of the whites means calamity to the Indians.

I so often longed for the companionship of womankind that I often took my sewing and sat by old Sally's camp fire, trying to imagine I was visiting some od friend, talking to her to the limited extent of my "Chinook" vocabulary and taking notes of the Indian method of family government.

There were six children in the family at this time, but as the years passed by they numbered ten. At present there was Tom, Holatchiah, Mathia, Illead, Miladee and Lewison.

The simplicity of the Indian mother's life, although she performed much hard labor, allowed her more time to devote to the care of her children than the average white woman. A great deal of soft moss is used in packing the little baby on its board. This moss takes the place of the linen used in civilized life, and saves much washing.

Her mind unburdened by the cares and perplexities of civilized housekeeping and social customs, she enters more into the child's life, cultivating its affections by sharing its joys and griefs. The Indian child is noticeably free from the quarreling and strife so sadly prevalent among the so called civilized children, and is, I believe, the result of this closely interwoven life of the mother and child.

Old Joe and Sally were so far civilized they were members of the Catholic Mission at the Lummi reservation.

When their sixteen-year-old son Tom was dying with consumption, the poor child said to me, "I do not feel bad to die, only I haven't 'ict bit' (one ten cents) to pay the priest to pray me out of purgatory."

I taught Sally to make light bread. However, as game and fish were very plentiful, and every Indian had his patch of potatoes, or "wapatoes," as they called them, and of which they were very fond, they ate very little bread, and when they did were inclined to like their own method of bread making best—mixing the flour with cold water into a stiff dough, it was flattened between the hands and baked in the hot ashes.

The Indians had to acquire a taste for Boston food. Mr. Tenant's wife, Clara, told me that the first Boston bread she ate, which had been brought on a ship to Port Townsend, made her very sick, and the first tea she drank made her vomit, and they threw all they had into the bay.

When La Bonta returned from his visit in Whatcom, he was accompanied by Miss Moore, his former teacher, and a friend of the family.

Miss Moore was a lover of nature, equally with myself, and her enthusiastic admiration of our wild environments satisfied even my partial heart. Her visit was a source of pleasure to us all, especially to me; and shortly after we were much pleased to learn that she had become the wife of Mr. T. W. Coupe, who had taken up a claim adjoining us, and when his house was completed she came to her new home, and thus the second white woman made her advent in the Nooksack valley.

Mrs. Coupe was an excellent teacher, and later on was elected superintendent of schools of Whatcom county, and Mr. Coupe county treasurer, which positions they held for a number of years. Their little boy, Russell, was the first white child born on the Nooksack river. When Russell was about two years old his Aunt Gertrude, from York, Pennsylvania, came to visit them. Miss Moore remained with her relatives two years, and then became La Bonta's wife, and they settled on an excellent piece of government land directly across the river from our home.

The next man that made his way up the river in canoes, with his wife, two children, pigs and chickens, was Mr. Lindsy. He found a piece of land about seven miles below us that took his fancy, and on which he decided to make their home; but how the family and their effects were to be conveyed to their new possessions was the next question. There was no road, and with all they help they cold procure they were six weeks in hewing an opening through the heavy primeval forests and building a little cabin, near where the flourishing town of Clearbrook is now located.

During the six weeks the family remained with us, and I assisted Mrs. Lindsy in preparing the lunches for the workers.

Unfortunately they built their cabin on low land, and one night during a freshet Mrs. Lindsy was roused by hearing the cat, as she thought, splashing in her pail of water, Springing out of her bed, to her dismay she found herself standing knee deep in water. This was more than they could endure, so they immediately returned to their home on the bay. However, in the course of time, they took up another claim in the same vicinity, and, profiting by former experience, they built their house on high land.

Before I had become well acquainted with the Nooksack tribe of Indians, I did not feel perfectly safe, for our experiences during the Indian war were still fresh in my memory.

The upper chamber, where the children slept, had but one door and one window, and when Mr. Judson was obliged to be away over night to this chamber I carried the gun, and barricading the door and window, would feel more secure.

The presence of these little orphan children in our home was a comfort to me at these times, for I thought that while caring for them the Indians would not be so likely to harm us.

Still, fear often knocked loudly at my heart's door, especially when listening to the appalling noises from the Indian camp on the opposite side of the river, as they made night hideous "momocking tomanamus" (making medicine) to heal their sick ones, or firing their guns to kill the "skiyou" (evil spirit) that they claimed they saw prowling around their lodges.

They believed that these "skiyou" were possessing their suffering ones, and they resorted to these means to drive them away.

CHAPTER XL

Annie wrote that she and her husband were going to attend the state fair at Salem, Oregon, and invited me to accompany them, which I decided to do, and visit my mother who had, after my father's death, moved to Forest Grove, Oregon, to educate her boys. I was longing to see my mother, who had been ill with nervous prostration for several years.

Railroads were still unknown in this far west. At Whatcom we took the boat for Olympia, and it was noon the next day when we steamed into the harbor at Olympia.

My heart was filled with conflicting emotions as I viewed the familiar scenes I had left so reluctantly three years before. I loved Olympia—my life there had been very pleasant. The school bell was ringing for noon, and it thrilled my heart like the voice of a dear old friend.

I looked across to Swantown, dear Lucretia's home. Sweet memories of bygone days were before me, mingled with dark clouds of sorrow and pain. Standing on the steamer's deck, my overcharged heart found relief in a flood of tears. With the scene of so many pleasant recollections lying before me, I realized with painful intensity the utter loneliness of my life on the river.

Before proceeding any farther on our journey, we made dear Father and Mother Judson a visit. We found mother very frail, 'though not confined to her bed. Very early, before light, one morning we took the four-horse stage for Monticello, a distance of seventy-five miles, changing horses four times on our route.

We reached Pumphrey's a midnight, where we changed for the last time, and remained a few hours for rest.

Starting the next morning before daylight, in order to reach Monticello in time to take the Portland steamer.

It was a decidedly sleepy company of fifteen passengers that took stage at Pumphrey's that chilly October morning. Although most crowded, everyone seemed to be on his best behavior. Someone struck up "Marching Through Georgia," all joining in the chorus. Other songs succeeded, and with laughter and singing, all drowsiness was dissipated and the dreaded "mud mountain" was crossed almost unnoticed.

The last mile of the route lay along the river bottom, making it very laborious for the poor horses, that seemed on the verge of giving out. How we pitied them, as they exerted every nerve in their quivering bodies to haul the heavy load through the deep sand. Some of the more compassionate of the men got out and walked, which lightened up the load so much that we were enabled to reach Monticello in due time to take the steamer for Portland; and from there we finished our journey by stage to Forest Grove.

My mother would be greatly surprised to see me, as she had not heard of my coming. When I went into her room I saw that she did not recognize me at first, so I stooped over the bedside, kissed her face and said, "Ma, don't you know me?" when again and again she exclaimed in an excited and pathetic voice, "Oh, Phoebe, Phoebe, I can't believe that it is you."

We were equally rejoiced to be together once more.

Seeing her so helpless, I decided at once to take her home
with me.

My brother Edward conveyed us over the rough way
in his comfortable carriage, and at Whatcom we found Mr.
Judson waiting us with a mattress for a bed in the canoe;
and thus we comfortably conveyed her to our home on the
Nooksack.

She remained with us ten years and two months, until
her death.   During all these years her night lamp never
failed to burn.

Daniel McLellehan, the only white man in the neigh-
borhood when we settled here, was a warm hearted kindly
neighbor.   Not long after our arrival he was taken suddenly
ill.   Realizing that he could not live, he begged us to take
charge of his children and find comfortable homes for
them in white families.   These were John, Horace, Norah
and little Dan.   The latter was only a few months old, and
remained with his mother, who went back to live with her
Indian friends, while we took the other children into our
home.   We found a home for Horace, but he was not contented and soon returned to us—so we kept them all.

Nina, their mother, often came to visit them.   When
baby Dan was two years and a half old, Nina was taken
sick and sent for me.   I found her lying in the lodge of her
brother, Chief Yelkanum Seclamatum..   Nina was in the
last stakes of consumption.   She told me "how much she
loved her children," and that "her heart was warm towards
me for taking care of them."   She said "she wanted them
to be good children."

I don't think a mother with the advantages of civilization could express more anxiety that her children should be taught to do right than did this dying child of nature.

At Nina's death Dan's uncle, Chief Seclamatum, brought him to us. The only English words the little fellow could speak were "swear words," and, strange to say, he knew where they applied, never using them except when angry. He was very homesick for a while, and cried piteously for "accouyah" (mamma).

Nora, the boys' sister, was but three years old when she came to live with us. She was a delicate child, and continued to be frail as she grew up into a modest, retiring young lady, beloved by all—especially by her brothers.

She died, when twenty years of age, of consumption, that she had inherited from her mother.

Nora's death was very beautiful. I had many sweet conversations with her about her heavenly home, and she was perfectly resigned to go and dwell with her dear mother, whom I am sure was waiting to welcome her dear child home. The last day of her earthly life she said to me, "Ma, I heard such beautiful music this morning." I still had hopes that she would recover, but, surrounded by her weeping brothers, with a lovely smile on her face and in her eyes, dear Nora left us.

To the affectionate memory of Nora McClanahan, who died in Lynden on Sunday, March 8th, 1891, aged twenty years and eight months, by her friend, Mrs. Mary Beavers.

There's another mound in the graveyard,
  Another dear one lies,
Crowned with beautiful flowers,
  Under the changing skies.

Gone in the golden morning,
  In the fair, sweet flush of dawn:
In the midst of her girlish dreaming,
  Her hopes and her visions gone.

Fair was the beaming promise,
  That arched the opening way,
Into the pure, bright regions
  Where her glad feet should stray.

When girlhood's rosy brightness
  Should deepen the flush of youth,
Into the fuller splendor
  Of womanhood's light serene.

Thy brief, bright journey ended,
  With its labors few and light,
The shade of the cross vanished
  In thy radiant upward flight.

CHAPTER XLI

In 1874 we began to think that our numbers demanded a post office. But to have a post office, we must have a name, and to me was conceded the honor of selecting one. Some suggested that it be called "Judson," but I thought Lynden a much prettier name, and Lynden it is.

This name had pleasant associations, because of a story Eason Ebey read to us while on a visit to their home on Whidby island; also from the poem beginning "On Linden, when the sun was low"—only changing the "i" to "y," because it looks prettier written so.

We circulated a petition, and in due time the Nooksack mail route was established, with Lynden as the terminal post office.

Samuel Caldwell was our first mail carrier, carrying it once a week on horseback, a distance of twenty-five miles, over the old trail that was cut through from Whatcom to the upper Nooksack crossing during the gold excitement on the Fraser river.

Mr. Judson was appointed postmaster, and for several years our bookcase held all the Lynden mail.

Now and then a stranger landed from a canoe on the bank of the river, and, wandering up to the lone cabin on the hillside, inquired the "distance to Lynden."

It was hard to tell whether most pleased or disappointed when informed that "this is Lynden."

The next accession to our numbers was the family of Enoch Hawley, consisting of wife, two sons, one daughter, and Miss Rachel Craven, the sister of Mrs. Hawley. We gladly welcomed this intelligent, enterprising family, who performed their part in the development of the country. Mr. Hawley opened the first store in the Nooksack valley.

By this time a number of single men had taken up claims in the surrounding country. What could we have done without these bachelors to pioneer the way through the swamps and dense forests where it was impossible to take a family. I felt a deep sympathy for these bachelor boys in their loneliness, cut off, as they were, from home comforts and associations. My sympathy found expression in opening our family circle and giving them a real home dinner on Christmas day.

Two of these enterprising bachelors, Watson Smith and Joe Stowbridge, boarded with us until they got their cabins built and a trail opened to their ranches.

Mr. Stowbridge was a good musician, and from him our little George took his first lessons on the violin.

During the time Mr. Hawley was building his house Miss Craven occupied one of our rooms. Watson Smith was charmed with her social qualities, and fully appreciated the energy and enterprise of her character. It was not long before a warm friendship sprang up between the two, which culminated in the first wedding on the Nooksack river. This wedding was a great event to us. The bride was attired in a white dress, trimmed with sprays of the beautiful trailing mytrle which grew so abundantly in the wild woods; white kid gloves and slippers put the finishing touches to the bridal costume.

One of our bachelor ranchers, Samuel Caldwell, Esq., performed the marriage ceremony.

The next morning, putting on her coarse shoes and short dress, after two hours of hard labor, climbing over and under logs, and creeping through the brush, the bride arrived at her new home, where she set to work with all the energy of her nature to make "the wilderness blossom like the rose."

"There are wives—and wives;" some are satisfied to be a drone in the hive, looking upon the husband as the only medium through which their pride and ambition may be gratified. Others, like our friend, unite with the husband to build up a home.

For years she packed the butter and eggs, a distance of two and a half miles, to the store, and carried the family groceries home, crossing Fish Trap creek on the footlog.

When old age began to creep upon them and the "gem city" of Lynden was incorporated, they sold their ranch where they had passed so many years of hard labor, transforming the backwoods wilderness into a profitable farm, and took up their residence within the city limits.

Watson Smith has passed to the great beyond. Mrs. Smith, or "Aunt Rachael," as she is familiarly called, is still among us, beloved by old and young, and admired and respected by all the country around.

Mr. and Mrs. Hawley, and their youngest son, Lec, have all passed away. Lida is the wife of Mr. Burthason, one of our most enterprising and industrious farmers. Emett, who had the honor of being our first city marshal, resides among us with his wife and fine large family of sons and daughters.

Mr. O'Neal and family were the next ones to join us. Six-year-old Robbie was their only child, though they afterwards adopted a baby girl only a few weeks old, and named her Jennie.

Mr. O'Neal took up land on the other side of the creek. A large fallen tree spanned the creek, and many a trip I have made across its rounded surface to visit our new neighbors. Mr. and Mrs. O'Neal still occupy the old homestead. Robert is our genial postmaster, and, with his much admired wife and five rosy children, make the old home cheerful. Jennie, her husband and two little girls are living in their pleasant home a few miles below us on the river.

Very soon our numbers were again augmented by the arrival of Mr. William Slade and family, consisting of wife and three sons. Mr. Slade settled near Mr. O'Neal's, on the other side of Fish Trap Creek. Being very industrious and energetic people, they soon had a large hole in the wilderness and a comfortable home erected. Henry and Harvey were young men, and a few years later Harvey visited his home in California, and returned with a fair young bride.

We were still so few in number that we felt like one family, and we gladly accepted this young stranger as one of us.

All of these early settlers who shared with us the privations and trials of pioneer life seem more like family relations than chance acquaintances.

Nearly two years after Allie Slade's advent among us, a little baby girl came to bless their home. As a rule, new babies possess little beauty, except in the eyes of fond parents; but little Theda was unusually pretty from birth. She was a bright, good baby and grew to be a great comfort to her parents. When Theda was nearly a year old Miss

Kathie Moore, of York, Pennsylvania, came to Washington
to visit her sister, La Bonta's wife.

I will here insert a poem written by her about little
Theda, which fitly describes the luxuriance of our vegetable
growth:

THE BABY'S THRONE

The baby's throne was, oh, so green,
  And, oh, so cool and round:
And baby clapped her tiny hands,
And thot that e'en in fairyland
  Can such a seat be found.

And who can guess the baby's throne?
Was it a great moss buried stone?
Or was it on the apple bough
Where robin swings—is swinging now,
Or was it by the reedy pool
Where shadows lie so dark and cool?

No, none of these my little queen,
Was thus enthroned upon her green:
The day was warm and mamma dear
Was working in the garden near;
And baby Theda, full of play,
Was always getting in her way.

'Till mamma had a happy thought,
Her baby in her arms she caught,
And set her on a cabbage head,
That, green and cool, great leaves outspread,
And baby laughed and clapped her hands,
The gayest queen in all earth's lands.

Now little maid, don't shake your head,
My tale is false, you are afraid.
Why, don't you know in this far west,
All nature with great wealth is blessed?
A cabbage eighteen feet around
Is no rare sight on this charmed ground;
And baby Theda, dainty queen,
Could creep upon her throne of green.

Harvey and Allie, with their interesting family of four boys and two little girls, reside among us.

This is the world of sorrowful parting, and Harvey and Allie were called upon to lay away their eldest born. When little Theda was nine years old she closed her blue eyes upon the scenes of earth.

Henry Slade married the daughter of one of the later settlers. When their two boys were eight and ten years of age, a little baby girl was added to the family, and Henry said, "Oh, we will call her Gladys, because the boys have a little sister and we have a little daughter."

They, too, have parted with their treasure, and have laid her to rest with her cousin Theda in the beautiful plot of ground set apart for the Lynden cemetery.

CHAPTER XLII

A young editor from Olympia, who was on a recuperating and prospecting expedition, penetrated the wilds of the Nooksack valley, and for a few days made his home with us. As he sat toasting his slippered feet one day, the children, who had gone for the cows, came rushing back exclaiming, "There are three great cougars right down here in the river bottom." What a commotion this report raised. The men sprang for their guns and made a dash for the river bottom. I never saw anyone more excited than the editor. The slippers flew from his feet, his boots were on in a trice, and he was off like a flash in the wake of the hunters.

They succeeded in killing two of the animals, and brought them to the house, and fatally wounding the third, which was found dead the next day.

They were powerful, ferocious looking creatures, and no doubt would have wrought havoc among the stock.

It was a new and exciting experience for the editor, and he was very exultant over the success of the chase. The incident made quite an interesting item for his paper.

Early in the autumn of 1875 the typhoid fever was very prevalent throughout the country. Three of our family were down with it at the same time. The nearest physician was at Whatcom, but as I do not believe in using drugs that did not trouble me. However, La Bonta was so weakened by terrible night sweats I thought I must get something to break them up, and sent to Whatcom by Mr. Coupe to get some medicine for that purpose.

The physician, who was a drinking man, asked "twenty

dollars" for a small phial. Mr. Coupe told him he was "sure we would not be willing to pay that price." He then reduced it to "fifteen." Mr. Coupe brought it to us, but by the time it reached me I had succeeded in breaking up the "sweats," so we returned the "costly phial" unopened to the physician.

The continued loss of sleep, in addition to the care of my mother, brought me to death's door. There came a day when I realized that for my brother Henry and George hope was vain.

Weakened by long vigils and the hard work, I sank under the pressure. All day Mr. Judson worked over me, applying various restoratives, and I'm sure it was due to his untiring efforts that I was restored. There was a terrible pressure on my brain, and I thought I never could go to sleep again, and that if sleep did come it would be the sleep of death.

I told Mr. Judson that I could not recover, and tried to plan everything to make it as easy as possible for him and the family. I was so confident that I was about to leave this world that I even selected a spot for my resting place. The house was kept as quiet as the grave. How it was managed I cannot understand—towards morning I dropped off into a deep slumber and dreamed that I was in my heavenly home. Everything was so gloriously beautiful— thousands of happy faced children sported around me, and my dear ones for whom I had given up all hopes, were among the number. I was supremely happy.

After a time in my dream I was taken to the river bank, where I saw three new canoes that had never been launched, and a woven covering of withes seemed to indicate that they were not ready to be occupied. As I slowly awoke from my slumber, before I opened my eyes, I still thought I was in the heavenly land.

My bed faced the window, and the first objects that greeted my fully awakened eyes were the great fir trees that cast their shadows over my earthly home. Surely, I thought, this cannot be heaven. Oh, how dark and dreary this earth life appeared. How heavy the burdens; must I take them up again? Then came the thought, how much I am needed here; my helpless mother and all these little children were dependent on my care, and I was thankful that I had been spared to lift my share of the burdens of life.

I took the "three unlaunched canoes" of my dream as a good omen. I rapidly recovered and was soon able to assume my post by the sick ones, with renewed hope and courage, and in due time had the joy of seeing them restored to health.

CHAPTER XLIII

In the fall of 1874 the first election of Lynden precinct was held in our house. It was quite a jubliee occasion, and I remember I got up a royal turkey dinner for the voters.

Mr. Judson was elected one of the county commissioners. The day was a rainy one. Our rains usually fall gently, but this was one of the hardest rains we had experienced in the territory. A warm south wind was blowing, which rapidly melted the snows in the mountains. Our young stock was running in the river bottoms, and so absorbed were the men in this first election that they did not notice the sudden rising of the river until it was too late to go in search of them that night.

Before morning the river was so high that the only way to reach the stock was by canoe. They found no trace of them, but found a number of bears swimming in the water, snapping and snarling as they all endeavored to clamber upon a cottonwood log that sank under their weight.

When the canoe came in sight, they immediately left the log and made for the canoe. In their fear of drowning, mistaking it for another log (the men had no gun) all were motionless. As the bears approached Mr. Judson sat in the bow, axe in hand, and as the animals came up to the canoe he succeeded in killing one old one and two half grown cubs; another old bear took refuge in a cottonwood tree. The men constructed a raft by the tree, where two of them remained on guard, while another came to the house for the rifle. They were successful in killing that one also.

But our poor stock—thirteen head belonging to Mr. Hawley and ourselves, were drowned.

Like lightning the news spread among the Indians, the country around that "looket ichoot" (four bears) were "memaloosed" (killed), and before night Joe's camp was fairly alive with their tillicums" (friends) and what a jolly night they made of it. They gourmandized until morning.

Some of the white settlers sampled the "cubs," and one of them still claims that it was the best meat she ever ate.

Eason and Annie made us a present of a fine blooded sheep. That was the beginning of a flock. Now that we had wool, my thought turned towards a spinning wheel. We ordered one from the head of the Sound, at Tumwater, where they manufactured the large, old fashioned kind. I had learned the rudiments of spinning when a child, and by practice soon mastered the art. And many a long winter evening was cheerfully passed picking, carding, spinning and knitting before the open fire.

We found that, with so many feet to clothe, that making our own stockings and socks was a great saving.

Besides providing stockings for my own family, I knit many a pair for the bachelor ranchers—they were much better than any they could buy. The demand for my yarn and socks was greater than the supply. For my lambs wool stockings I spun the yarn "cross banded" single thread and very fine. When knitted loosely and colored black, they were as nice, and much softer, than merino stockings.

My wheel was a great curiosty to the native women. Many a roll they have spoiled for me in their attempts to learn to spin.

They had a unique way of making yarn from the wool

of mountain goats. They picked the wool, and without
carding, rolled it on the bare leg, that had been well lubri-
cated from the hip down with bear's oil; the left hand held
a stock, which took the place of the spindle, on which they
wound the yarn as they rolled it with the right hand.

Their primitive method of knitting socks was to make
them straight, allowing the foot to make its own heel. I
taught Sally my method of heeling and toeing the sock, and
she took a great deal of pride in knitting them the "Boston
style."

They still adhere to the primitive method of spinning.
The yarn not being twisted tightly, is very soft, and
"Siwash" socks are in demand among the "Bostons," and
are always found for sale at the stores.

One day while Joe was working for Mr. Judson in the
field, Lewison came to his father and reported a new baby
in the camp. Joe left his work at once and went home to
see the new addition to his family., I went right over as
soon as I heard the news to see if I could render any assistance, but found Sally busily engaged in getting the dinner, as though nothing unusual had happened. The new
baby was already strapped to its little baby board and
swaddled in a quantity of soft moss, which takes the place
of the linen used in civilized life.

The Indian mother rocks her baby, but her method is
different from that of her white sister. The top of a young
tree, or sapling, is bent over, and to this the board on
which the baby is bound is suspended. The mother holds
a string that is attached to the board by which she keeps
this Indian cradle in motion—a veritable illustration of
the old song, "Rock a by baby on the tree top."

Sally bore four children after we moved here, but she only pressed the head of the first one.

Twins are very rare. In my more than fifty years' association with the Indians I have never known of a pair of twins.

In a conversation with Chief Seclamatum several years ago, he said it was their custom, in the event of the birth of a pair of twins, to drive the mother from the camp, and when she returned she brought only one child.

Since the Indians have become Christianized, all of their supertitious cruelties have been abolished.

The old Indian doctor was a noted character among the tribes, who looked upon him as a deity.

The Indians are very prompt to call upon newcomers, not that the form of etiquette demands it, but simply through curiosity; and very soon after our arrival on the river this old medicine man favored me with a call. I was greatly pleased with my visitor, and thought I had found a congenial spirit among the Indians. He told me "he had known God ever since he was a little boy" and talked so familiarly about the Great Spirit that I was completely captivated. We spent two or three hours in conversation. I gave him a lunch and a pressing invitation to repeat his visit.

However, one evening, not long after the doctor's visit, hearing a doleful din from Sally's camp, we went over. One of Sally's girls was sick, and there was the old doctor, surrounded by his "tillicum" performing his heathenish incantations, throwing his body into disgusting and inconceivable contortions, making the most hideous grimaces imagin-

able, at the same time giving vent to swine-like grunt-
ings and groanings.

As I witnessed the pretentions of this conjurer, my
exalted admiration of his "spiritual attainments" underwent a sudden transformation.

All the Indians in the camp were, with much solemnity,
beating a board, pan, or anything they could find on which
to keep time to a weird chant that rose high above the din
of the tattoo. These charms were to fascinate the "skiyous" that they imagined infested the sick girl. The
"skiyous" (evil spirits) the old doctor pretended to catch,
crowd into his gun and shoot through the roof of the lodge.

Fortunately for the doctor, the girl got well, as it was
customary, should the patient die, to kill the doctor, unless
he could prove that some one had bewitched the sufferer—
then the accused was killed, instead of the doctor.

Two young Indians, called "Felix" and "Jack of Clubs,"
who worked for us, were victims of this inhuman custom.
The old Indian doctor continued his devil fighting practice
among the Indians until one Fourth of July, while the citizens of Whatcom were celebrating the national holiday.
While firing the first cannon that was brought to the
bay by Captain Roeder, it exploded, killing two Indians in
their wigwams, and one of them proved to be the "old doctor."

Great was the excitement and wailing among the tribes
until they were made satisfied that the explosion was an
accident, and the county had paid them well for their loss.

Not long after the death of the old Indian doctor, Holachie, Sally's eldest daughter, was taken very sick. They
thought she was dying, and sent to the Lummi reservation

for the Catholic priest to come and confess her. However, her sickness was not unto death, but when the priest left he carried away Joe's cow and gun with him as remuneration for his priestly office. When I inquired of Sally what service he had rendered to rob them of the chief of their earthly possessions, she replied that Holachie confessed to him that her "tum tum" (heart) was "hias mesachie" (very bad), that she had "capswallowed" (stolen) and "clemmenwet" (lied) and by his prayers to the "Sothalic Tyee" (Great Spirit), he had made her "close" (good).

I tried to make her understand that God loved Holachie, and that if she would pray to Him herself He would answer her prayers, without "money or price." As I talked to Sally about God's great love for *all* His children, the Indians, as well as the whites, she repeatedly exclaimed "nauwitka" (yes) in such heartfelt tones that I knew she was drinking in the truth.

CHAPTER XVIV

Late one Saturday night two men knocked at the door. They proved to be the Rev. Mr. Tate, an English missionary from Chilliwack, B. C., and his friend "Captain John," a native preacher of the Methodist denomination. They had come to hold meetings with the Indians, and were the first Protestant teachers to come among them.

Early the next morning messengers from the camp carried the news in every direction, and before nine o'clock our house was filled to overflowing with these unpolished aborigines, eager to hear the new gospel. They had bestowed no extra care to make themselves presentable for the occasion. Their crude, filthy clothing, unkempt hair and bare feet were a great contrast to a beautiful apparelled civilized assembly.

But the Indians felt no disgrace, for they had no pride in that direction, and when they began taking part in the devotional exercises of the meeting in a childlike spirit, my aversion towards these poor heathen vanished. Sally was one of the first converts—her testimony affected me to tears.

Though she gave it in the Indian tongue, I could understand that she said she rejoiced in this free religion, and that she had learned it from me.

Many other conversions followed. In their innocence and simple childlike faith, they grasped the truths of the gospel more readily than many who enjoyed the advantages of civilization. Truly, I thought, "we must become as a little child before we can enter the kingdom."

On pleasant days we would take the melodeon out under the trees, and many times there were a hundred or more Indians in the yard.

Mr. Tate always preached to them in the native tongue, which he had learned to speak fluently. He also translated a number of gospel hymns into their language. These they learned readily and sang with great spirit. I was much surprised to learn that they possessed so much of the spiritual element in their nature, and deeply regretted that I had not conversed more with them on that subject.

I had learned that "God is no respecter of persons" and that "He will bless *all* who gather together in His name."

Mr. Tate worked a number of needed reforms among the Indians. It was their custom to keep their dead above ground. The bodies were usually wrapped in several pairs of blankets and placed in boxes on scaffolds built for that purpose. Rude wooden images of wild beasts and birds, which they imagined watched over the departed, also guns, clothing, cooking utensils, and various other valuables were left for their use; which made a grewsome resting place for their dead. After the Bostons took possession of their country these articles were defaced rendering them useless.

Old Skaleel, an ancient Indian, who claimed to be as old as Mount Baker, lived with his family a few miles north of us, in the timber. Old Skaleel never wore any garments; he was "too old a dog to learn new tricks," and always made his appearance wrapped in the traditional blanket.

Well he might vie with hoary Mount Baker in age, for his mummylike form was suggestive of nothing more human than a tanned hide.

His eldest son, "Lapuse" (a name given him by the Indians for stealing a hoe) looked to be a centenarian. Lapuse was noted among the settlers for his begging and thieving propensities. Peter, another son, was accidentally shot, and lay very ill for a long time. Mary, his young sister, came to us nearly every day asking for "pie" for her sick "owe" (brother). The word pie was about the extent of her English vocabulary. When there was no pie, something else answered just as well. Peter recovered, but Mary was taken suddenly sick and died. The box containing her body was placed high on a tree. The boys belonging to the family of some new settlers, hearing there was money in the box, pulled it down and scattered the contents.

No greater crime could be committed against an Indian than to desecrate the resting place of his dead, and these "stick Indians" (so called because they lived back from the river, in the heavy timber) were greatly enraged at this wanton desecration of their sacred dead.

They came out to our house, and oh, what a "pow wow" ensued. I was really frightened for I did not know what would be the result. I think they made more ado than did the Alaska Indians over the theft of their "totem pole." We gave them our full sympathy and succeeded in pacifying them.

These grewsome resting places of the dead produced very unsanitary conditions, and Mr. Tate persuaded them to place their dead beneath the ground.

Another reform was in introducing the marriage ceremony, and abolishing polygamy. So a day was appointed, in which all the Indians were to be legally joined in wedlock. A plurality of wives was only the prerogative of a chief or a "tyee" (man of wealth). It had been the habit of Chief Seclamatum to change his wife whenever so inclined. The marriage ceremonies were to be performed at one of the meetings at our house, and Mr. Tate was taken by surprise when the old chief stepped before him, leading a young and pretty maiden to be his bride. Eyeing him severely, Mr. Tate told him "that would never do," he must get his old wife and be married to her." This was a hard pill for Seclamatum; he earnestly demurred. However, Mr. Tate refused to marry him, and he reluctantly reinstated old Fanny, his wife.

One of the first camp meetings ever held on the upper Nooksack was marked by a tragedy.

While returning home the canoe containing Mr. and Mrs. Tennant, Elder Lesourd and two or three other ministers, Chief Seclamatum, his son George, with his wife, infant and little girl, ran against a sunken rock and split in two, plunging them all into the Nooksack's icy current. The Indians, forgetting themselves, devoted all their energies to the rescue of the ministers; some of them had a narrow escape. Chief Seclamatum's little granddaughter was drowned. The mother swam ashore with the infant, then spent so many hours in the water assisting in the search for the child, that at length, when the lifeless body was found, she was so exhausted and frantic with grief that she did not long survive her little daughter.

We all attended the funeral of the little girl in the chief's camp. Elder Lesourd spoke many comforting words, through an interpreter, and we mingled our tears with those of the girl's stricken parents.

As the Indians marched to the burying ground, carry-

ing the little casket, they sang in their native tongue,
"Shall We Gather at the River?"

A number of camp meetings soon followed in the wake
of the missionaries. Our Olympia friend, Mr. Tennant, was
converted at the one first held near his place at Ferndale.
We attended the meeting and spent the night at his lovely
home. His yard was beautifully laid out and filled with
the choicest flowers, in which he took much pride, for he
was quite a botanist and his soul delighted in the beauties
of nature. Their home was a model of neatness and comfort.

Mr. Tennant treated his Indian wife with all the defer-
ence due a cultured white woman. He began preaching at
once, and always took her with him to the general confer-
ence.

One of his first appointments was at Lynden, and here
they built a cozy little home, where they spent the remainder of their lives. Mr. Tennant was an able minister and
filled many appointments throughout the surrounding country. Clara, as he called his wife, was a princess, the daughter of a Lummi chief, and the pride of her tribe; a woman
of large physique, and of an unusually strong character,
strikingly deficient in beauty, but of a bright and lively disposition.

Many an interesting tale has Mrs. Tennant told me of
her childhood days; what a large tribe they were; how
they lived in almost constant fear of their enemies, passing much of their time in subterranean dwellings, which
were connected by tunnels. She said they had a vast number of these underground houses, to which they retreated
in time of danger, stealing out occasionaly for supplies of

salmon and game, which was very plentiful in those days. It was their custom to hold a grand annual "potlatch." For several days, and sometimes weeks, friends from far and near would join them, and the time was passed in feasting and various amusements, among which gambling was a prominent feature, for the red man is as passionately fond of gambling as his pale brothers. Beaver's teeth passed current as coin; ponies, blankets, guns and all available property changed hands at these times.

One such gala occasion a Northern Indian, one of the bitter enemies of the Lummis, stealthily clipped a lock of her father's hair. This was considered an omen of great misfortune, and caused dire dismay throughout the tribe. The old chief took it greatly to heart—he, in common with his tribe, believing that an evil spirit would take possession of his body, and that he would lose his life as a result of the stolen lock of hair. The threatened doom so prayed upon his mind that in a few days he sickened and died.

The little Indian girl faithfully performed her part with her brothers and sisters in nursing her father in his last illness. With a portion of her inheritance, she afterwards went to Victoria and bought two little slave boys from the Northern Indians. These slave boys grew up and were faithful servants for many years.

Two boys were born to Mr. and Mrs. Tennant. One died in its infancy. Bayard grew up to be a beautiful, intelligent boy of eighteen. Every advantage and luxury that money could buy were lavished upon this youth, but the dread white plague, consumption, claimed him as its victim. He was sent to southern California, but all in vain. His mother mourned for her boy every moment of the separation, and he for his mother. When all hope was gone, he was brought home. A canoe awaited him at the mouth of the river. Life was almost extinct, but the poor boy seemed determined to live to see his mother once more. The longing of his heart was gratified, but he only lived a few hours after reaching home. His mother's grief was deep. Her long black hair grew white in that night of anguish. She has many times told me he would have lived if they had kept him home and employed an "Indian medicine man."

How lovingly she tended his grave, keeping it bright with beautiful flowers. I have heard her say that "Bayard often came and comforted her when she was grieving for him."

After Mr. Tennant's death "Clara" remained a widow for a number of years. She had been a true and faithful wife; during Mr. Tennant's last sickness no one could minister to his wants so acceptably as she.

At the age of seventy years she was wooed and won by our ancient Indian friend Chief Sallakanum Seclamatum, commonly called "Indian Jim" by the white settlers. Mrs. Seclamatum only lived a few months after her marriage, dying very suddenly of pneumonia. I called to see her the day of her death. She was very particular in giving directions about her funeral. She wanted to be dressed in black silk, placed in a handsome casket, carried by white pallbearers to the Methodist church, where her husband had officiated, and from whence he was buried. It was her desire to be laid to rest beside her husband and children in the Lynden cemetery. Her wishes were faithfully fulfilled.

She had lived so frugally (industriously knitting socks for sale), that people thought she had no means but her landed estate, and great was their surprise to find eighty dollars in her purse under her pillow, besides two thousand in her trunk. In addition, she left property to the amount of twelve thousand, which the chief and her brother and sister inherited.

CHAPTER XLV

The lack of locality in my mental composition has brought to me more than one laughable experience.

One bright spring morning I started off on my Indian pony, Gypsy, to visit a pioneer friend, Mrs. Harkness, who lived at the upper Nooksack crossing, seven miles away. Through the road was but a narrow Indian trail, I had perfect confidence in "Old Gyp"; she was a trained Indian pony, and could jump a fallen tree and walk a foot log like a man. I jogged along at a slow pace, letting the pony take its own gait, drinking in the pure air, exhilarated by the evidence of opening spring that met my view on every hand. The bursting bud, the tender green of the springing grass, enlivened by the bright blossoms of the flowering currant that greets us so early in the spring, the little lambs frolicking in the field, and last, but not least, the dark green of the foothills of old Kulshan, from which the warm sunshine had melted the snow.

About two miles from our house I passed the McLellahan ranch and spoke to a man who was ploughing in the field. About a mile farther on the trail diverged, branching around a clump of evergreens and coming together again on the other side. The faint trail was all clear, so long as my thoughts were intent upon it; but, lost in pleasing reveries, I did not notice that old Gyp, on coming to the place where the trails untied, took the homeward track. Indian Job's homestead would be the next on my way. As I drew near what I supposed to be his home, I was greatly surprised that the Indian had made so much improvement. A fine young orchard, well fenced fields, a comfortable looking house in the place of the "'wigwam," and here was even a gate. I rode up to it and called loudly for Job; there was no response, so I rode on, thinking that the next time I saw the old Indian I would give him unmeasured praise for the progress he had made in adopting the customs of civilization. Presently I came to a man ploughing in a field, and then it dawned upon me that this was the McLellahan ranch, and old Gyp had doubled on her track and was taking me back home. Knowing I would never hear the last of it, if I went home, I wheeled old Gyp around, and taking her guidance into my own hands, reached the crossing without further adventure, in time to make a short but pleasant visit with my friends.

One of the foothills of Mount Baker, domelike in shape, rose considerably higher than its fellows. As we were looking out and admiring the beauties of our surroundings one day, Mr. Judson said, "I intend some day to go to the top of that mountain and build a great fire that you can all see." And I said, "When you go, I'm going, too," and so it fell out, one August day, taking old Joe and Sally, with blankets and provisions enough for a week, we set out. Fortunately for my outing, Miss Annie Smith, who had come from the east to visit her sister, Mrs. O'Neal, consented to take charge of the home during our absence. Miss Smith afterwards became my brother Henry's wife.

The first part of the journey was accomplished by canoe. That was a very easy part for me, and, as the canoe was impelled swiftly along by the paddles of the stalwart Indians, my cup of contentment seemed full, and I was thrilled with enthusiastic excitement.

The prospect that lay before held nothing but delight.

Such a trip as this had been the longing of my heart for many years, and I completely yielded myself to the pleasures of the hour.

We camped the first night near old Lockkanum's wigwam, not far from the river. A large fire was built under the wide spreading cedars and we began preparations for supper. Old Sally procured a fine salmon, which she dressed without the use of water. Wiping it perfectly clean with ferns and grass, she set it up on sticks, to roast before the fire. A more delicious fish I never tasted. I have since repeatedly tried her method, but never succeeded in cooking a salmon that I relished as the one old Sally cooked by the camp fire, probably because I did not have the same "sauce."

One of Sally's old "tillicums" (friends) from Lochkanum's came over and spent the evening with us, and we engaged her services for the trip. I shall never forget how happy the Indians were around the camp fire that night. The trip appeared to be as much a treat to them as to me. They fairly bubbled over with joy, laughing and talking like a company of happy children, as they cracked and ate the hazel nuts they had gathered on the way. When night came old Sally took the initiative in gathering fir boughs and enormous ferns to make a bed for me; and when a blanket was spread over these impromptu springs, it proved a most restful couch.

The novelty of the situation kept me awake for some hours, which I spent gazing up through the network of branches that canopied my resting place, into the beautiful starlit heavens, and listening to the cheerful crackling of the camp fire, which the Indians kept blazing all night.

Early morning hours found us astir, for a hard day's tramp lay before us. Up hill and down dale we scrambled. Old Sally seemed to consider me her special charge, always offering a helping hand in what she considered the hard places. As we proceeded the undergrowth grew more dense, sometimes almost impentrable, and in these places it took the united effort and skill of Sally and Mr. Judson to disentangle and pull me over the great logs and up the steep, rocky ascents.

We rested and took our lunch by a beautiful mountain stream. When night came and we pitched our camps, how my aching bones and bruised flesh enjoyed the rest.

The next day the way became more open, and about noon I was rejoiced to hear the Indians, who were a little in advance, shout, "Latate, Latate" (the head, the head). We had reached the coveted height. A strange feeling of exultation thrilled my being at the thought of standing where white man's foot had never trod. The top of the mountain was a broad table land, with a scattering of trees and no undergrowth. It was a pleasant change after long hours spent creeping through the thick brush under the heavy timber.

Here we had a magnificent view of the surrounding country as far as the eye could reach.

Port Townsend lay to the southwest. A trim steamer was creeping across the waters to Whidby island. Away to the north flowed the Fraser river, like a broad ribbon, dividing the landscape. There, too, we could distinguish a tiny steamer.

Mountains and foothills lay about us in all directions. To the southeast Mount Baker, the highest peak of the

Cascade range, reared its kingly head high above all the rest, cold and grand. Our own little home lay due west, though there was nothing by which we could distinguish the spot; and as I thought of the rough way that lay between, how I longed for a balloon, that I might take a bee line over the tree tops to my home.

We remained here two days, completely captivated by the scenery with which we were surrounded. It seemed, while elevated above the sordid cares of earth life—resting and drinking in the pure mountain air—we were that much nearer heaven. And I remarked to Mr. Judson, "Some day, when this country is settled, this will be made a delightful summer resort." Thirty years have passed, and now this mountain is all staked off into gold mining claims.

The only large game we saw was a bear, which they shot at but missed. We feasted on the red and blue huckleberry that grew in abundance, and the young grouse Sally broiled, like the salmon, on sticks before the fire, and were just as appetizing.

The descent of the mountain was accomplished with much more ease, and celerity than the ascent. We took a different route on our homeward way, descending the spur, or backbone, of the mountain, the view of different points was so fascinating that we often tarried to enjoy the magnificence of the scene.

Towards evening we entered a beautiful valley and pitched our camp by a little stream. I was surprised to see old Polly, who had all the time been so jolly, go off by herself and sit down by the little creek that rippled along so merrily, singing on its way to the sea, seemingly wrapped in deep meditation. Polly paid no attention to camp duties.

Presently she raised her voice in mournful wails of sorrow, and continued to utter her cries of grief for an hour or more. When she returned to the camp her clothing was wet with tears.

Old Sally was full of sympathy for Polly. She had torn her dress, and bringing a needle and thread, Sally sat down by her and mended it—a most practical demonstration of sympathy.

I inquired the cause of Polly's grief, and found she had been recalling bygone days. In spite of their nomad life, I have noticed the love of home and friends is a pronounced characteristic of the Indian nature.

This lovely valley had been her father's favorite camping ground. Here, a little child, she had played with her brothers and sister. This valley had been covered with her father's ponies. A trap in the creek supplied them with an abundance of salmon and trout, and here she had, as a wife and mother, passed many happy years. Now they were all gone and she was a lonely "lummai" (old woman), obliged to pack for a living.

Poor old Polly! My heart went out in sympathy for the poor lonely old soul.

The next day we reached home. In spite of bruised flesh, strained muscles and scratched skin, our expedition had been one of unalloyed pleasure. The trip had fulfilled my expectations, and more, too. Besides the pleasant recollections I seemed to have received a new lease of life, and I took up home duties with fresh interest and enjoyment.

CHAPTER XLVI

Some bright gleams radiated through my lonely life in the Nooksack valley. The very brightest lay in the days spent on the bay with my long cherished friend, Elizabeth Roeder. Our visits at first were made by an Indian canoe, as the river at that time was our only thoroughfare.

Our greetings in the early days were signalized with shouts of joy, but in later years, when sorrow had laid its heavy hand upon our lives, these joyful salutations were changed to tears of mournful sympathy.

The occasional hour stolen from burdensome care to indulge in a pleasant walk to some lone consecrated spot, deep in the forest, where we could uninterruptedly relive our girlhood days, away back in Ohio, on the shores of Lake Erie, were precious moments.

On one of my trips across the bay the water was so rough it splashed into the canoe. I had the Indians let me ashore, and I walked nearly all the way from the Lummi reservation to Whatcom, a distance of six miles, following along the beach until I found an easy grade to climb the bank into the road.

When I reached Fort Bellingham I was refreshed with a cup of tea by the kind hearted Mrs. Tuck, one of the early pioneers of Bellingham Bay. I did not tarry long to rest, but hastened along over the rough way as fast as I could walk, arriving at Elizabeth's home a little before dark, and, going in quietly by the back way, gave my friend a happy surprise.

Each time I visited the bay it wore new beauties. As I gazed upon its broad expanse, dotted with many canoes (almost the only vessels that traversed its waters at this time) I indulged in pleasing visions of the day when this commodious harbor (one of the best in the world, where, it is said, a whole fleet could lie in safety) should be crowded with white-sailed ships from all nations.

A sunset on the bay is a glorious scene. The following beautiful lines convey but a faint idea of the loveliness, which must be seen to be appreciated:

> *A sunset on Bellingham Bay*
> *I watched not long ago,*
> *The fairest picture that nature could paint*
> *On water and sky, I know.*
>
> *The sun, just sinking beneath the waves,*
> *In haste for his nightly rest,*
> *Had flushed with a rosy glory*
> *The heights of the deep, wide west.*
>
> *And the water lying beneath it,*
> *All lulled in a peaceful hush,*
> *Smiled up to the glowing heavens,*
> *And caught in its depths their flush;*
>
> *'Til the stretch of the shining water*
> *And the stretch of those heavenly heights*
> *Were glowing and flaming with crimson*
> *In myriad shadows and lights.*
>
> *A sail on the distant water*
> *Shone out like a faint, white star,*
> *And the glinting of snowy gulls' wings*
> *Was flashed to me from afar.*

Then strangely and slowly and surely
  The glory began to fail,
The light died out of the water,
  The glow in the heavens grew pale.

Ah, lovely the shifting of colors,
  Of tintings, of shadows, of light,
'Til the water grew purple and silver
  And twilight hung, waiting for night.

Then out from the shades of the gloaming,
  Her light trailing far on the sea,
Shone Venus, the star of the evening,
  The fairest of planets to me.

Nature has pictures most lovely
  In earth, and in sky, and in sea,
She has shown in all moods and aspects
  Her beautiful pictures to me.

But there's nothing among all her treasures
  Of sky and of rich water-way
Surpassing the picture she showed me
  That evening on Bellingham Bay.
                              —Kathie Moore.

As the country settled up, and there was no physician within reach, I was often called upon in cases of sickness. This climate being so healthy, I am happy to say, there was little need of a physician, except in cases of accident or increases of population.

In those early days, before we had good roads or bridges, I had many rough and thrilling experiences.

Towards evening one day a man came to me in great haste to go to his sick wife. I climbed into the buckboard and we drove off with all speed. In a short time the sky was overcast with clouds and a heavy storm came on. In spite of every effort, by the time we reached the heavy timber it was dark. I never realized such intense darkness before in my life—it could almost be felt, and the rain came down in torrents. We had no lantern, as we expected to reach our destination before dark, but the unlooked for storm upset our calculations, and there was nothing to do but to press on. It was not long before the horses got off the road and fell down across a log. The situation was appalling, although the horses did very little struggling. The driver's horse was hitched to the back of the buckboard. Imagine my sensation when, as I climbed out the driver said, "Be careful, the horse behind us is a kicker." In vain we tried to light a match to shed some light on our situation. So I climbed out, not knowing where my feet would land. The driver managed to mount the led horse, which carried him home, a mile or more.

As I stood in the pouring rain, dense darkness and thick brush, not knowing what moment the fallen horses might struggle to their feet and trample me beneath them, or a cougar pounce upon me, the minutes seemed like hours. To pass away the time I counted the seconds in a minute, and when the horses stirred I talked soothingly to them. Finally I saw a faint spark of light glancing through the heavy timber; needless to say, my heart leaped for joy. Soon voices were audible and I knew relief was at hand.

In spite of these hindrances, I am glad to say, I reached the suffering woman in time to render the needed assistance.

The little town of Northwood now stands on the very spot of that night's fearful experience.

Another time a man, whose mind was unbalanced, came for me, and Mr. Judson said, "No, you must not go," but I felt that poor suffering woman must not be left in the forest alone without help. So I spoke to one of my most valued friends, the wife of Prof. Swim, who felt as I did, and readily offered to accompany me. The fire was running in the woods, and on account of the fallen timber we were obliged to leave our conveyance a full mile and a half from the house and pick our way through the burning forest.

The insane man was powerfully built, and wild in appearance, and every step of the way we were afraid we would meet him. However, mercy's call must not be unheeded, and we resolutely pressed on to the house.

We found the poor woman suffering much pain, and to add to her distress her insane husband paid several visits to her room during the night, threatening to kill her. It was a terrible experience to all.

How thankful we were the next morning to leave our patient quite comfortable in the hands of a kind courageous neighbor, while we set out to retrace our steps to the buggy.

We have not gone far when we heard a loud shout, and our hearts sank with fear when we looked back and saw the burly form of the insane man hastening after us. We had no inclination to heed his command. I picked up a club and hastened on faster than ever, but in spite of our haste he overtook us. Much to our relief, he only wanted to make some simple inquiry. He was soon after removed to an asylum, where he died.

Crossing the river in the darkness, in a shovel-nosed canoe, by the light of a lantern, when the waters were booming and filled with enormous floating logs, a touch from one of which would have sent us into the icy waters, was not pleasant. I usually sat in the bow of the canoe, holding the lantern—and my breath, too.

These are but some samples of the hazardous experiences of the early settlers, before the days of roads and bridges. And I recall them with a sense of satisfaction that I was given the strength needed to answer these many and vexed experiences among the pioneer sick; and that I never lost a patient, young or old. I attribute a great measure of my success to the fact that I seldom used drugs—always trusting in God, the true physician, and in nature to do the work.

CHAPTER XLVII

Old Sally's only sister, Kate, from the Lummi reservation, often came to visit her. Sally seemed devotedly attached to her sister, who was much younger than herself; and when she learned that Dick, Kate's husband, was very unkind, she would not allow her to go back to him, nor Dick to come to her.

One day, as we were returning in a canoe from a visit to some new neighbors about seven miles up the river, we met a canoe load of Indians, who informed Sally that Dick, her brother-in-law, was in Seclamatum's camp. Sally said not a word, but her paddle made the water fly. When we reached the chief's camp she grounded the canoe, swiftly strode up the bank and entered the wigwam, seized Dick by the hair and silently dragged him out, cast him irefully to the ground. Still silent, she resumed her place in the canoe and took up her paddle as though nothing unusual had occurred; but Dick was thoroughly convinced that when old Sally said "he should not see Kate" she meant it, and, as far as I know, he accepted his fate without further protest, for he never visited the camp again.

Mr. Judson advised the Indians to sever their tribal relations and take advantage of the law entitling them to a government claim. Accordingly, a number followed his advice. He accompanied them to LaConner, at that time our county seat, to "file" on their claims. The journey was made by canoe, and this is how it came about that we lost our nearest neighbors, for old Sally and Joe took a homestead about two miles from us. Sally seemed highly pleased at the prospect of owning a piece of their old hunting grounds that could not be taken from them by the "Bostons." They built a snug little house, with windows and doors, purchased a cook stove and other furniture, and began housekeeping like "white folks."

Sally came to our garden to get flowers and shrubbery, and although wild blackberries grew all around in great abundance, she thought she must have some cultivated ones in her garden.

Not long after they were settled in their new home Lewison, their only remaining son, a boy of twelve, was taken very ill, and the night of his death Sally sent for me. I was aroused about midnight by a messenger, with an Indian pony for me to ride. It was a very dark night. My guide led the pony and carried the lantern.

I found Sally surrounded by her friends and completely overcome with grief. I never saw a white mother express greater love for a child, or more sorrow for its loss, than this poor, uncivilized child of nature. My presence seemed to remind Lewison of lessons, as he had attended school at our house, for he immediately asked for his book. As soon as his mother understood what he wanted, the book was brought. He turned the pages with trembling hands and strained his dying eyes in a vain attempt to decipher the familiar words. With the dawning of the morning his life went out, and Sally's grief was pitiful to witness.

Child though he was, Lewison had united with the church, and gave evidence of a Christian spirit. One day he and one of his schoolmates were quarreling. I happened to be in the yard, and, calling Lewisoin to me, told him "that was wrong. Christians must not quarrel," and he at once offered his hand, and made friends with his companion.

Sally mourned, without ceasing for many days. One day she came to me, early in the morning. As soon as she entered the door, not waiting to sit down, she exclaimed, "I have seen Lewison. I was digging potatoes yesterday," she said, "and was crying for my boy, when Lewison came to me and said, 'Don't cry any more for me, mamma, for I'm safe and happy.'"

When I think of the peace and comfort that shone from those dark features, it brings to mind the scripture, "As one whom his mother comforteth," for surely God had comforted this sorrowful heart, as only a mother can comfort.

Not long after Lewison's death Sally and Joe mourned the loss of two of their daughters, and at the present writing poor old Joe and one grandchild are all that are left of this large family.

I stood by Sally's death bed and felt that I had lost a true, loyal friend, whom I expect to meet in a better world.

When the plan for the Lynden Stickney's Indian school was proposed, Seclamatum donated to it twenty-five acres of his land. Mrs. Stickney, a devoted missionary from the east, gave one thousand dollars to build a school and home on the land, placing it under the auspices of the Woman's Home Missionary Society of the Methodist Episcopal church.

All the Indian children of the Nooksack valley were gathered into this home, the children proved intelligent and learned rapidly. Seclamatum's granddaughter, Sarah, and her husband, George, were both educated and married from this school. They were a very interesting couple, and their wedding was quite an event in the annals of the school, which occurred while Mr. Stark, wife and daughter were superintendent, matron and teacher of the home and school. Many of the Lyndenites were invited to attend, and assisted in preparing the bridal dinner, which was quite an elaborate affair. Dollie, my foster daughter, who had developed a great talent for dressmaking when quite young, made the bridal robe and adornments. The bride made a pretty appearance, as the groom gallantly escorted her down the stairs to the parlor, where they were united in wedlock by the minister of the Lynden Methodist church.

The bride and her friends were seated at the first table, which was beautifully decorated and crowned with a handsome bridal cake.

This school has been a great benefit to the Indian children. They have not only been given a thorough common education, but have been trained to become industrious farmers, tidy housekeepers and skillful needlewomen.

Seclamatum often receives letters from his granddaughter that he brings to me to read for him. They are so intelligent and legibly written that I can hardly realize they are from a native woman. It is with a sense of pleasure that I look upon the fifteen or twenty pupils from the Stickney Home as they file into church on a Sunday morning. In neatness of dress and correctness of deportment they are not a whit behind their fairer brothers and sisters, Indeed, in justice to the Stickney young people, I must say the department credit marks would be on their side. The contrast between these native children and those which attended the first missionary meeting held in the Nooksack valley is pleasingly noticeable.

Stickney Home still flourishes under the able supervision of the Rev. Mr. and Mrs. Brown.

CHAPTER XLVIII

Our first industry was hoop-pole making. What a stir it created in the uneventful tenor of our lives when a Seattle firm contracted with us for poles, and sent a half dozen men, or more, to get them out. We hailed their advent among us as the entering wedge to more prosperous times. They all boarded with us, and what lively evenings ensued. As there were several fine singers among the company, my little melodeon, with Dollie as organist and soprano, was in great demand. The foreman, Miles Rittenberg, being one of the musicians, their mutual love of music soon created a bond of sympathy between them.

The crew remained all winter. In the spring the little steamer "Gem," the first that ascended the Nooksack, was sent up from Seattle to carry away the hoop poles and workers.

Miles had found so strong an attraction here, that he decided to cast his lot with the Lyndenites. The following May he and Dollie were married. He opened a cooper shop, our first permanent industry. Dollie became the village dressmaker, and her talents are still in constant demand.

When their daughter, Lettie, a sprightly, curly-headed little dumpling, was five years old, she decided one day, in spite of frequent admonitions, that she would take a look down into the well. Placing the washboard against the high well curb, she climbed up and leaned over to take a peep into the dark depths. Her mother came to the door just in time to see the wind catch her short skirts, and fling them into a miniature balloon, carry little Lettie head foremost into the well. Her little brother, Will, who was play-

ing in the yard, rent the air with shrill screams of terror
as he saw his little sister disappear into the well. His cries
quickly brought papa to the scene. All was silent in the
well. With fear-filled hearts the parents leaned over the
curb. To their great joy they saw little Lettie clinging
to the well bucket, which fortunately was down when she
fell.

Miles was a man who never grew excited, or lost his
self control. Camly and decidely he spoke to the little one
thirty feet below him in the icy waters. "Lettie, put one
foot into the well bucket (it was too small in circumference
to admit both feet) and hold on to the chain tightly with
both hands, and papa will draw you up." Lettie obeyed;
slowly and carefully the chain, on which hung the precious
little life, was wound upon the windlass. Not a sound
passed the little lips; there were no tears on the dimpled
cheeks; the brave, brown eyes gazed trustfully upward into
the loving faces bent so anxiously above her. The mother
stood with extended arms, ready to snatch the child from
her perilous position. Just before she was drawn within
reach Lettie looked up into her papa's face and said, re-
proachfully, "Papa, what for you dig the well so deep?"

Though trembling and cold, little Lettie received no
injury from her head foremost trip to the bottom of
the well. Her mother washed the sand from her curly
head, and, after a good nap, she got up as bright as ever.
The feeling of the parents at the miraculous escape of their
little daughter can better be imagined than described.

It was about this time that I received a letter from the
wife of the dear brother who was drowned when the Port
Angeles customs house was swept away. She with her

daughter, Lottie, and her youngest son, Walter, had left
their Ohio home, and were on their way to make us a long
visit. I was so thankful they could finish their journey by
steamer instead of the tottleish canoe.

At last the day set for their arrival dawned. How
anxiously I listened, as the day drew to a close, for the
whistling of the steamer. It was about dark when we
heard her labored panting just below "Devil's Bend." At
last the puffing ceased, and then we knew that she had
anchored below the point for the night.

I had no thought of waiting till morning to see the dear
ones from whom I had been so long separated. A glorious
moon cast its silvery radiance over all nature, as Mr. Judson and I drove along the river bank to Devil's Bend.

They were in the cabin when we reached the steamer,
with no thought of seeing us until the next day. I did not
stand upon ceremony, but quickly entering the little cabin,
Maria and I were locked in each other's arms.

Maria and Elizabeth Roeder were foster sisters, and
as dear to me as my own. Together we played on the shores
of dear Lake Erie; together we sat in the little brick schoolhouse; and together we shared the dangers and privations
of early pioneer life, they having followed us the year
after.

Maria, with her three little ones, had returned to her
father's home after the customs house was swept away
and her husband drowned, and now we were once more re-
united. It was one of the happiest moments of our lives;
how we laughed and cried as we embraced and reembraced;
while her daughter Lottie, now a young lady, sat by par-
taking in our joy with smiles and tears of sympathy.

The time flew rapidly by, midnight came before we were aware of it, and Mr. Judson, though in full sympathy with our happiness, at last informed me that it was time to return. But Maria protested and earnestly pleaded that I should remain and share her berth the remainder of the night. Needless to say, sleep was a stranger to the inmates of the little cabin that night.

The current was so strong the little "Edith" made several attempts before she succeeded in rounding the sharp point of Devil's Bend the next morning. As she approached the landing, we saw Horace coming with the team to meet us. When the whistle sounded (the first the horses had ever heard) they became frantic with terror, and started on a wild stampede homeward.

We watched them tearing along the bank, fearing every moment they would plunge over the bank into the river. Horace, who was but fourteen, held bravely to the lines until the horses leaped over the bars, leaving the wagon behind them. Horace escaped with only a few bruises; the wagon and harness were more or less demolished, but we were thankful Horace suffered no serious injury. I was so pleased with his bravery that I handed him a silver dollar, which was considered big money in those days.

It was but a short walk across the field to the little log house on the hillside, where we spent many happy weeks together, for they made us a long, delightful visit.

CHAPTER XLIX

For four years, from 1883 to 1887, the territory of Washington enjoyed impartial suffrage. I took my turn on petit and grand jury, served on election boards, walked in perfect harmony to the polls by the side of my staunch Democratic husband, and voted the Republican ticket—not feeling any more out of my sphere than when assisting my husband to develop the resources of our country.

At the polls, men were respectful; voting places were kept clean and free from loafers. The women, as a rule, allowed character, rather than party, to influence their votes. Party spirit ran high, but the women worked nobly, leaving no stone unturned, and during these four years local option carried in Lynden. It was not because of failure, by any means, that we were deprived of equal rights, for it was a grand success; in so much that a prominent politician remarked that if the women were allowed the ballot they would be compelled to nominate good, competent men for office, and so we were disenfranchised, except in menial service.

The government offered many inducements to persuade its people to emigrate to wild, unsettled regions, thousands of miles from home and civilization, where they risked their lives, suffering severest trials and privations and spending years of arduous toil to make the rough places smooth. Then this same government sends licensed rum to cast its baleful shadow over the fair land, like a trail of a venomous serpent, leaving ruin and desolation in its path—more to be dreaded than the wild beasts and wild men of nature.

Oh, yes, Uncle Sam was very liberal in allowing us equal rights with the sterner sex in taking up land, paying taxes and sharing in their perils and labors; but when it comes to covering this fair land (which we have so dearly purchased and helped to make blossom like the rose) with licensed saloons, we have no voice in the matter. He would have us bear the disgrace, poverty and heartrending sorrow in silent tears, without protest.

Better far a log cabin in the primeval forests, surrounded by savages and wild animals, than a palace with all its luxuries, shadowed by this dreadful "hydra-headed monster, rum."

When our territory was admitted into the Union in 1889, we immediately came into notice. Our climate, fertility of soil, timber, fisheries, mines and other natural advantages offered great inducements to homeseekers, who came pouring in across the continent, over the different haum) from a straggling hamlet speedily bloomed into a good sized city, at present numbering 22,632 inhabitants. railroad lines. Embryo cities sprang up in all directions throughout the new state. Whatcom (now called Belling-

Lynden, notwithstanding her almost inaccessible location, and being the most northwestern town in the state (only four miles from the British line) responded to the new life manifested in more favored localities.

We donated a number of acres of land to Messrs. Robinson and Maltby, owners of a saw mill, and soon the hum of the saw and plane and the scream of the mill whistle awakened the silence, attuned heretofore only to the voices of nature. The ringing of axes and the crashing of great trees, as their proud heads hit the dust, the shouting of teamsters to the oxen, as they drew the great logs to the mill—combined to create a scene of activity and bustle cheering indeed to the ones who had waited so many years, Macaber-like, for "something to turn up."

Although it grieved me to see the great forests despoiled, I realized it was one of the "needs be" in the path of progress.

The little log schoolhouse across the creek had served us many years for all public meetings, elections, literaries and religious services; but, with the advent of the "saw mill" we began to devise ways and means to erect a neat little church.

The settlers from the surrounding country, all with one accord, without sectarian spirit of

> *"So many Gods, so many creeds,*
> *So many paths that wind and wind,*
> *When all this old world needs,*
> *Is just the act of being kind"*

cheerfully turned out and felled the mighty monarchs of the forest, to be converted into lumber at the saw mill.

To help prepare the dinners for the volunteer workers who were wielding the axe and the saw, was my part of the free will service. Long my ears had yearned for the sweet sound of the "church bell" calling to the house of worship, and, as the first tones from the little belfry floated over the firs and cedars of Lynden's forests, my heart was thrilled with a sweet and solemn joy.

I realized that my "ideal home" was one more step nearer completion. A more enchanting spot upon which to rear it could hardly be surpassed on earth. The soil so productive, the scenery most magnificent, and the climate all one could desire; the mild Chinook winds warming the atmosphere in the winter season, and the refreshing breezes from the ocean played over the snow clad mountains—tempering the warm sunshine in the summer season.

Surely nature could be no more lavish with her gifts; our environments were as pure as when created by the hand of God.

No gambling dens, no saloons, nor even a drug store where that "dark beverage of hell" could be procured— had come to cast its debasing gloom over this capitvating landscape where our "ideal home" had now begun to materialize.

Selecting a spot on the plateau, a few blocks north of the old log house, we began felling the great fir trees. So closely they stood together that ninety of these lords of the forest were brought to the ground to make room for the new house.

They were not all felled by the axe—some were brought down by fire. With a large augur two holes were bored into the tree—one sloping slightly upward and the other downward, to make them meet, thus creating a draft. After a few burning coals were dropped into the holes, it usually required four to five days to burn them down. Often they burned only to the sap, leaving a hollow shell, when a few strokes of the axe would bring them to the ground—some of the largest ones making the earth tremble, as though shaken by an earthquake. Felling them was a small part of the work. Their giant forms now cumbered the ground and must be disposed of in some manner, and the auguar was again called into use, holes were bored at regular intervals the whole length of the tree. In the holes fires

were set to burning, which were kept blazing night and
day until the tree was consumed. In due time the ground
was cleared, and the house, a square roofed, two story
building stood completed. It was not a mansion by any
means, but a commodious, comfortable and pretty home.
After our long sojourn in the backwoods, home would
not be home without a firelpace, so our "ideal home" contained two ample hearth stones, where the fir bark fires
continued to brighten and cheer the dark winter days.

Mr. Judson took great pleasure in laying out the two
acres we reserved for grounds. Choice fruit and ornamental shade trees, beautiful shrubs and flowers, replaced the
giant firs and dense underbrush of old.

Now we just realized what a beautiful building place
we possessed, and all declared that on this plateau our city
must be built.

George had graduated from the Territorial University
at Seattle, and married a fellow student, also a graduate of
they university. They settled in Lynden, and, as county
surveyor, George laid out the townsite. Our streets were
broad, and the lots of a generous size. We donated land
for churches, parsonages, public and normal schools, printing office, blacksmith shop, and also for various private
purposes. Aggressive work began at once on the townsite.
The stately firs and wide spreading cedars, under whose
branches the wild animals had roamed and the Indian
erected his wigwam, and performed his mysterious en-
chantments for unknown centuries, now found their lofty
tops brought low.

Great columns of smoke and flame ascended day and
night from the many high piled log heaps. The nightly

spectacle presented by the many glowing fires was grand, as well as inspiring.

The ground was rapidly cleared; new buildings sprang up in all directions, and everything wore that indescribable air of excitement and thrill that accompanies the carving out of a town in the wilderness.

Mr. Judson erected two large store buildings, with halls overhead. The largest bore the dignified name of "Judson Opera House."

In this hall, years after, we celebrated our golden wedding.

The Northwest Normal School brought in an intelligent class of people. A public library was established, and our literary advantages were many and varied. The Judson opera house was in great demand for lectures and entertainments of various characters.

Among the first gatherings in this hall, I remember, was a surprise party on my sixty-fourth birthday. The company numbered about one hundred and fifty friends. The following is a clipping from a Whatcom paper:

A PIONEER'S SURPRISE

"Friday, October 25th, about twenty-five friends of Mrs. Judson, from Whatcom, proceeded to Lynden to celebrate her sixty-fourth birthday anniversary. The affair was a complete surprise to Mrs. Judson, who, it is needless to say, enjoyed it thoroughly. Mrs. Judson crossed the plains in '53, locating at the head of the Sound, where she and her husband resided 'till '70, when they moved to their present home at Lynden. For two years Mrs. Judson was the only white woman in this county north of Bellingham Bay. Among those present were representatives of four generations of the family all calling Mrs. Judson mother. A number of tokens of esteem were presented to Mrs. Judson, among others being a beautiful silk quilt, the work of some of the ladies present. Upon one of its largest pieces, printed upon white satin, was the following poem, composed by Miss Kathie Moore, dedicated to Mrs. Judson:

BIRTHDAY THOUGHTS

In the heart of the great west country,
  Where the white man ne'er had trod,
A lonely little family
  Raised an altar to their God.
And here, while summers dawned and died,
  While winters came and went,
To the cabin in the wilderness
  Sweet household joys were sent.

There were little ones around the hearth,
  Sweet girls with winning ways,
And boys who learned to walk like men,
  Through life's most adverse days.
But sweetest in the litte group,
  That made the home-life fair,
Was "Mother," with her brave, true heart,
  A mother everywhere.

For other homes sprang up meanwhile,
  Upon the land around,
But she was "Mother" everywhere,
  Where e'er a home was found.
And even red men sought her aid,
  And what was still more sweet,
They found a true and tender heart,
  Where love and kindness meet.

And thus she lived a life of toil,
Of sacrifice and care,
But such a life as noble hearts
Wish they might help to share.
And so the years have crowned her life,
With that most perfect good,
The love of all who cross her path,
And noble womanhood.

And still the autumns came and went,
In all their harvest worth,
And brought this happy natal day,
Her birthday—sixty-fourth.
And thus we cannot wonder
That this autumn day so fair,
Brought thoughts from all the country side,
Where she is held so dear.

While hearts sent happy wishes,
Busy hands were swift to do,
Setting in with dainty stitches,
All the tender thoughts they knew.
And, behold! the silken fabric,
Like an autograph of friends,
Lies outspread, a birthday greeting,
Till her life's great mission ends.

CHAPTER L

Soon after we moved into our new house four orphan nephews and nieces came to cluster around the hearth and brighten our home.

The golden-haired, rosy-cheeked, five-year-old twins, Elsie and Edie, Joel, a manly boy of eight, and baby Don. This was our fourth family, and glad we were that there was room in both home and hearts for these orphaned little ones. These children remained with us until they went out to make homes for themselves. Joel and the girls are congenially married. Don still makes his home with me, a bright young man of eighteen.

From their earliest years a platonic friendship existed between Don and Dollie's youngest boy, Horace Rittenberg, and many an escapade did these two youngsters engage in. Before they were out of their dresses, Dollie left them while she ran into a neighbors. It was a cold rainy day. Taking advantage of her absence, the children played in the water and got their feet wet. When she came home she found them dancing around the kitchen, minus shoes and stockings. The room was filled with a peculiar pungent odor. Hastily opening the oven door, she saw four odd looking little black balls reposing on the upper grate. "Why, what is this?" exclaimed Horace's mother. "Oh," answered Don (who usually was the spokesman for the two) "we're drying our shoes." Sure enough, they were "dry," and Mr. Rittenberg carried shoeless Don home on his back.

Living within a few blocks of each other, constantly together, still this did not satisfy their ardent souls.

Don came to Mr. Judson one day with this pathetic appeal: "Uncle Holden, won't you buy Horace, so he can come and live with me and be my brother?" Uncle Holden's eyes twinkled, and he replied: "Yes, Don, you go down and tell his father I will give him a good fat pig for Horace." Away trotted the six-year-old pair, not doubting that the desire of their hearts would be satisfied. Soon the woebegone little men returned, and Don mournfully announced that "Mr. Rittenberg would not trade Horace for a pig." However, they both brightened up when we said Horace might stay and spend the night with Don.

I often smile as I think of a moving tableau that met my eye as I looked out of the window one sweltering hot day. Don had been down playing with Horace, and while barefooted had stepped on a bee, which left its stinger in his foot. Horace, with his heart full of sympathy, got his little wheelbarrow to wheel his wounded comrade home. On they came, over the rough road, through the yellow sunshine, little Horace puffing like a young porpoise, the sweat rolling down his face, while Don lay on his back in the wheelbarrow with his white bandaged foot pointing skyward.

The friendship of the two boys has continued unbroken, and grown stronger with the years, reminding me of David and Jonathan of old.

Before we fully realized such a possibility, we found ourselves an incorporated city, with H. A. Judson its first mayor.

From Lynden's first paper, the "Pioneer Press," the following notice is clipped:

"Lynden's prayer for the right to incorporate has been granted. Two tickets were nominated for the city officers, both representing good men, decidely opposed to the liquor traffic, bawdy houses and gambling dens within the corporate limits. Of the Hon. H. A. Judson, the nominee for mayor of Lynden, we cannot refrain from penning a warm tribute of praise, prompted by the sincerest regard and respect for the man who will, without doubt, be the first mayor of Lynden. By his keen practical sympathy in all worthy public enterprises, he has justly earned the right to be Lynden's first mayor. His name will be a source of strength for Lynden, and he will worthily represent her municipal government. Lynden has no citizen on which she could more fittingly bestow the highest and most responsible office in her gift than Holden A. Judson."

CHAPTER LI

Every prospect seemed pleasing, and I thought to settle down to the quiet enjoyment and the comforts and pleasures brought by advancing civilization, but prosperity is not sorrow proof.

George and Eason Ebey, Annie's husband, were in the mountains working their gold claims. They had been gone from home but two weeks when the sorrowful tidings were brought to us that George was no more. The following from the home paper contains a brief sketch of his life:

"George Holden Judson, son of Hon. H. A. and P. N. Judson, was born at Grand Mound, near Olympia, December 19, 1859, and died at Glenore May 19, 1891, aged 31 years, five months and two days.

"He came with his parents to Whatcom county twenty-one years ago and grew up to manhood in Lynden. In 1878 he entered the Territorial University at Seattle, receiving in December of that year, a fine unabridged dictionary as a prize for superior scholarship—Judge Burke making the presentation speech. On May 25, 1882, he graduated in the scientific course, having taken all but one year in classical course. He graduated on the birthday of Miss Flora A. Phelps, who had attended the same school and graduated the year previous—a niece of the president of the university. To Miss Phelps he was married November 16, 1882, at the home of her parents in Waterloo, Iowa. They came to Lynden the following January, where they have since resided. By profession he was a civil engineer, and was elected that same year (1882) county surveyor, and again elected in 1888, by a large majority. In 1888 he was elected to the first legislature of the state of Washington, and, with the assistance of his colleague, Hon. William R. Moultray, succeeded in getting a bill through the lower house to establish the Lynden Normal school as a state institution. The Pioneer Press in an editorial at that time, said:

"'A few weeks ago we noticed the work of the Normal school, and showed that its work was first class. Since that time a bill has been introduced in the house of representatives by Mr. George Judson to locate a State Normal school at Lynden. When the news reached Lynden everybody was enthusiastic in their praises of Representative Judson. People of Whatcom county have long known Mr. Judson as an honorable, upright young man, and an untiring worker in the interests of his county.'

"These are some of the facts of his public career, but who shall write the inner history of his modest, manly soul? He was so retiring in his disposition, thinking much and deeply, but reticent in expressing his thought. Only the friends of the home circle, where he was best known, understood his true worth, and they loved him with a great love. Truly, he was his father's pride, his mother's joy, the idolized brother of two loving sisters, and of his elder and only brother. Such was the tender attachment between these brothers that it is a remarkable fact that not even a ripple of discord ever marred their lives. He was the treasure of a large circle of friends, and when he fell their hearts were filled with a great desolation. Over and over the mother exclaimed: 'No one knew what he was to me— how much I loved him,' and in a few moments lived over the life of her darling boy, the interesting letters he had written her while at school; the time, when after a little separation, they met and both wept for joy; the many incidents of his life crowding thick and fast—she realized that he had lived a great deal in those thirty-one years.

"And how crushingly the blow upon the devoted wife, left with three little children, Allan, Leilla and Raymond. With a sublime faith, born of the conviction that 'God had taken him,' and that she must be brave to care for and train her children, she bore up heroically under this unexpected and great bereavement.

"Mr. Judson was a great lover of music—at one time a member of the Lynden band and a leader of an orchestra. His wife was a musician, and accompanied him on the piano, or organ, while he played the violin; and to each this was one of the pleasantest recreations of home.

While in the legislature his little son Allan, age six years, and daughter Leilla, nearly five, printed a letter to him. He never said anything about the letter, but they were found among his papers in a sealed envelope, addressed to himself, with a translation of them, the best he could make, written out. On his last return home, before his death, he came on the sixth birthday of his little Leilla, who was filled with joy, calling it one of her 'surprises,' and the best of them all.

"He loved the beautiful in nature and art, and the noble thoughts of our best authors and poets. He desired to make home a lovely place, and had partly completed a convenient and commodious residence in the southwestern part of Lynden, and had sent for seeds and a variety of plants to beautify the place; but he has been called away, we believe, to a better home, even the heavenly.

"On May 7th he started from home, arriving at Glenore, his mining camp, May 9th. He had not been well for some time; said to a friend before he left that he thought he had something like the la grippe. On Tuesday, May 12th, not feeling able to work, he went deer hunting, and, as heretofore stated in the Press, lost his balance in climbing a large fir tree and fell upon a sharp knot, which pierced through the flesh in his thigh to the bone. The wound, however, began to heal, and if he had been well when hurt, he would probably have recovered; but the hurt, combined with his sickness, doubtless caused his death. He lived a week from the time he was hurt. A few days before he died he dictated a letter to his father, hoping that he would be able to start home soon; but Tuesday, May 19th, at 3 P. M., he died, speaking to his brother-in-law, Mr. Ebey, just a few seconds before, saying that if anything happened to him to see after the interests of his wife and children. Mr. Ebey and his son Allen, to whom he was tenderly attached, were with him, ministering unto him and doing all in their power to make him comfortable. They were surprised and overwhelmed with grief at his sudden and unexpected death. The next day at 3 A. M. he was carried down from the mines; then in a canoe, on the Skagit river, sixty miles to Sedro; from thence on the train to Whatcom, arriving on the evening of the same day.

"Here the Knights of Pythias (of which order he was a member) met the body at the depot, passing up the streets beneath the electric lights, with their departed brother. One spoke of the scene as thrilling and pathetic. The next day, accompanied by a delegation of the Knights, and other friends from Whatcom and the Crossing, he was brought to Lynden and borne beneath the parental roof, just two weeks from the day he left and promised to return.

"The funeral services were held in the M. E. Church at 2 P. M., prayer was offered by Rev. B. K. McElmon, and scripture reading from Psalms, 23, 1st Thessalonians 4th Chapter 13-18; also Rev. 22, 1-7. Sermon from John 14, 1-2-3 by Mrs. M. F. Beavers; also brief biographical sketch. At the close a large concourse of friends took a last look at the beloved sleeper. A universal sorrow pervaded the community, that one so young and promising, and filling such a large place among us, should be called away so soon.

"It was a great comfort to the stricken relatives that they could gaze once more upon the dear face and form, looking so natural and peaceful, and place the beautiful flowers above the pulseless heart that had loved them so fondly in life. He was buried in the Masonic cemetery, in the spot he himself had selected on Decoration Day, 1890. The last rites were performed by Rev. B. K. McElmon.

"For some time there seemed to be a pathetic sadness filling his mind, a still gentle feeling manifested in his intercourse with friends; and he reading the Bible with renewed interest. While attending university, he, with a large number of students, professed faith in Christ as his Savior, and united with the Congregational church.

"Though he may not have been actively engaged in religious works, and had his faults as well as virtues, yet it is evident he never lost sight of these religious principles. He was very temperate in his habits, using no liquors of any kind, and not even tobacco.

"With Mr. Ebey, with whom he was intimately associat-

ed, he talked over his business affairs. Even before he was
hurt he spoke of the little there was in the riches and pleasures of this world. A number of little incidents and conversations led this friend to say, 'His soul realized he was
going.'

"He was quite a reader, and often selected for his mother,
and she for him, such reading as indicated the loftiest moral
sentiments.

"We can close this brief sketch in no more fitting way
than to record here his favorite hymn, 'Go Bury Thy Sorrow,' and the following poems. They will give a deeper
insight into the soul life of the quiet, modest man. He
played this hymn so often, and did so while visiting his
mother just before leaving home for the last time. How
beautiful and appropriate to the lonely hearts now bowed
in a great sorrow. The poem, 'A Legend,' was the only one
pasted in a new scrap book. This he did himself, hurriedly,
and not in the usual neat manner he exhibited in everything
he did, but seeming to feel it must go in at that time.

"Oh, sorrowing friends, doubtless he was putting away,
even then, from his heart, with the assistance of the Divine
Spirit, all evil, and soon to hear and join the song of the
angels.

"The poem entitled, 'Like a Grain of Mustard Seed,' he
carried in his vest pocket, dropped it out while doing some
work on the roof of his house, and requested his wife to
pick it up and take care of it. She afterwards gave it to
him, and found it among his papers.

"How sweet to remember that the heavenly kindom had
birth in his heart in youth, and in these last moments renewed preparation going on for a life of endless praise.

A LEGEND

"There has come to mind a legend, a thing I had half
    forgot,
And whether I read it or dreamed it, ah, well, it matters
    not.
It is said that in heaven at twilight a great bell softly
    swings,
And man may listen and harken to the wonderful music that
    rings.
If he puts from his heart's inner chamber all the passion,
    pain and strife,
Heartache and weary longing, that throb in the pulses of
    life—
If he thrusts from his soul all hatred, all thoughts of wicked
    things,
He can hear in the holy twilight, how the bell of the angels
    rings.

"And I think there is in this legend, if we open our eyes to
    see,
Somewhat of an inner meaning, my friend, to you and me,
Let us look in our hearts and question, can pure thoughts
    entertain
To a soul if it be already the dwelling of thoughts of
    sin?
So then, let us ponder a little, let us look in our hearts and
    see
If the twilight bells of the angels could ring for us, you
    and me?

LIKE A GRAIN OF MUSTARD SEED

"In words we love to hear and read,
    The Master told us long ago,
His kingdom is a little seed,
    The least of all the grains that grow.

"*But planted deep within the mind,*
It sends out branches broad and high,
Wide reaching love for all mankind,
And lifted thought that seek the sky.

"*And even as it spreads and thrives,*
The birds of heaven find shelter there,
To build their nest and fill our lives,
With songs of joy and peace and prayer.

"*O Christ, Thou sower of the seed,*
From whence immortal harvests spring,
Our open hearts before Thee plead,
To us this blessed promise bring.

"*Thou didst walk the field of earth,*
To give new life from nature's ways,
Now give this heavenly kingdom birth,
In all our hearts for endless praise."

CHAPTER LII

Eason and George were close friends and congenial companions. He did not long survive the death of George.

A few years later death again cast its shadow athwart our path, and took our youngest, Mary. Life seemed to hold all that was desirable for Mary—wealth, a kind and indulgent husband, and two bright little children. She, with her family, visited the World's Fair at Chicago. After their return her health declined rapidly. On her last visit home she told me that she would soon be with George, whom she dearly loved and sorely missed.

When she left us for her home I gave her a bouquet of beautiful roses. I see her now, as the carriage rolled away, and though she looked so much like the white roses she held in her hand, I could not bring myself to believe she would soon be taken from us.

The twentieth of June, 1899, many friends from far and near gathered in the "Judson Opera House" to celebrate our golden wedding. It was a very enjoyable occasion. We were both in good health and spirits, rejoicing in the prosperity of the country, and the evidence of love and affection from all.

The following verses, written by La Bonta's wife, who was in California, were read by a friend to the assembled company:

TO MY DEAR FATHER AND MOTHER

How sadly sweet are the pleasures of today,
That memory brings to the pondering heart—
The falling tear and the bitter sting,
How faintly they loom in that far away past.

Of this life, the pathway that lieth behind,
  'Tis the sunshine we see as we gaze on the past,
The shadows are faint as we backward look,
  And o'er the sharp stones a brightness is cast.

The golden vales that fleck the way,
  Along the checkered journey of life,
Are sunny and fair tho' oft passed by,
  For with sorrow and care is rife.

The sunny hours of merry child life,
  As we played by the rippling forest stream,
And houses built in the shifting sand,
  Come back with a fairy golden gleam.

Tho' here a crumbling ruin stands,
  And there a shattered column lies,
And blackened stones now mark the spot
  Where flames once gladdened dancing eyes.

O'er all the tinted lichen lies—
  The ivy green doth clinging creep,
And thro' the softening haze of time
  Bright roses cover chasms deep.

Our steps we never can retrace,
  And time's frail bridge on which we tread,
Sinks back into eternity
  At every step, as on we're led.

Then forward let our watchword be,
  Our wasted time we can't redeem,
As earnest work e'er lies before
  As that we passed far up the stream.

I thank the God that rules the skies,
For all the bright and joyous days,
On that fair roadway stretched behind,
Wound in and out along its ways.

They are the last to sink from sight;
Their sweetness still upon us gleam,
When angry tho't and smarting pain,
Are buried deep 'neath Lethe's stream.

The past is gathered and garnered in,
Once ours, now ours no more,
Unspeak we no word, undo we no deed,
The future lies open before.

The golden glory on mountain and hill,
Proclaim the night's repose—
The golden wedding's softened light
Gleams near life's journey's close.

May you journey on together until you reach
    the end,
And the brightness of your presence unto this
    earth long lend.

             Lovingly your daughter,
               GERTRUDE JUDSON.

In four short months after the golden wedding, the parting time came, the time we had so long dreaded, yet knew some day must be, when one would be left to finish the journey of earth's pilgrimage alone.

Mr. Judson had been failing for several months, and for some time sought to conceal from me the seriousness of his condition; but one Sunday, as we two sat before the cheerful fire in our cozy sitting room, he said, "I have just

asked the Lord to spare me three days longer, and I would
be ready to go, and I have received the answer."

He set to work to arrange his affairs; his manner was
cheerful and composed as though only preparing for an ordinary journey.

His first act was to write a farewell letter to our two
remaining children, Annie and La Bonta, the two who had
shared all the dangers and privations of our pioneer life,
and were now residing in California. The three days of
probation were closely occupied with business, but I noticed
that he would occasionaly drop his work to walk out on
the front veranda and gaze around, as though bidding farewell to the work of his hands.

He was not confined to his bed until the last day;
cheerful and happy, contented to go, and solicitous of my
welfare to the last moment.

From among the many tributes to his memory, I have
selected the following:

LIFE OF A PIONEER

"A neighbors' tribute to the late Hon. H. A. Judson.

"Looking back to the time when our townsite was an
almost unbroken wilderness, memory recalls a letter received some sixteen years ago in a far eastern state, a letter
which bore the post mark of Lynden, Washington.

"The letter contained a graphic description of towering
forest trees; of the river and Mount Baker, guarded by
green foothills, and stated that the post master of the place
was H. A. Judson, who, with his family lived near the little
log building which was store and post office combined. For
years Mr. Judson held the position, removing to the build-

ing now occupied by Smith and Waples, and finally to the larger one built by him near the family residence.

"During all the years since that time many have been the recipients of kindness at the hands of these pioneer residents of our valley.

" 'Patient vigils keeping' tells the story of the last weeks in the life of Mr. Judson. Only to those who have passed through the same experience does it come with full significance; but all hearts have been touched with tender sympathy as messages came from the home where all things were being put in readiness for the transition to the home beyond.

"In June of the present year the golden wedding anniversary of Mr. and Mrs. Judson was celebrated in their hall, as the home would not accommodate all those who gathered to rejoice with them on that occasion.

"October 28 the same friends, with many others, met in the same place to tender the last token of respect to all that was mortal of Mr. Judson.

"His latest care and thought was for the one who had never faltered in life's journey by his side, beginning away in the eastern land and prefaced by long toilsome journey across the plains.

"During the lifetime of Mrs. Judson we hope to read in her contemplated work of reminiscences of that long journey, and of the varied experiences and incidents to the present time.

"What better monument can she build in memory of those who penetrated the trackless plains and forests and laid the foundation for the homes builded thereon?

"Lynden, November 6, 1899."

H. A. JUDSON

"Who was he? What was he? Who he was and what he was were one and the same thing. It is as impossible to tell who a man is without telling what he is as it would be to tell what a watch was like without describing it.

"We don't know all about him, but we do know that when we came to this country sixteen years ago, and everything was new, and there was no public roads worth the name, and logs and stumps and forest seemed unconquerable, and we were homesick and uncertain, that H. A. Judson stood there, not only with encouraging word, but with kindly act, to make the task more light and the way more plain.

"He knew things about the land office business with which we were not familiar; he knew all about the land, and what he did for us he did for hundreds of others.

"He was a neighbor, friend and legal adviser for most of the first settlers in the region of Lynden, and to them the town will not seem like itself without him in it.

"H. A. Judson was the father of Lynden, and his wife was its mother. Most of we early settlers have cheered ourselves by their fireplace and rested under their hospitable roof. It seems only yesterday that we traveled the narrow river trail that led to the little post office where he officiated and greeted us with kindly word; but now he is dead, and the old place can only remind us of him and bring to memory the warmth of the past, which will be his epitaph upon the hearts of his old neighbors who survive him.

"What need for us to tell how he married kind-hearted

Phoebe Goodell, away back in Ohio in 1849; of their journey together across the continent to Olympia in 1853? For
we cannot go over that seven months' drive with them
again if we would. Two kind hearts were one in them, and
that was why they beat in unison to make a cheerful home
for more than fifty years.

"To say that he served his country and commonwealth
in a legislative capacity adds no proof to our evidence of
his worth; and to say that one forever young in heart died
in Lynden, Washington, October 26, 1899, aged 73 years,
does not mean that his kind influence shall ever die."

CHAPTER LIII

After the last sad rites my friends insisted on taking me from the cemetery to the home of my granddaughter, Mrs. Victor A. Roeder, of Whatcom. From thence I was persuaded to visit my children in California, and I did not see my home again for six months; but even though with my children, in the land of orange flowers and the birds, how my lonely heart longed for the dear home place —for the fireside where I, with my husband, after the dangers and struggles of pioneer life, had enjoyed so many peaceful days.

I returned to Washington by train and enjoyed the garden-like scenes of California, but when we entered the wild, uncultivated regions of Oregon and Washington, and I gazed upon the familiar sight of unbroken forests, fallen logs, dense underbrush, swamps and swails, I felt that I would gladly again begin pioneer's life, could I once more have my husband by my side.

My home coming was very pleasant. Many friends had gathered in my old home to greet me. Cheerful fires blazed on the hearth, and the table was spread with an abundance of good cheer. I appreciated it all; but there was a void that friends could not fill.

It was spring. Nature was attiring the shade trees of maple, locust and mountain ash that surrounded the home, in her spring time robe of tender green; the lilacs and laburnams were just putting forth their white, purple and yellow blooms; every tree and shrub around the home voiced the care and taste of the one who had planted them.

The only shade upon my pleasure was that my husband had not lived to enjoy it with me. But I am glad that he lived to see his labors crowned with a measure of success— the almost uninhabited country blossom with fruitful farms.

But very few of the advance guard of pioneers have lived to see their fond hopes realized.

Captain Roeder and Elizabeth, our dear Ohio friends, are among those of our most intimate friends and relations who have passed away to the spiritual realms.

My twin sister, Mary, is still with us. We spent our seventieth birthday together on Bellingham Bay.

Mrs. Eldridge, Mrs. Lysle and Mrs. Biles, dear compatriots, still survive. We four have passed the same number of milestones on life's journey, exceeding the allotted "three score years and ten."

Mrs. Eldridge and Mrs. Roeder were the first white women to settle in Whatcom, when it was a vast, unbroken forest, not a road or trail, and no communication with the outside world.

During the Indian war they were posted in the old "block house," located on the brow of the hill, near the present corner of Sixteenth and D streets, in what was then called the little town of Whatcom, but not the City of Bellingham.

We would they had all lived much longer to enjoy the fruits of their labors.

To me it is a source of great satisfaction to see the silent wilderness grown pregnant with human life, and dotted with beautiful homes.

Iron bridges spanning the rivers have taken the place of the rope ferries. Substantial wooden bridges have replaced the old time foot log, and the rough corduroys given way to broad plank and graveled roads. Various industries have been established. The whistle of the saw and shingle mills is heard in every direction. Electricity has supplanted the tallow dip, and annihilated time and space. And the slumbering echoes of hoary Mount Baker are awakened by the shriek of the locomotive.

CHAPTER LIV

The first day of January, 1904, we welcomed the first train from Bellingham to Lynden. It was an occasion of great rejoicing to the Lyndenites. Many invitations had been sent to our friends throughout the surrounding country to come and rejoice with us.

Messrs. Kildall and Waples, the chief merchants, furnished entertainment and refreshment for the guests, whom it is estimated numbered three thousand. Congratulatory speeches were made by the mayor, lawyers and other prominent citizens of Bellingham. Mr. Cline of Lynden also favored us with a very interesting and vivid description of the trials and hardships of early days in comparison with the comforts and conveniences of civilization. The Lynden and Bellingham bands vied with each other in discoursing inspiring strains. It was the largest and most enthusiastic assemblage in the annals of Lynden.

About this time I was surprised and greatly pleased to receive the following letter from Superintendent J. J. Donovan of the B. B. & B. C. Ry. Co.:

"Dear Madam:

"It gives me great pleasure to hand you herewith this annual pass, good during the year 1904, between all the stations of this road. I do not know that I have ever had the pleasure of meeting you personally, though I did know Mr. Judson when he was alive, and everybody in this part of the country who has lived here any length of time knows of your pioneer experience in going into the forest when Whatcom county was very different from what it is now, and it gives me much pleasure, as one of the later comers, representing the railroads that followed the blazes made by the pioneers, to send you this evidence of esteem on our part.

"I have learned from a friend that you are contemplating a visit to town next Saturday to stay for a few days. I regret that our regular trains are not yet running to Lynden, owing to the failure of the steel company to send the rails which were ordered many months ago, but I have requested Mr. Branin, who has charge of the trains, to have a coach at the county road about 11:30 and a train will bring this coach over to Hampton and put it on our regular train, reaching Whatcom at 1:05 P. M.

"If for any reason you should be unable to come in on Saturday at 11:30 A. M., please telephone me, so that I need not send a car unnecessarily.

"Wishing you many years of continuance of your useful life, I remain, with much respect,

"J. J. Donovan,

"General Superintendent."

I gladly availed myself of his kindness. After having traveled so long by the "shovel nose" canoe, over the rough corduroys, drawn by plodding oxen, and later by the jolting stage—as I sat in the comfortable coach, gliding smoothly over the rails, I felt like a bird let loose. One dream of my life was at last realized.

CHAPTER LV

After all, the trials and hardships that have been our lot while journeying through the wilderness, I would not exchange my "buried" life, as it has been called, for the "wear and tear" of the fashionable society woman who must fulfill her social obligations, with no fruit to show as the result of her hard labor.

Many times, when talking with dear Elizabeth, over those bygone days of solitude, when we were drawn together in pleasant, helpful, loving relations, with our innocent little ones perfectly safe amid nature's haunts, from the corroding influences of advanced civilization, we realized that those were our happiest days, though we failed to realize it at the time. For many years the sunshine of life was undimmed by the direful shadow caused by man's greed for gold, that stifles all human sensibilities of the soul, and makes man willing to trample his brother into the mire.

Alas, for fair Lynden! The "queen of the Nooksack Valley," with her prosperity, a dark cloud arose threatening to enshroud her beauty. To the horror and dismay of the "Gem City" mothers and sisters, they learned that two strangers had applied for a saloon license within our borders. With hearts all aflame with love for husbands, sons and fathers, we rallied to the rescue. We visited by ones, by twos, and in companies, the different members of the city council, and pleaded for the safety of our loved ones; but all in vain—our pleadings, prayers and entreaties —greed of gold carried the day, proving the truth of the old adage, "The love of money is the root of all evil."

And the saloon, with its woeful influence, was planted in our midst. I have lived long enough to realize that unless the government prohibits the manufacture of that curse of the world—that fell destroyer of mankind, "rum," it will be utterly impossible to rear on this mundane sphere an "ideal home."

How refreshing for the weary pilgrim, amid the toil and turmoil of this life, to pause a moment and look with the eye of faith into that "promised land" where sorrowing and sighing are unknown.

Since the transition of my dear ones to the "home of the soul" I am more deeply impressed that the dream of fifty years ago, away back on the plains in the emigrant wagon —that "we had built our ideal home on the wrong side of the river" was not a meaningless phantasm of the brain.

Slowly, all these years, I have been learning that only the spiritual is real; and as I near the river's brink that "ideal home" grows more and more real and beautiful.

Already my pathway is brightened by glimpses of immortal life, and "I fancy but thinly the vale intervenes between that fair city and me."

Over the river, "in the sweet fields of Eden, where the tree of life is blooming," I know there awaits me my "ideal home."

THE CONQUEST OF THE WEST

(A poem written for Mrs. Judson by Miss Katherine Moore which aptly portrays the experiences of the early pioneers whose courage and steadfastness subdued the wilderness and brought civilization to our great West.)

Long years ago, one summer day,
A band of pilgrims took their way,
With hopeful hearts and spirits bright,
Across the land; through cloud, through light,
Through untried ways, through dangers great,
They journeyed forth with hearts elate,
From out the wilderness to wrest
From savage man and savage beast,
A home—to hew, to build, to toil,
To win a living from the soil.

They turned away from homes so dear,
From friends to true, from rest, good cheer,
They faced the risk of fire and flood,
Of desert vast and pathless wood,
Of savage foes, of famine dread,
Yet eagerly they westward sped.
The caravan slow wound its trail,
Through vistas fair of hill and dale,
With wooded river, lake serene,
Where skies were blue, where earth was green.

But gradually a change, all new,
Transformed the land they journeyed through.
The forest vanished, streams ran dry,
No grass grew 'neath the burning sky,
And weary, dreary was the way,
As on they plodded, day by day;
For famine stalked them—side by side,
The sturdy man and infant died,
The cattle fell and perished there,
And hope seemed given to despair.

Across the plains of alkali,
The train crept on. The lurid sky
Was almost hidden by the dust
That rises from that sun-baked crust,
To choke and stifle. Still they pressed
On, still onward, in their quest;
Around them ever birds of prey
Swung round and followed all the way.
Though they marked with graves new laid
The track their weary march had made,
Still they journeyed, 'till one day
Dust and desert passed away.

Once again green branches waved,
Once again cool water laved;
Blooming fair on every hand
To the verdant promised land,
Where primeval forests vast,
Dense and deep their shadows cast.
Here they tarried—on this spot
They would choose to cast their lot,
Here the little hero band
Brave, undaunted, made their stand.

Small, indeed the band had grown,
E'er they reached this blooming zone;
But with noble heart and mind,
Sorrows past, were left behind,
And they set with eager haste
To make a dwelling in this waste.
There the ringing axes swung,
Little cabin houses sprung,
Little garden plots soon smiled
Where the brush was thick and wild.
Time sped on, and new made fields
Soon were blest with bounteous yields.

Ah, but dangers great and sore,
Hovered, ever, at the door.
Not a night but watch was kept
While the weary workers slept;
Not a day, but, as his guard,
While her husband labored hard;
The wife must ever by him stand
With the musket in her hand,
Lest upon them foes should fall,
Murdering and burning all.

Every instant they must be
Ready from their homes to flee,
Should some trusted Indian friend
Secret warning to them send.
Then the dreaded Indian war
Spread its horrors through the year.
In that terror stricken wild
Not an instant safety smiled.
Houses built with such loving care
Smoked in ruins everywhere;
Fields were wasted, and the blood
Of murdered families stained the wood.

Ah, those dreadful times are o'er—
Vanished, to return no more!
Often as I sit in dreams
Of the past, my story seems
So unreal! Can it be
That strange life belonged to me?
Looking down through streets so fair,
Handsome villas everywhere,
Fields and gardens smiling nigh,
Trolley cars swift passing by,
Little children dance along
Now with shout, and now with song.

Where is all the deadly fear
That once filled the region here?
Where the forests, dense and high?
Where the wild beasts, growling nigh?
Where the cruel Indian brave
From whose hand no power could save?
Did I live in those dread days?
Did I tread those dangerous ways?
Did I toil those wilds to clear?
Did I help these homes to rear?

Was it I who dared to stand
With the musket in my hand,
Guarding while the men were all
Working on the block house wall?
Can it really be that I
Saw those pilgrim martyrs die?
Lost dear friends among the slain?
Soothed the hearts bowed down with pain?
Are these dreams, or can it be
Such a life belonged to me?
Musing thus, it all doth seem
Like a wild and troubled dream.

Peacefully the twilight falls,
Sweet and clear the church bell calls,
O'er yon snow-capped mountain's crown
The first faint star is gleaming down.
Can earth show a scene more fair
Than this spot to me so dear,
Carven from the wilderness?
Joy its portion, now, and peace,
But 'twas purchased through long years
With the blood of pioneers.

CONCLUSION

I wish the reader to understand that upwards of seventy years have elapsed since my husband and myself, our little daughter Annie (now Mrs. Ebey), and son La Bonta, born en route, crossed the continent in an emigrant wagon. Through these many years, first in the territory and later in the state of Washington, we have passed through many trials, through sorrow and hardships, only to learn that "perfect love casteth out all fear," and all the evil fortunes we have experienced have been as nothing compared to the blessings we have enjoyed. God was with us all the way, leading us to this beautiful Nooksack valley, abounding in picturesque scenery with its background of snow-capped mountains—a continual feast for the soul. Here we found the place to build our "ideal home" and it is here I am still living in my ninety-fifth year, under the shade of the wide spreading maples my husband planted after clearing the ground of the many huge majestic fir trees that so thickly studded it, a slow and laborious task with the unscientific implements in use in those days.

Words cannot express the happiness I have enjoyed living in my humble home, amid these beautiful surroundings, with my two eldest children, Annie and La Bonta, who tenderly care for me. My grand, great grand and great great grand children, my adopted ones and my nephews and nieces living in Washington and California often visit and cheer Grandma Judson, making the pioneer home joyful with their presence.

THE END

CPSIA information can be obtained
at www.ICGtesting.com
Printed in the USA
LVHW052116210722
723977LV00007B/276

9 780803 275591